THE
GLUTEN-FREE
COOKBOOK

THE GLUTEN-FREE COOKBOOK

ENJOY THE FOODS YOU LOVE

Penguin Random House

Senior editor Alastair Laing
US consultant Kate Ramos
US editors Jenny Siklós, Margaret Parrish, Rebecca Warren
Project art editor Katherine Raj
Managing editor Dawn Henderson
Managing art editor Christine Keilty
Art director Peter Luff
Senior jacket creative Nicola Powling
Production editor Raymond Williams
Production controller Claire Pearson
Creative technical support Sonia Charbonnier

COBALT ID
Editors Marek Walisiewicz, Sarah Tomley
Art editors Paul Reid, Darren Bland, Rebecca Johns

Recipe photography William Shaw

Important The recipes contained in this book are to be followed exactly as written. The Publisher is not responsible for your specific health or allergy needs that may require medical supervision. The Publisher is not responsible for any adverse reactions to the recipes contained in this book. Every effort has been made to ensure that the information contained in this book is complete and accurate. However, neither the publisher nor the authors are engaged in rendering professional advice or services to the individual reader. Professional medical advice should be obtained on personal health matters. Neither the publisher nor the authors accept any legal responsibility for any personal injury or other damage or loss arising from the use or misuse of the information and advice in this book.

This American Edition, 2015
First American Edition, 2012
Published in the United States by DK Publishing
1450 Broadway, Suite 801, New York, NY 10018

A catalog record for this book
is available from the Library of Congress.
ISBN 978-1-4654-3450-0

DK books are available at special discounts when purchased in bulk for sales promotions, premiums, fund-raising, or educational use. For details, contact:
DK Publishing Special Markets, 1450 Broadway, Suite 801, New York, NY 10018, SpecialSales@dk.com

Colour reproduction by Media Development & Printing Ltd
Printed and bound in China

For the curious
www.dk.com

MIX
Paper from
responsible sources
FSC™ C018179
www.fsc.org

This book was made with Forest Stewardship Council™ certified paper – one small step in DK's commitment to a sustainable future. For more information go to www.dk.com/our-green-pledge

CONTENTS

INTRODUCTION

Changing to a gluten-free diet is a great opportunity to eat well and take control of your health.

This introduction will explain why going gluten free may be the right choice for you, and will guide you through all the stages required to eliminate gluten from your food and plan healthy, balanced gluten-free meals: at home, on the go, and dining out.

You will also find all the information you need to start cooking with gluten-free ingredients. A gallery of gluten-free grains and flours explains each one's particular qualities and how best to use them in dishes, while recipes with step-by-step photographs demonstrate how to bake delicious bread and cakes, and make perfect pastry and pasta using gluten-free flour.

EATING WELL ON A GLUTEN-FREE DIET

Finding out you have a gluten intolerance can prompt mixed feelings. Relief that finally you're taking control of your health, but probably also concern that adopting a gluten-free diet might mean cutting out many of your favorite foods and accepting a less enjoyable, less flavorful diet. Yet nothing can be further from the truth and this book is here to prove you can eat fantastically well on a gluten-free diet.

DISCOVERING NEW FLAVORS

Far from being a life sentence of disappointing food, cutting out gluten is a wonderful opportunity to explore new dishes made with grains and flours you may never have heard of before. Going gluten free is also the perfect excuse to release the home baker in you. A new generation of preblended flours, combined with the magic of xanthan gum, has transformed gluten-free baking, so that with our step-by-step instruction and specially created recipes you will still be able to enjoy all your favorite bakes.

EATING FOR HEALTH

Going gluten free is also about recovery. When first diagnosed, you are likely to be suffering the effects of poor nutrient absorption, which could include fatigue, joint pains, and various conditions related to vitamin and mineral deficiencies. By cutting out gluten your body will begin to recover gradually; it can take time, so be patient and stick with a gluten-free diet. It is also crucial to assess your diet to ensure it is balanced and that you're getting enough of the full range of nutrients. In the following pages, we outline the principles of a healthy, balanced diet and identify nutrients you should be eating more of. Recipes employ a nutrient boost icon to highlight health benefits, and each features calorie and nutrient analysis so that you can plan a balanced, calorie-controlled diet.

We have selected a broad range of recipes to provide all the meal inspirations for healthy eating, but it should be emphasized that this is not a "diet" book of calorie-restricted recipes. Pies, cakes, pastries, and desserts are the dishes that people who give up gluten can miss the most, yet they tend to be high in calories. In creating gluten-free versions we have been guided by taste, not calorie counts, but just because they're gluten free doesn't mean you should be eating pies and cakes all the time! You'll find plenty of healthy recipes to choose for every day, and the guidelines will show you which dishes to enjoy as a rare treat.

GUIDELINES PER SERVING

- ●●○ Calories
- ●○○ Saturated fat
- ●●○ Salt

Spiced lamb and hummus wraps (page 188)

Ricotta and squash ravioli with sage butter (page 138)

Red velvet cupcakes (page 314)

Chocolate cheesecake (page 296)

FOUR STEPS TO GLUTEN FREE

GET AN APPOINTMENT

If you suspect you may have a problem with gluten but have not yet been diagnosed, read pages 12–15 to learn more about symptoms and conditions, and make an appointment to see your doctor to discuss your concerns. Meanwhile, you must keep eating gluten foods for the medical examination to be effective. If you are diagnosed, ask your doctor to make an appointment for you to see a registered dietitian, who will give you detailed advice about changing to a gluten-free diet and how to ensure it is healthy and balanced. They can also tell you about any vitamin and mineral supplements you might need to take, and will provide you with a list of gluten-free products available on prescription.

GET ORGANIZED

Once diagnosed, it's a good idea to join an organization for people with celiac disease and other gluten issues. They will be able to provide you with up-to-the-minute medical advice, contacts to local support groups, a list of products containing gluten, and details of restaurants that offer gluten-free meals. Next, spend some time examining what you normally eat, identifying where gluten needs to be cut out, and making a menu plan for the week ahead (see page 24). When you're tired at the end of a busy day, you are much more likely to make mistakes with your diet. Planning in advance gives you time to think about what you are going to eat and check that everything is gluten free.

If you think you may benefit from cutting gluten out of your diet, these four steps and the pages that follow will take you from initial diagnosis to your first gluten-free meal.

GET SHOPPING SAVVY

Contact the supermarket where you regularly shop and ask for a list of gluten-free products, or look online. Some supermarkets may even offer a guided tour around the store with a dietitian. If there is a particular product you'd like to see stocked, don't be embarrassed to ask the manager: "free from" is an increasingly lucrative market and it makes business sense for supermarkets to build up their range. You should also get to know your local health food stores and the specialized websites that sell some of the more difficult-to-find gluten-free flours, grains, and other products. International food stores, particularly south and east Asian and Mexican, will also sell a whole host of gluten-free foods.

GET IN THE KITCHEN

You've planned what you're going to eat and sourced all the ingredients, but before you start cooking, you need to turn your kitchen into a gluten-free zone, or at least an environment where the risk of gluten contamination is minimized (see pages 30–31). With the kitchen properly organized, you are ready to cook and will find that the recipes in this book, in addition to being utterly delicious, have been designed to be easy to follow. Extra help can be found on pages 38–47 where step-by-step recipes demonstrate how to make gluten-free bread, cakes, pasta, and pastry. If you're new to cooking, though, you may find it useful to enroll in cooking classes: look out for gluten-free courses.

WHY GO GLUTEN FREE?

CELIAC DISEASE

The most common reason to follow a gluten-free diet is in order to treat celiac disease (CD). Often referred to as an allergy or intolerance, celiac disease is, in fact, an autoimmune disease that occurs when the body's immune system reacts abnormally to gluten and produces antibodies that attack its own tissues. CD affects 1 in 133 adults in the US, although some experts believe that only 1 in 8 people with the condition are clinically diagnosed, which means around 3 million people in the US may have the disease without knowing it. The number of people suffering from celiac disease has quadrupled in the last few decades. This can be partly attributed to greater awareness and better diagnostic techniques, but this does not fully explain the rise.

DIAGNOSIS AND TREATMENT

Celiac disease can occur at any age: symptoms may first appear when a baby starts eating wheat-containing cereals (see page 25), but they can also occur later in life. The disease runs in families and studies show that if a family member has the condition, there is a 1 in 10 chance that a close relative will develop the disease. There is no cure or medication for CD and the only remedy is a strict gluten-free diet. Even a tiny amount of gluten, from particles of flour contaminating a work surface, for instance, is enough to cause problems for some people.

SYMPTOMS OF CELIAC DISEASE

The symptoms of celiac disease can vary from one person to another and can range from mild to severe. Symptoms include:

diarrhea
excessive gas and/or constipation
nausea
vomiting
stomach pain
cramping
bloating
tiredness
headache
mouth ulcers
alopecia (hair loss)
skin rash
unexplained weight loss

Left untreated, celiac disease can increase the risk of other conditions, including infertility, repeated miscarriages, osteoporosis, and depression. Although weight loss is a common symptom of celiac disease, it is not always the case and many people are of normal weight or even overweight when they are diagnosed.

DON'T STOP EATING GLUTEN... YET!

If you suspect you or a family member may have celiac disease do not immediately start cutting gluten from your diet. It is essential to keep eating foods that contain gluten for six weeks before being tested for celiac disease, otherwise you could get a false negative result.

CELIAC DISEASE EXPLAINED

The wall of the small intestine is lined with fleshy projections called "villi," responsible for absorbing nutrients into the body from food. Celiac disease leads to damage of the villi that seriously diminishes their ability to absorb nutrients.

DAMAGE TO SMALL INTESTINE

Healthy intestines

Nutrients passing through the intestines are absorbed through the villi walls into blood vessels

The tonguelike shape of the villi maximizes surface area for absorption

Intestines showing celiac damage

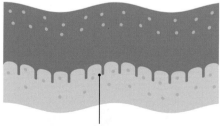

Inflammation causes damage to villi that are unable to absorb nutrients so effectively

The first thing your doctor will want to do is take a simple blood test to check for antibodies to gluten. The next step is a referral to a hospital to see a gastroenterologist who will perform a procedure called a biopsy, which allows the doctor to take a small sample from your intestinal lining for detailed examination. If you are diagnosed with celiac disease your doctor may then refer you to a registered dietitian who will be able to advise you on a gluten-free diet. Some people start to feel better soon after they start on a gluten-free diet; for others it can take several months: everyone is different.

NON-CELIAC GLUTEN SENSITIVITY

While the best-known reaction to gluten is celiac disease, recent research has identified a new, less severe, condition called non-celiac gluten sensitivity. This produces symptoms similar to celiac disease—especially non-intestinal ones such as joint pain and headaches—usually hours after eating gluten-containing foods. Non-celiac gluten sensitivity does not seem to involve the immune system or cause damage to the lining of the gut. If you think you may be affected, do not immediately stop eating gluten (see left). First consult your doctor to rule out celiac disease, then seek advice on a suitable gluten-free diet. Research suggests that there may be six times as many people suffering from non-celiac gluten sensitivity than with celiac disease—and the majority are unaware of the problem.

DERMATITIS HERPETIFORMIS

Dermatitis herpetiformis (DH) is a skin condition characterized by intensely itchy blisters on the buttocks, back of the neck, scalp, elbows, knees, and back. It affects about 1 in 10,000 people in the US, is more common in men than women, and typically appears between the ages of 15 and 40 years. Like celiac disease, it is caused by gluten and managed with a strict gluten-free diet.

OTHER MEDICAL CONDITIONS THAT MAY BENEFIT FROM A GLUTEN-FREE DIET

The use of gluten-free diets for other conditions remains controversial, but many people with conditions listed here feel that experimenting with a gluten-free diet for a trial period may be worth trying. However, no one should embark on a gluten-free diet without first consulting a doctor.

OTHER CONDITIONS WITH A POSSIBLE LINK TO GLUTEN

AUTISM

Although scientific evidence is limited, some children with autistic spectrum disorder (ASD) may benefit from a gluten- and casein-free diet. Much more research is, however, required.

MULTIPLE SCLEROSIS (MS)

Multiple sclerosis is an autoimmune disease and people with MS have a greater risk of suffering from celiac disease, although the use of a gluten-free diet for people with MS remains controversial.

LUPUS

Lupus is another autoimmune disease where the body's immune system becomes hyperactive and attacks healthy tissue. Since celiac disease is also autoimmune, lupus sufferers may be at greater risk of developing it.

IRRITABLE BOWEL SYNDROME (IBS)

The symptoms of celiac disease and irritable bowel syndrome are very similar, and a recent survey carried out by Coeliac UK revealed that nearly 60% of people with celiac disease had previously been incorrectly diagnosed with IBS.

CHRONIC FATIGUE SYNDROME

There is anecdotal evidence that some people with chronic fatigue syndrome find their symptoms improve by adopting a gluten-free diet. It certainly doesn't work for everyone, but may be worth a try.

MISCARRIAGE AND INFERTILITY

Evidence suggests undiagnosed celiac disease could be one cause of infertility and repeated miscarriages. The proportion of women attending fertility clinics found to have undiagnosed CD is greater than in the general population.

STILL UNSURE?—A QUICK Q&A

There are a lot of uncertainties and myths about choosing a gluten-free diet, especially if you feel it's unlikely you are a celiac sufferer or have no symptoms. This Q&A aims to answer some of the most common questions.

! DON'T SELF-DIAGNOSE

Home testing kits and allergy tests available in some health food stores or by mail order are not reliable ways to diagnose celiac disease. If you suspect you have the condition, the first thing you should do is make an appointment with your doctor.

Should I change to a gluten-free diet to lose weight?

Some weight-loss diets advocate avoiding carbohydrates, but there is no scientific evidence to suggest that cutting out gluten helps people lose weight. Weight loss is a common symptom of celiac disease (CD), and when people who have lost weight as a result of undiagnosed CD switch to a gluten-free diet, they often regain the weight they lost.

I often feel tired and bloated after eating. Will I benefit from a gluten-free diet?

Bloating and lethargy are common symptoms associated with celiac disease, but they are also symptoms of other medical conditions and can be caused by lifestyle factors, such as eating too fast. A gluten-free diet is not necessarily the answer. Keeping a food diary may help you to identify other factors. If symptoms persist, discuss with your doctor.

Is it possible to be suffering from celiac disease yet not have any symptoms?

Although uncommon, it is possible. Some experts now talk about a "celiac spectrum." At one end of the spectrum are people who have all the classic symptoms of the condition, while at the other end, people may not be aware of any physical symptoms but may still have damage to the lining of the small intestine. The best advice is to consult a doctor.

Is it beneficial to reduce wheat in my diet even if I have no related medical condition?

Many people eat wheat at breakfast in the form of cereal, again at lunch as a sandwich, and yet again in the evening, for instance, as pasta. Some alternative practitioners believe this overreliance on a single food is a bad idea and can lead to an intolerance or allergy to that food. For this reason it might be a good idea not to rely too heavily on wheat.

ELIMINATING GLUTEN

WHAT IS GLUTEN?

Gluten is a protein found in wheat, rye, and barley and in foods made from these grains, such as cakes, pastry, bread, and pasta. Gluten has qualities useful for cooking and baking, including elasticity, an ability to hold water, and a tendency to hold shape and harden in high heat.

WHAT DOES GLUTEN DO?

It is the gluten in flour that gives bread and baked goods, such as cakes and muffins, their characteristic texture and structure. When flour is mixed with water the gluten becomes elastic, turning the mixture into a soft, stretchy dough that can be kneaded and shaped. Carbon dioxide produced by yeast or baking powder is trapped within the dough and held there by the gluten, enabling breads and cakes to rise and giving them their "airy" texture. Thanks to a miraculous little ingredient called xanthan gum, however, it's possible to mimic the action of gluten in doughs made with gluten-free flours. And by carefully mixing the different gluten-free flours available, and adding additional flavors and glazes, it is possible to recreate the taste, texture, and appearance of all your favorite bakes in gluten-free form. See pages 38–47 for flour blends and illustrated techniques.

GLUTEN-CONTAINING GRAINS

Cultivated grains containing gluten are limited to wheat, spelt (an ancient form of wheat), barley, and rye. Triticale, a hybrid of wheat and rye, also contains gluten and can be found in some health food stores, but is mainly used as an animal feed.

Can I eat oats on a gluten-free diet?

Oats contain a protein similar to gluten but it doesn't seem to cause the same adverse reaction. Celiacs wishing to introduce oats into their diet should start by adding small amounts, but children and severe sufferers should consult a nutritionist first. Oats are often contaminated with gluten during processing, so buy gluten-free brands.

MAIN GLUTEN-CONTAINING PRODUCTS

All biscuits, breads, cakes, chapattis, crackers, muffins, pastries, pizza bases, rolls, and cookies made from wheat, rye, or barley flour

Wheat noodles and pasta

Wheat-based breakfast cereals

Meat and poultry cooked in batter or bread crumbs, e.g., breaded ham, or chicken or veal cutlets

Fish or shellfish coated in batter or bread crumbs, e.g., fish cakes, fishsticks

Yogurts containing granola or cereals

Vegetables and fruit in batter, bread crumbs, or dusted with flour

Potatoes in batter, bread crumbs, or dusted with flour, e.g., potato croquettes

Soy sauce

Ice cream cones and wafers, desserts made using semolina or wheat flour

Stuffing made from bread crumbs

WHEAT *Triticum spp.*
Wheat varieties often have different names: Emmer, Kamut, Einkorn, Faro, Farrina, and Dinkel are all types of wheat. Bulgur wheat (pictured), couscous, and semolina are also made from wheat.

BARLEY *Hordeum vulgare*
Pearl barley can be added to stews and barley flakes are sometimes added to granola. Beer, barley waters, and malted milk drinks all contain barley.

RYE *Secale cereale*
Rye bread and pumpernickel are popular in Germany and eastern Europe. Rye is also used to make flat breads and crackers.

SPELT *Triticum spelta*
An ancient form of wheat that has seen a resurgence in popularity in recent years as a health food. Used in baked goods and beer.

FINDING HIDDEN GLUTEN

Eliminating gluten from your diet is not as simple as cutting out obvious sources of gluten, such as bread and pasta. Wheat and other gluten-containing grains are often used as ingredients in other foods, and in some cases foods that are naturally gluten free can become contaminated with gluten during processing or storage. For this reason, it's important to check the label on certain products and choose brands certified gluten free where contamination is a risk, such as with oats and polenta. Mobile technology can help too—apps that allow you to scan food items when you are shopping to check if ingredients are gluten free are available for both iOS and Android devices. These apps keep you informed while on the go.

CHECKING THE LABEL

The names of some additives used by the food industry can hide the fact they are derived from gluten grains and may not be safe. Look out for the following:

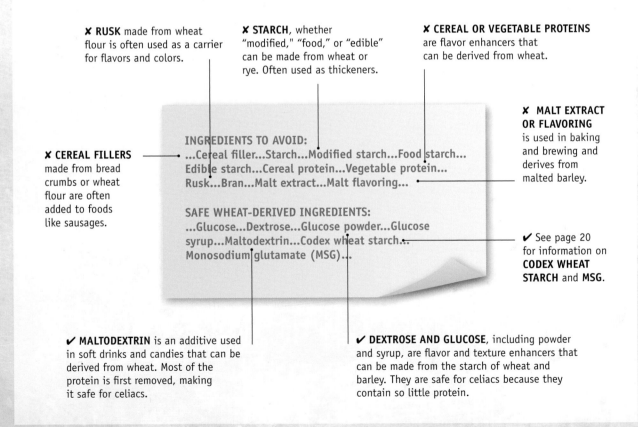

✗ **RUSK** made from wheat flour is often used as a carrier for flavors and colors.

✗ **STARCH**, whether "modified," "food," or "edible" can be made from wheat or rye. Often used as thickeners.

✗ **CEREAL OR VEGETABLE PROTEINS** are flavor enhancers that can be derived from wheat.

✗ **MALT EXTRACT OR FLAVORING** is used in baking and brewing and derives from malted barley.

✗ **CEREAL FILLERS** made from bread crumbs or wheat flour are often added to foods like sausages.

INGREDIENTS TO AVOID:
...Cereal filler...Starch...Modified starch...Food starch...Edible starch...Cereal protein...Vegetable protein...Rusk...Bran...Malt extract...Malt flavoring...

SAFE WHEAT-DERIVED INGREDIENTS:
...Glucose...Dextrose...Glucose powder...Glucose syrup...Maltodextrin...Codex wheat starch...Monosodium glutamate (MSG)...

✔ See page 20 for information on **CODEX WHEAT STARCH** and **MSG**.

✔ **MALTODEXTRIN** is an additive used in soft drinks and candies that can be derived from wheat. Most of the protein is first removed, making it safe for celiacs.

✔ **DEXTROSE AND GLUCOSE**, including powder and syrup, are flavor and texture enhancers that can be made from the starch of wheat and barley. They are safe for celiacs because they contain so little protein.

PRODUCTS THAT MAY CONTAIN HIDDEN GLUTEN

Check closely the packaging of food products listed here for the presence of hidden gluten.

✔ GRAINS AND FLOURS

Sometimes naturally gluten-free grains are milled with wheat, barley, or rye and are thereby contaminated with gluten. These include: buckwheat, chestnut, chickpea, gram, millet, mustard, oats, polenta, potato, quinoa, rice, sorghum, soy, tapioca, teff, and urad dal

✔ BREAKFAST CEREALS

Buckwheat, corn, millet, and rice-based breakfast cereals and those that contain barley malt extract or oats

✔ PRESERVES AND SPREADS

Lemon curd, peanut and other nut butters

✔ FRUITS AND VEGETABLES

Fruit pie fillings and processed vegetable dishes made with sauces, such as cauliflower cheese

✔ DRINKS

Cloudy carbonated drinks, chocolate milk, malted milk

✔ SOUPS AND SAUCES

Canned or packet soups, sauces in jars and packets

Blended seasonings, gravy granules, stock cubes, curry powder, curry paste

Mustard products such as English mustard

Dressings, salad cream, and mayonnaise

✔ DAIRY AND FATS

Coffee and tea milk substitutes

Fruit and flavored yogurts or dairy desserts

Soy desserts, rice milk, soy milk

Some soft, spreadable cheeses

✔ BAKING INGREDIENTS

Cake decorations, marzipan, ready-to-use frosting

Baking powder, baking soda

Suet, vegetarian suet

✔ NUTS AND SAVORY SNACKS

Dry roasted nuts, popcorn (not homemade), potato and vegetable chips, pretzels

Baked beans and other beans in sauce

✔ POTATO PRODUCTS

Frozen fries and potato wedges, instant mashed potatoes, potato waffles, ready-to-roast potatoes

✔ MEAT AND FISH

Any meat or poultry marinated or in a sauce, burgers, meat pastes, pâtés, sausages

Fish pastes, fish pâtés, taramasalata, and fish in sauce

✔ MEATLESS ALTERNATIVES

Marinated tofu, ground soy meat, falafel, vegetable and bean burgers

✔ CAKES AND COOKIES

Store-bought meringe, macaroons, and granola bars are likely to have come into contact with gluten-containing cakes

✔ CONFECTIONERY AND DESSERTS

Chocolates, ice cream, mousses, and all kinds of candies, especially licorice candies

TO EAT OR NOT TO EAT?—A QUICK Q&A

You should now have a good sense of which foods to avoid completely and which to check first, but there will inevitably be many more questions as you examine your diet. Here we try to answer the most common ones. For a comprehensive list of safe products, it is a good idea to consult the Celiac Disease Foundation website.

Is it safe to eat foods cooked in the same oil used to fry foods coated in gluten batters or crumb coatings?

No. The oil can be contaminated with gluten from batter used to coat fish and other foods. Check for gluten-free evenings, however, which are becoming popular with some fast food outlets, when they use gluten-free batter and clean oil to prevent cross contamination.

Are products labeled as wheat-free suitable for someone on a gluten-free diet?

Not necessarily. Wheat is not the only gluten-containing grain and the product may still have rye- or barley-based ingredients, or oats contaminated with gluten.

Is monosodium glutamate (MSG) gluten free?

MSG is a flavor enhancer used in many ready meals, stock cubes, and savory snacks and can be made from wheat. However, during processing, the gluten protein is completely broken down, so MSG is safe for people with celiac disease.

What is codex wheat starch?

Codex wheat starch is added to processed foods to improve their taste and texture. Though made from wheat, it has been processed to contain less than 20 parts per million (ppm) of gluten. Research shows this tiny amount of gluten is not toxic to celiacs.

Do some medicines and supplements contain gluten?

Most medicine and drugs prescribed in the US are gluten free. Although they can sometimes contain wheat starch as a filler, it is highly processed and safe for anyone on a gluten-free diet. If you are buying non-prescription medicines and supplements, however, you should check with a pharmacist.

Can I use malt vinegar?

Although malt vinegar is made from barley, the end product only contains a trace amount of gluten, well below the level that is safe for most people with celiac disease, and is fine to use. Balsamic, cider, sherry, white wine, and red wine vinegars are all safe.

NATURALLY GLUTEN-FREE FOODS

The idea of cutting gluten out of your diet can seem slightly daunting, but all the foods listed here are naturally gluten-free and can still be enjoyed.

MEAT, POULTRY, AND FISH

All fresh meats and poultry ● Cured pure meats, plain cooked meats, smoked meats ● All fresh, dried, and smoked fish, fish canned in brine, oil, or water, and shellfish

FRUIT, VEGETABLES, NUTS, AND SEEDS

All fresh, frozen, canned, dried, and juiced pure fruits and vegetables ● Vegetables pickled in vinegar ● All plain potatoes, baked, steamed, boiled, or mashed ● Plain nuts and seeds, all legumes (peas, beans, lentils, corn)

DAIRY, EGGS, AND FATS

All milk (liquid and dried), all cream (half-and-half, heavy, whipping, sour, and crème fraîche), buttermilk, plain yogurt ● Butter, cooking oils, lard, margarine, reduced and low-fat spreads ● Cheese, eggs

RICE, QUINOA, & OTHER GLUTEN-FREE GRAINS AND FLOURS

All grains, flours, and flour mixes labeled "gluten free," including: amaranth, buckwheat, cassava, chestnut flour, chickpea flour, corn, cornstarch, fava bean flour, gram flour, millet, mustard flour, polenta (cornmeal), potato flour, potato starch, oats (see page 17), quinoa, rice, rice bran, rice flour, sago, sorghum, soy flour, tapioca, tapioca starch, teff, and urad flour—see pages 32–7 for more information

GOOD-BYE TO PASTA, BREAD, CAKES, PASTRY, AND COOKIES?

As more people follow a gluten-free diet, the food industry has responded to their needs by developing an expanding selection of gluten-free products, including cakes, cookies, pasta, ready-made pastry, and bread. Of course, there's no need to rely on ready-made products: you can use commercial gluten-free flour blends—or blend your own (see page 38)—to bake at home, adapt favorite recipes, and try new ones. Some store-bought bakes are better than others, but none can match the taste of homemade.

A BALANCED GLUTEN-FREE DIET

Choosing a balanced diet is important for everyone and a gluten-free diet can be very healthy due to the emphasis placed on fresh and unprocessed foods. A balanced gluten-free diet should include plenty of fruit and vegetables, moderate amounts of lean protein, healthy unsaturated fats, whole grains and unrefined gluten-free carbohydrates, and minimal amounts of saturated fats, salt, and sugar.

TACKLING NUTRIENT DEFICIENCY

Untreated celiac disease can lead to nutritional deficiency in iron, calcium, magnesium, and zinc. When you start on a gluten-free diet make sure it contains foods rich in these nutrients. Standard breakfast cereals and bread are often fortified with these nutrients, as well as B-group vitamins and fiber, but gluten-free versions are rarely fortified and alternative sources should be sought.

IRON

Needed for the manufacture of red blood cells.
Good GF sources of iron include lean red meat, eggs, quinoa, dried fruit, lentils and chickpeas, baked beans, dark green leafy vegetables.

CALCIUM

Needed for strong bones, especially important for children, teenagers, and young adults.
Good GF sources include yogurt, milk, cheese, canned fish eaten with their bones (e.g., sardines), almonds, sesame seeds, tofu.

MAGNESIUM

Helps maintain muscle and nerve function, a healthy immune system, and strong bones.
Good GF sources include nuts and seeds, beans and legumes, brown rice, dark green leafy vegetables.

ZINC

Essential for growth and development, a healthy immune system, and wound healing.
Good GF sources include lean red meat, poultry, eggs, shellfish, beans, and nuts, especially Brazil nuts.

FOLATE
Involved in the production of red blood cells. Found in oranges, green vegetables, chickpeas, legumes.

IRON
Found in red meat, beans, and legumes. The body can more easily absorb iron from nonmeat sources if eaten in conjunction with foods rich in vitamin C.

DIETARY FIBER
Helps to keep the intestine healthy and prevent constipation. Sources include lentils, beans, legumes, quinoa, buckwheat, brown rice, fruit, and veg.

B VITAMINS
Have many vital functions. Sources include potatoes, broccoli, and bananas.

VITAMIN B12
B12 is important for a healthy nervous system and is found in fish, lean red meat, and eggs.

CALCIUM
Found in milk, yogurt, cheese, canned sardines. Choose low- and reduced-fat dairy products when possible.

PLANNING YOUR DIET

Planning a menu for the week ahead enables you to check that everything is gluten free. Aim to eat a wide variety of foods to supply all your nutritional needs, opt for healthy dishes with the occasional treat, and try to prepare fresh meals if possible. Here's a sample 7-day menu plan for guidance and inspiration.

	BREAKFAST	LUNCH	EVENING MEAL
DAY 1	✔ Glass of fruit juice ✔ Gluten-free oatmeal with fresh or dried fruit and nuts (page 53)	✔ Masala dosa and a green salad (page 234) ✔ Fruit yogurt	✔ Lemon and asparagus pasta (page 136) ✔ Lemon sorbet and fresh berries
DAY 2	✔ Glass of fruit juice ✔ Breakfast blueberry muffins (page 74)	✔ Gluten-free toast with hummus ✔ Fresh fruit salad	✔ Creamy chicken crumble (page 180) ✔ Rice pudding
DAY 3	✔ Glass of fruit juice ✔ Granola with apple crisps (page 54)	✔ Quinoa, fava bean, and dill salad (page 124) ✔ Fresh fruit	✔ Haddock and turmeric rice (page 161) ✔ Gluten-free fruit crumble (page 291)
DAY 4	✔ Glass of fruit juice ✔ Gluten-free bread with jam or honey (pages 38 and 216)	✔ Gluten-free minestrone soup with a gluten-free roll (pages 107 and 218–19) ✔ Fruit yogurt	✔ Chicken and parsley pot pies (page 260) ✔ Fresh fruit salad
DAY 5	✔ Glass of fruit juice ✔ Gluten-free granola with fresh fruit (page 52)	✔ Beet and ginger soup (page 110) ✔ Caraway seed bread spread with low-fat soft cheese (page 228)	✔ Sweet and sour chicken with green beans (page 177) ✔ Gluten-free ice cream with fresh fruit (page 299)
DAY 6	✔ Glass of fruit juice ✔ Breakfast berry bars (page 76)	✔ Gluten-free baked beans (page 70) on gluten-free toast ✔ Yogurt with fruit	✔ Mee goreng (page 150) ✔ Banana and gluten-free custard (page 286)
DAY 7	✔ Glass of fruit juice ✔ Scrambled eggs on gluten-free toast	✔ Soba noodle and shrimp salad (page 128) ✔ Fresh fruit	✔ Salmon en croute (page 166) ✔ Gluten-free apple and blackberry pie (page 280)

GLUTEN-FREE DIETS FOR CHILDREN

Cooking for children on a gluten-free diet requires special planning to ensure they get all the nutrients they require, and you will need to meet with carers or school staff to ensure they stay gluten free away from home. When your child is diagnosed, try to explain the condition in terms they understand and involve them in planning their new diet. Encouraging your child to help with the preparation of meals is another good way for them to learn about and enjoy eating gluten free. Children can get upset if they are singled out as being different and it is important to keep their diet as "normal" as possible, while still excluding gluten. A celiac child doesn't have to miss out on all the fun: you will find plenty of recipes in this book perfect for parties, whether you are hosting or sending your child along with their own gluten-free treats to share. And we have highlighted easily adaptable, kid-friendly recipes for every day, which all the family can enjoy. As soon as they are old enough, it's important to give children the independence to manage their own diet.

GREAT
FOR KIDS

Do I need to take vitamin supplements?

The intestinal damage caused by untreated celiac disease frequently leads to many nutritional deficiencies. When you are first diagnosed, your dietitian will probably recommend taking a vitamin and mineral supplement. In serious cases, it may even be necessary to have vitamins injected. Check with your dietitian before taking supplements and make sure the supplements are gluten free.

INTRODUCING GLUTEN INTO A BABY'S DIET

Cereals containing gluten should not be introduced into a baby's diet before they are six months old, but there is no reason to delay the introduction any later than six months. Once a baby begins eating solids, gluten should be included regularly, since celiac disease can only be diagnosed once gluten is established in the diet, and if your child does suffer from celiac disease it's better to discover sooner rather than later.

GLUTEN-FREE DIET AND LACTOSE INTOLERANCE

Lactose intolerance is a common consequence of untreated celiac disease (CD) because the enzyme lactase, which is needed for the digestion of lactose (a sugar found in milk), is made in the area of the intestine that is damaged by gluten. Without lactase, lactose passes unchanged into the large intestine where the bacteria that naturally live there metabolize it, and in the process produce large amounts of gas. Symptoms of lactose intolerance include bloating, stomach cramps, diarrhea, and flatulence and usually occur 30 minutes to 2 hours after eating or drinking milk products. Lactose intolerance associated with CD is usually temporary because, once established on a gluten-free diet, the intestines start to heal. However, it can take up to two years for lactase production to return to normal. Lactose intolerance is treated by avoiding or restricting lactose in the diet. Lactose can occur in unexpected sources, such as fries, cookies, and some medicines, which you wouldn't think contained milk, so always check labels carefully. Dairy products provide a lot of calcium in the diet and you will need to replace them with plenty of non-lactose sources. You should also discuss the need for supplements with your doctor.

NON-LACTOSE SOURCES OF CALCIUM

NUTS AND SEEDS ▶
Almonds, hazelnuts, Brazil nuts, and walnuts are all particularly high in calcium, as are sunflower seeds and sesame seeds.

◀ DRIED FRUITS
Dried fruits tend to contain more calcium than most fresh fruit. Figs are a particularly rich source, but apricots, dates, and prunes also provide good amounts.

HARD CHEESE ▶
Traditionally made, aged hard cheeses, such as Parmesan, contain only small amounts of lactose and may be more easily tolerated.

GREEN LEAFY VEGETABLES ▲
Leafy greens such as broccoli, cabbage, kale, and chard are calcium-rich, but avoid spinach, which contains a chemical that interferes with the absorption of calcium.

GLUTEN-FREE DIET AND DIABETES

Celiac disease and dermatitis herpetiformis are both more common in people with type 1 diabetes. This is probably due to a shared genetic risk for both conditions. Celiac disease associated with diabetes is often the latent type that exhibits no symptoms and is often only discovered during screening. Unexplained hypoglycemia (low blood sugar) and poor blood sugar control, particularly in young children, can be a symptom of undiagnosed celiac disease. If you have both type 1 diabetes and celiac disease, it is even more important that you see a registered dietitian regularly, and one who specializes in both conditions, as each requires ongoing review and management. When first diagnosed with celiac disease, a person with diabetes will need to monitor their blood sugar levels more closely, as once the intestine starts to heal, it will begin to absorb more carbohydrate, and insulin levels often need to be adjusted to reflect this. The principles of a healthy diabetic diet are the same for people who also have a gluten intolerance, the only difference being that unrefined carbohydrates must obviously be non-gluten (see opposite).

The American Diabetes Association (www.diabetes.org) has a range of useful literature designed for people with both diabetes and celiac disease.

PRINCIPLES OF A HEALTHY DIABETIC DIET

◀ GET YOUR 5-A-DAY
Aim to eat a minimum of 5 portions of fruit and vegetables each day.

EAT MORE HEALTHY FATS ▶ Replace saturated with unsaturated fats, found in foods including nuts, seeds, avocados, and olive oil.

REDUCE SALT INTAKE ▶
Use strongly flavored ingredients such as chiles to replace salt.

◀ REDUCE SUGAR INTAKE
Wean yourself off sugar or replace it with lower-GI alternatives such as fructose.

EAT MORE UNREFINED CARBS ▶
Choose low-GI gluten-free carbs like brown rice.

GLUTEN FREE ON THE GO

EATING AT A RESTAURANT

Eating out may seem a little daunting when you first start on a gluten-free diet. Follow a few simple ground rules, however, and there is absolutely no reason why you can't enjoy dining out at restaurants just as much as before.

6 TIPS FOR DINING OUT

 ASK AROUND If you have joined a celiac group, ask local members if they can recommend restaurants in your area that cater to gluten-free diets.

 LOOK ONLINE Many online review sites now list gluten-free restaurants. You will also often find menus published online to check ahead.

 GET IN TOUCH Contact the restaurant at least 24 hours before you intend to visit, to check whether they are properly set up for gluten-free cooking.

 DON'T BE SHY Emphasize to the restaurant just how important it is for you to remain gluten free. Try to talk to the chef to confirm what's in each dish.

 CHECK THEIR SET-UP Explain that even a tiny amount of gluten flour is harmful and ask if they have kitchen systems to guard against cross contamination.

 BYO If you want to bring your own gluten-free bread to eat at the start of the meal, ask ahead and confirm again with the waiter when you arrive.

How do I stay gluten free traveling abroad?

What about takeout?

At fast-food outlets you need to be certain everything you ask for is cooked in fresh oil. Prepared meats are usually not suitable and if they use frozen fries these are often coated in flour. Many dishes from Indian takeout will be fine to eat, provided they use fresh ingredients and whole spices. Watch out for soy sauce in Chinese food.

If you have joined a celiac organization, it should be able to provide you with country-specific leaflets about gluten-free eating abroad, including language translations with useful phrases to help when you are dining out. It's always worth packing emergency gluten-free snacks, however, and items such as pasta and bread in your suitcase.

GLUTEN-FREE PACKED LUNCH

A growing number of cafés are beginning to offer gluten-free choices, but they are few and far between and you may pay extra for the privilege. Packing your own lunch and snacks is often the best option, and providing your child with a packed lunch will help reassure you that they are eating well and staying gluten free away from home.

NUTS
A handful of nuts provide healthy fats and protein. Avoid roasted nuts, which can contain flour.

DRIED FRUIT
Ready-to-eat dried fruit, such as apricots, are a good source of dietary fiber, but do contain concentrated sugars, so go easy.

FRESH FRUIT
An apple or other piece of fresh fruit is the perfect gluten-free and healthy choice for snacking.

BREAKFAST BARS
Granola bars made with oats and crispy rice are great for breakfast on the go or a midmorning snack (see pages 75–6).

SANDWICH
Baking your own bread for sandwiches will make eating them a treat, not a chore. Bake a few loaves at a time and freeze them for several weeks' supply (see pages 38–9 and 216–19).

HOMEMADE SWEET TREATS
Treat yourself to a homemade cookie or slice of cake a couple of times a week: teacakes are a healthy, low-fat option (see pages 328–9 and 332–9).

6 SNACKING TIPS FOR KIDS

1 SEND THEM PREPARED Make sure you always send your kids off with plenty of gluten-free snacks in case there is nothing else suitable to eat.

2 OFFER VARIETY Children can quickly get bored with eating the same snacks, so try to provide them with a changing menu across the week.

3 GO NATURAL If your child is concerned about feeling different, include naturally gluten-free snacks like cheese portions, sesame bars, popcorn, and smoothies.

4 MAKE AT HOME Cakes and cookies are easy and fun for children to bake at home, and they will be excited to eat a snack they've made themselves.

5 DON'T SPOIL THE PARTY Secretly bring some gluten-free snacks and treats when you drop off your child at a party, so they don't miss out on a party bag.

6 TEACH INDEPENDENCE Make sure older children know what to look for on the ingredients list, so they can choose suitable snacks for themselves.

SETTING UP A GLUTEN-FREE KITCHEN

One of the most important things you learn when you are first diagnosed with celiac disease is that even tiny traces of gluten can be enough to cause problems. This means that if you are preparing both gluten-free and ordinary meals, you will need to set up a "dual use" kitchen and adopt some simple cleaning and food preparation habits to prevent food becoming contaminated with gluten.

DEEP CLEAN

When first going gluten free, empty out all cupboards and clear surfaces, then scrub the kitchen thoroughly from top to bottom, to get rid of any gluten flours and crumbs that might be lurking in unseen places. Repeat the process regularly throughout the year.

KEEP IT SEPARATE

Use a separate board for cutting gluten-free bread and other baked goods. Plastic boards are easier to clean than wooden ones, which have tiny pores where crumbs will remain.

PACK IT AWAY

Store both gluten and gluten-free dry goods, like flour and pasta, in separate airtight containers and, if possible, keep in separate cupboards. Make sure everything is clearly labeled as gluten free or not, and if you need to retain cooking instructions you can tape the relevant part of the label to the container. Always keep extra plastic containers on hand for fresh items like cookies, cupcakes, and leftovers. Chilled and frozen items with a contamination risk should also be placed in separate containers or labeled plastic bags.

KITCHEN TIPS

- ✔ If you share a kitchen with non-celiacs, make sure everyone understands the rules.

- ✔ If you're preparing two meals, prepare the gluten-free version first to avoid any possibility of cross contamination.

- ✔ Gluten is invisible to the naked eye, so always wipe down surfaces before you start cooking.

- ✔ For the same reason, it's advisable to wash pans and other equipment with detergent and hot water before using, or keep separate sets.

- ✔ Gluten remains in oil after frying, so always fry gluten-free first or, better still, use fresh oil.

- ✔ To avoid contamination from oven racks, baking sheets, and griddle pans, cover first with a fresh piece of aluminum foil.

BREAD MAKERS

If you intend to make your own gluten-free bread, a bread maker can be a convenient way of ensuring a steady supply. Look for models with a special setting for gluten-free breads and cakes. You will need to keep the machine exclusively for gluten-free baking.

COLOR CODE

It can be difficult to wash away all traces of gluten from equipment like colanders, serving tongs, and serving spoons, and you may find it helpful to keep a set exclusively for gluten-free cooking. Buy color-coded sets so it's absolutely clear which is gluten free.

BAG YOUR TOAST

Ideally, you should keep separate toasters for gluten-free and ordinary bread, but if space is an issue you can use toaster bags to prevent cross contamination.

DON'T DOUBLE DIP!

Always use separate, clean knives and spoons when, for example, spreading butter and jam onto toast. Don't return the same cutlery to the jar or spread or you will contaminate it with gluten-containing crumbs.

GLUTEN-FREE GRAINS

A trip to a good health food store or a large, well-stocked supermarket will reveal a huge range of gluten-free grains that are nutritious, tasty, and extremely versatile. Exploring the many nongluten grains can transform going gluten free into an opportunity to discover a new world of tastes and textures.

BUCKWHEAT *Fagopyrum esculentum*

Despite the name, buckwheat is not related to wheat and does not contain gluten: it is a seed from a plant that is a relative of rhubarb. Buckwheat groats are buckwheat kernels stripped of their inedible outer coating and then crushed into smaller pieces. Unprocessed groats are slightly bitter, so before you cook them it's a good idea to toast them in oil for a few minutes; this removes the bitterness and brings out a pleasant, nutty flavor. Buckwheat groats can be used as an alternative to couscous.

RICE *Oryza sativa*

There are many different varieties of rice including basmati, sticky, red, brown, and risotto, all of which are gluten free. In addition to being served plain as an accompaniment, rice can be used to make sweet and savory dishes such as pilaf, risotto, and rice pudding. It can also be made into rice flour, noodles, pancakes, spring roll wrappers, and rice cakes. Brown rice is a wholegrain cereal and contains more vitamins, minerals, and fiber than refined white rice, from which the germ and bran are removed.

OATS *Avena sativa*

Compared to other cereals, oats contain higher levels of both protein and fat. They also provide useful amounts of B vitamins and the minerals calcium, magnesium, iron, and zinc. Oats are rich in beta glucan, a type of soluble fiber that can help to reduce high blood cholesterol levels. Whole oats or oat groats take 1¼ hours to cook, retaining their shape but turning creamy. They make a delicious addition to meat or vegetable stews, and precooked oats can be baked into coarse-grain bread doughs.

AMARANTH *Amaranthus spp.*

A seed rather than true grain, amaranth is rich in protein and provides useful amounts of calcium, iron, and magnesium, with more fiber than other gluten-free grains. Amaranth has a slightly peppery, nutty flavor and sticky texture. It can be cooked as a cereal, ground into flour, popped like popcorn, sprouted, or toasted. The seeds can be added to stir-fries, soups, and stews as a thickening agent.

SAGO *Metroxylon sagu*

Extracted from the spongy center of tropical palm stems grown in Papua New Guinea and Southeast Asia, sago is virtually pure carbohydrate and offers very little protein, vitamins, minerals, or fiber. Sago pearls are small grains similar to tapioca and can be used to make desserts. Sago can also be ground into flour, which can be used to make pancakes, baked goods, noodles, or for thickening stews or gravies.

QUINOA *Chenopodium quinoa*

Sacred to the Incas, quinoa has been cultivated in South America since 3,000 BCE. It is extremely high in protein and provides useful amounts of phosphorus, calcium, iron, vitamin E, and B vitamins, as well as fiber. With a delicious nutty flavor and pleasant texture, quinoa can be boiled and used instead of rice for salads or pilafs, to make stuffings, as an accompaniment to stews, or added to breakfast cereals. It is also available as flour.

MILLET *Pennisetum glaucum*

Millet is a small, round, yellow grain containing useful amounts of protein, vitamins, minerals, and fiber. A staple food in many parts of Africa and Asia, where it is eaten as a oatmeal or used to make bread, it has a fairly mild flavor and can be used in breakfast cereals or for dishes such as pilaf. It can be ground and made into flour for Indian-style breads like rotis.

WILD RICE *Zizania spp.*

Wild rice is not actually rice but the seeds of freshwater grass. It contains twice as much protein as rice, and higher levels of B vitamins, zinc, iron, and fiber. The long, thin black seeds have a distinctive nutty, slightly woody flavor, and a chewy texture. It can be cooked and served in the same way as ordinary rice, although it takes about 10 minutes longer to cook. Try mixing half and half with basmati rice.

KASHA *Fagopyrum esculentum*

Kasha, not to be confused with kamut, a variety of wheat, is the Russian name for a wholegrain cereal made from roasted whole buckwheat groats. Toasting the groats helps to remove buckwheat's natural bitterness and to bring out a sweeter, nuttier flavor. They come whole or crushed into a coarse, medium, or fine grain.

GLUTEN-FREE FLOURS

Wheat is not the only flour. Around the world, and often for thousands of years, people have been producing and using flours from an array of nonwheat grains, seeds, nuts, beans, and vegetables. Learn how to cook with them, get to know their distinctive qualities, and create your favorite blends for baking.

CORNMEAL FLOUR

Cornmeal flour is made from corn kernels that have been dried, soaked in lime water, washed, and ground into a coarse flour. Stoneground cornmeal retains some of the bran and germ of the dried kernels that standard milling removes, and thus tends to have a better flavor and nutrient value. Cornmeal flour is a good ingredient to use as a crumb coating for fried foods and in addition can be used to make corn tortillas (try to source the authentic Mexican variety masa harina), pancakes, muffins, and corn bread. Popcorn is made from a special hard variety of corn kernel and is a good gluten-free snack.

OATMEAL

Oatmeal is produced by milling the hulled whole oats. The grains are milled to different levels of fineness: coarse oatmeal can be used for stuffings, thickening soups and stews, and sprinkling in place of bread crumbs over dishes to be gratinéed; medium oatmeal is the most versatile for baking and gives an even coating to fried fish; fine oatmeal can be worked to a smooth texture suitable for pancakes, pastry, and gravies. Always chose oatmeals marked gluten-free, since they can be contaminated in the milling process.

CORNSTARCH

Not to be confused with cornmeal, cornstarch is the pure starch extracted from corn kernels. Almost tasteless and easily blended with liquids without the need for additional fat, the fine white powder is commonly used as a thickener for sauces but can be mixed with other flours for baking.

CORNMEAL (COARSE)

Coarsely ground cornmeal, also known as polenta, can be cooked as a savory accompaniment, either boiled to produce an "oatmeal" (wet polenta) or left to set then cut into slabs and fried or grilled. Coarse cornmeal can also be used in conjunction with other flours in baked goods, but instant or quick-cook varieties have a grittier, crunchy texture that is less appealing in cakes.

BUCKWHEAT FLOUR

Buckwheat is higher in protein than other gluten-free flours and has a strong, slightly sweet taste and speckled appearance. Japanese soba noodles are traditionally made with buckwheat flour and it is also good for making pancakes, blinis, and pasta.

TAPIOCA FLOUR

Low in protein and other nutrients, tapioca flour is almost pure starch and largely flavorless. It can be used by itself to make puddings and to thicken soups or sauces, or blended with other gluten-free flours for baking. Tapioca also makes a crisp, golden crust when used as a batter or "bread" coating for fried food.

CHESTNUT FLOUR

Made from the ground whole nuts, chestnut flour is high in fiber, healthy fats, and protein, and contributes additional texture, moisture, and a slightly sweet flavor to cakes and cookies. Chestnut flour is also good for making pancakes.

ALMOND FLOUR

Made by grinding blanched almonds, almond flour is high in fiber, healthy fats, and protein, and provides good amounts of calcium. Use it in gluten-free baking to add extra flavor, moisture, and texture, and for improving nutritional value.

SOY FLOUR

Soy flour is made from ground soybeans and comes in defatted, low fat, and full-fat varieties. An excellent source of protein and B vitamins, it has a strong "beany" flavor and is best used in combination with other flours.

BROWN RICE FLOUR

Brown rice flour can be used in the same way as white rice flour but it has a more grainy texture and stronger, nutty flavor that helps to provide a "whole-wheat" taste and texture when used in flour blends for baking.

POTATO FLOUR

Also called potato starch or farina, potato flour helps retain moisture and gives a fine, light texture to baked goods. It also makes an excellent thickening agent. Like cornstarch and tapioca, potato flour is high in refined carbohydrates and low in fiber and nutrients.

WHITE RICE FLOUR

White rice flour has a mild flavor and can be used as a sauce thickener in the same way as cornstarch: simply mix first with cold water before adding to the sauce and cooking until thickened. It is also used, particularly in Asian cooking, to make dumplings, pancakes, cakes, and sweets. "Ground rice" is also made from white rice and has a slightly grittier texture that helps give a crispy finish to pastries and cookies.

URAD DAL FLOUR

Milled from urad beans, urad dal flour is a protein-rich staple of South Indian cooking where it is used to make dosas, uttapams, idli, and papadums. The flour can also be used in conjunction with other flours in flatbreads, as a thickener, and added to soups and purees for additional protein.

CHICKPEA FLOUR

Also known as gram or besan flour, chickpea flour is high in protein and fiber, and has a distinctive "beany" flavor. It is widely used in Indian cuisine to make the batter for bhajis and pakoras, and in papadums and breads. Chickpea flour is also useful for thickening soups and sauces, but should be mixed with other flours for general baking.

SORGHUM FLOUR

Milled from grains of sorghum, a cereal crop, sorghum flour is a high-protein flour with a smooth texture and bland taste. It is best mixed with other gluten-free flours in small proportions to provide extra protein.

TEFF FLOUR

High in protein and fiber, and with a slightly sweet, nutty flavor, teff flour is made from the seeds of a grass native to Ethiopia. The flour can be used in combination with other gluten-free flours in baking. The whole seeds can be used to make oatmeal, added to soups or stews, or served as an accompaniment instead of rice, millet, or bulgur wheat. Teff also provides useful amounts of iron, calcium, magnesium, and zinc.

OTHER USEFUL INGREDIENTS

Going gluten free is a great opportunity for many people to bake at home for the first time. In addition to raising agents common to all baking, a gluten-free baker needs extra ingredients to help replace the elastic quality of gluten-containing flours.

GLUTEN-FREE BAKING POWDER

Used in cake baking, once activated by the liquid in a cake mix, baking powder undergoes a chemical reaction that produces carbon dioxide gas to help the cake rise.

GLUTEN-FREE BAKING SODA

Baking soda is similar to baking powder but requires the addition of the natural acid in ingredients such as buttermilk or yogurt to produce the same chemical reaction.

YEAST

Yeast is a living microorganism, which, when added to dough, creates the carbon dioxide that causes bread to rise. Available fresh or dried, fast-action dried yeast is probably the most useful for novice bakers.

XANTHAN GUM

Xanthan gum helps gluten-free doughs to bind together and adds some elasticity, making bread less crumbly and pastry easier to roll and handle. Buy it online, in health food stores, or large supermarkets. Guar gum has similar properties but can be more difficult to source.

ARROWROOT

A white starch made from the root of a tropical herb, arrowroot helps to bind ingredients together, adding body and texture to baked goods. It is also useful as a clear thickener for soups and sauces.

BAKING BREAD

Homemade gluten-free bread is far superior to store-bought. The right blend of flours is key, as is the inclusion of xanthan gum, which enables the dough to rise. Suggested flour blends for white and brown bread are included below, but you can experiment with your own mix, or buy preblended. If blending your own, scale up as required and store in an airtight container; keep only until the earliest use-by date of the flours.

MAKES	1 loaf
PREP	20 mins
	PLUS RISING
COOK	45 mins
FREEZE	3 months

oil for greasing
2¾ cups gluten-free
  white bread flour
  blend (see below),
  plus extra for dusting
2 tsp fast-acting
  dried yeast
1 tsp salt
1 tbsp granulated sugar
1 egg
2 tbsp vegetable oil
1 tsp vinegar
1 egg, beaten, for brushing

SPECIAL EQUIPMENT
9 x 5in (23 x 12cm) loaf pan

BREAD FLOUR BLENDS

Makes 4½ cups
White bread flour
2¾ cups white rice flour
⅔ cup potato flour
½ cup tapioca flour
½ cup cornstarch
4 tsp xanthan gum
Brown bread flour
2¾ cups brown
  rice flour
⅔ cup potato flour
½ cup tapioca flour
½ cup cornstarch
4 tsp xanthan gum

CLASSIC WHITE LOAF

This moist, springy loaf slices well for sandwiches and makes great toast, too. The bread will keep for 2–3 days wrapped in a plastic bag. Turn any leftovers into bread crumbs and store in the freezer to use in stuffings, coatings for fried food, and so on. If you like, double the quantities and bake two loaves at the same time, then freeze one.

1 Lightly oil the pan. Sift together the flour, yeast, and salt into a large bowl, then stir in the sugar. Measure 1¼ cups lukewarm water into a liquid measuring cup, add the egg, oil, and vinegar and whisk together with a fork.

2 Make a well in the center of the dry ingredients and add the wet ingredients. Draw the flour into the liquid with a wooden spoon, mix well, and then bring together with your hands to form a dough.

3 Turn the dough out onto a lightly floured surface and knead for about 5 minutes, or until smooth. To knead, hold the dough with one hand and stretch it with the palm of the other hand, then bring it back together, turn, and repeat.

4 Shape the dough into a rectangle roughly the size and shape of the pan and place it in the pan. Make 3 or 4 slashes on the top with a sharp knife. Cover with oiled plastic wrap and leave in a warm place to rise for 1 hour, or until doubled.

5 Preheat the oven to 425°F (220°C). Brush the top of the loaf with egg—this will help to color it, since gluten-free bread tends to bake to a paler color than standard bread—and sprinkle with a little flour.

6 Bake for 35 minutes or until the loaf is risen and golden brown on top. Remove from the pan, transfer to a baking sheet, and bake for another 10 minutes to crisp the crust. Remove from the oven and leave to cool on a wire rack.

BAKING CAKES

Gluten-free self-rising flour has made baking gluten-free cakes easier, helping to provide good lift and a light texture, although it is not all that readily available. As with traditional baking, it is crucial to beat thoroughly to incorporate air into the mix. To blend your own self-rising flour, add 3–4 teaspoons xanthan gum and ¼ cup baking powder for every 4½ cups of all-purpose flour.

SERVES	8
PREP	15 mins
COOK	25–30 mins
FREEZE	3 months
	SPONGES ONLY

12 tbsp unsalted butter, softened, plus extra for greasing
¾ cup granulated sugar
3 eggs
1¼ cups gluten-free all-purpose flour, plus 1 tsp baking powder, and ½ tsp salt
3 tbsp milk
1 tsp pure vanilla extract
5 tbsp strawberry jam
confectioner's sugar, for dusting

SPECIAL EQUIPMENT
2 x 8in (20cm) round cake pans

VARIATIONS

Orange
Omit the vanilla extract and milk, and instead add the finely grated zest and juice of 1 orange at the same time as the flour. Sandwich together with quality marmalade.

Chocolate
Replace ⅓ cup of the flour with cocoa powder and bake and cool as described. Sandwich together with gluten-free chocolate spread or fresh whipped cream.

VICTORIA SPONGE

This buttery, vanilla-scented sponge cake has a light, fluffy texture and (if it's not eaten in a single session!) can be stored in an airtight container for 3–4 days. Strawberry jam is a classic filling, but you can use whatever jam you have in the pantry. You could also fill with whipped cream and fresh fruit, but eat this version on the same day.

1 Preheat the oven to 350°F (180°C). Lightly grease the pans and line the bases with parchment paper. Cream together the butter and sugar with an electric mixer until the mixture is pale, light, and fluffy.

2 Add the eggs one at a time, beating well between additions, until the mixture is well combined and fluffy. If required, add 1–2 tablespoons flour with the last egg to stop the mixture from curdling.

3 Add the remaining flour, milk, and pure vanilla extract to the bowl. Mix in with an electric mixer for 1 minute until thoroughly incorporated and no trace of flour remains.

4 Take the prepared pans and divide the mixture equally between them. Spread the mixture out to the edges of the pans and use the spoon or a spatula to even the tops.

5 Bake in the preheated oven for 25–30 minutes. When ready, the cakes should look golden and spring back when lightly touched in the center; alternatively, a metal skewer inserted into the center of the cake should come out clean. Leave to cool in the pans for 5 minutes.

6 Carefully remove the cakes from the pans, peel away the lining paper, and cool completely on a wire rack. To finish, transfer one of the cakes to a serving plate, spread the jam over the top, and sandwich with the second cake. Dust with confectioner's sugar to serve.

MAKING PASTA

Making your own pasta is time-consuming but hugely rewarding, and the results are a world apart from the dried gluten-free pasta available to buy. If pasta is your passion, it is well worth investing in a pasta machine (or dusting off the one you've never used!). Set aside time to make a large batch and freeze in individual portions; fresh pasta freezes well and can be cooked straight from frozen.

MAKES 12oz (350g)
PREP 40 mins
COOK 3–4 mins

¾ cup tapioca flour
¾ cup cornstarch
3 tbsp potato flour
3 tsp xanthan gum
½ tsp salt
3 large eggs
2 tbsp olive oil
gluten-free all-purpose flour,
  for dusting

SPECIAL EQUIPMENT
pasta machine with
  tagliatelle attachment

FRESH EGG PASTA

Here the pasta dough is formed into tagliatelle. Other standard cutter attachments include spaghetti and fettuccine, but the rolled pasta can be formed into any shape or left flat for lasagne sheets and ravioli. If not using immediately, place the pasta on baking sheets dusted with cornmeal; cover with plastic wrap or a dish towel. Leave for up to 4 hours.

1 Sift the flours, xanthan, and salt into a large bowl. In another bowl, beat together the eggs and oil. Make a well in the center of the flours, then pour in the egg and oil mix.

2 Use a palette knife or round-bladed table knife to draw the flour into the liquid. Mix until it starts to bind, then finally bring it together with your hands to form a dough.

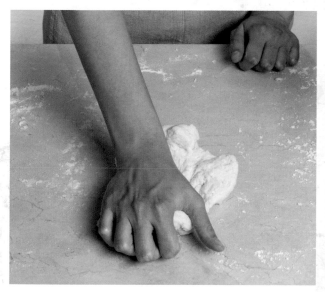

3 Transfer the dough to a lightly floured surface and knead gently until it becomes smooth. Wrap tightly in plastic wrap and leave to rest for 10 minutes. Unwrap the dough and divide it into 4 equal pieces.

4 Take one of the pieces of dough and, using a rolling pin, roll it out to a long strip, about 5in (12cm) wide and ¼in (5mm) thick. Set aside and cover with a damp, clean dish towel, as you repeat the process with the remaining dough.

5 Dusting well with more flour, pass each strip of dough through a pasta machine 4 times. Adjust the dial by a stop each time until the pasta is really thin; don't worry if a few holes appear. Dust and set aside each sheet.

6 Attach the cutter and pass the flour-dusted strips through the machine to form the tagliatelle. To cook, bring a large pan of water to a rolling boil, add the pasta, and cook for 3–4 minutes; the pasta should still have some "bite."

MAKING PASTRY

Though a little more delicate to handle than traditional pastry, with practice you will soon master the art of gluten-free pastry and the results are well worth the effort. The addition of egg and xanthan gum helps the dough to bind, making it easier to roll out and giving the cooked pastry a crisp, flaky consistency that is almost indistinguishable from pastry made with wheat flour.

MAKES 14oz (400g)
ENOUGH FOR A
MEDIUM TART CRUST

PREP 20 mins
COOK 20 mins
PLUS CHILLING

1⅓ cups gluten-free
all-purpose flour, plus
extra for dusting
1 tsp xanthan gum
pinch of salt
7 tbsp cold butter,
cubed
1 large egg, beaten

SPECIAL EQUIPMENT
9in (23cm) round tart pan,
ceramic baking beans
(optional, see step 5)

VARIATION

Sweet shortcrust pastry
Add 2 tbsp powdered
sugar with the flour
before blending into
crumbs. After blind
baking, brush the pastry
crust with egg wash
from 1 egg, beaten,
and bake for another
5 minutes to make
it crisp.

SHORTCRUST PASTRY

The pastry dough is here used to "blind" bake a crust for tarts and quiches, but it is also perfect for making single and double crust pies and tartes Tatin. If you get a few cracks and holes as you lift the pastry and line the pan, simply patch them up with excess pastry and "glue" together with a little water to seal.

1 Preheat the oven to 400°F (200°C). Sift the flour, xanthan, and salt into a bowl and mix. Add the butter and rub it in with your fingertips until the mixture forms crumbs. Alternatively, you can do this by pulsing the mixture in a food processor.

2 Add the egg and mix it in with a palette knife or round-bladed table knife. Gradually add 1–2 tablespoons cold water, a few drops at a time, mixing after each addition. Keep adding water and mixing until it just comes together to form a dough.

3 Transfer the dough to a floured surface and briefly and lightly knead until smooth. Wrap in plastic wrap and chill in the fridge for 10 minutes. Roll out the pastry on a lightly floured surface until it is about ¼in (5mm) thick and large enough to fill the pan.

4 Carefully wrap the pastry around the rolling pin, lift over the pan, and unroll the pastry. To line the pan, gently press the pastry into the base and sides, pressing it into the flutes if you are using a fluted pan. Trim the edges, repair any holes, and prick the base with a fork.

5 Line the pastry with parchment paper and weigh down the parchment with ceramic baking beans (or you can use ordinary dried beans, such as chickpeas). Place on a baking sheet and bake in the preheated oven for 15 minutes.

6 Remove the tart from the oven and carefully lift out the parchment and beans. Return to the oven for another 5 minutes to crisp up, then add the filling of your choice and bake as per recipe instructions.

ROUGH PUFF PASTRY

MAKES 14oz (400g)
PREP 30 mins
PLUS CHILLING

8 tbsp butter, wrapped
  in foil and frozen for 1 hour
  until hard
1 cup gluten-free all-purpose
  flour, plus extra for dusting
large pinch of salt
1 tsp xanthan gum

1 Sift the flour, xanthan, and salt into a large bowl. Unwrap the butter and, still holding it in the foil (this stops the heat of your hand from melting it), coarsely grate it into the flour.

2 Stir the butter and flour until well mixed. Gradually add ½ cup ice-cold water, stirring with a palette knife or round-bladed table knife until it forms a dough.

3 On a floured surface, briefly knead the dough into a ball, then wrap in plastic wrap and chill in the fridge for 10 minutes. Roll out the pastry to a rectangle 8 x 14in (20 x 35cm).

4 Mentally divide the pastry into thirds, or you could lightly score it with the back of a knife. Fold the bottom third of the pastry up over the middle third.

5 Take the top third of the pastry and fold it down over the bottom third. Lightly press together the edges to seal the "parcel."

6 Give the dough a quarter turn. Roll out again and fold as before, wrap in plastic wrap, and chill in the fridge for 20 minutes.

HOT WATER CRUST

MAKES 1lb 2oz (500g)
PREP 20 mins

2 cups gluten-free all-purpose flour, plus extra for dusting
2 tsp xanthan gum
1 tsp salt
3 tbsp milk
3½oz (100g) lard or white vegetable fat
1 egg

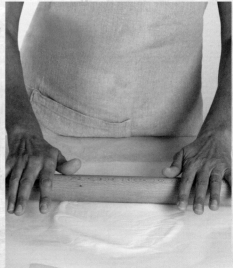

1 Sift the flour, xanthan, and salt into a large bowl. Gently heat 1 cup water with the milk and lard until just boiling. Pour the hot liquid into the flour and quickly beat with a wooden spoon until it forms a dough.

2 Turn the dough out onto a lightly floured surface and knead gently until smooth. This pastry can be sticky and difficult to handle, and when rolling out you may find it easier to roll between sheets of parchment paper.

RECIPES

The recipes in this book have been selected, devised, and tested to provide delicious gluten-free replacements to many favorite dishes normally made with gluten-containing grains, or where the store-bought variety often include added gluten. We have also sought to offer a wide range of options for dishes that use ingredients from grains that don't contain glutens, and some gluten-free versions of takeout favorites.

A "Guidelines per serving" chart is provided for each recipe, weighted according to the type of meal and the proportion of daily intake you should be getting from that meal. This tells you at a glance whether the recipe is high (3 dots), medium (2 dots), or low (1 dot) in calories, saturated fat, and salt—three key areas to watch for a healthy diet. If you choose a recipe that is high in any of these areas, aim to choose dishes that are medium or low in those areas for the rest of the day. Each recipe also has a "Statistics per serving" breakdown of the number of calories and amount of protein, fat, carbohydrate, sugar, fiber, and salt in the dish. So if you really need to crunch the numbers, you can make sure you're getting the exact balance.

Flours and other ingredients made from gluten-free grains, such as rice noodles and cornmeal, are assumed to be gluten free in the ingredients lists, but always check the label, since there can be a risk of contamination with gluten grains at the milling stage.

BREAKFAST
AND
SNACKS

MUESLI WITH TOASTED COCONUT

SERVES 6
PREP 15 mins
COOK 5 mins

GUIDELINES PER SERVING

● ● ● Calories
● ● ● Saturated fat
● ● ○ Salt

STATISTICS PER SERVING

Energy 557kcals/2322kJ

Protein 12g

Fat 34g
Saturated fat 14g

Carbohydrate 49g
Sugar 29g

Fiber 10g

Salt trace

The sticky dates add a toffee-flavored sweetness to this super-healthy mix of flakes, seeds, fruits, and nuts.

2½oz (75g) rice flakes
2½oz (75g) buckwheat flakes
2½oz (75g) milled ground flax seed
6oz (175g) soft pitted dates, chopped
2½oz (75g) sour cherries
4½oz (125g) Brazil nuts,
  roughly chopped

1¾oz (50g) sunflower seeds
3½oz (100g) dried
  unsweetened coconut
milk, Greek yogurt, and fresh seasonal
  fruit of your choice, to serve

1 Place the flakes, ground flax seed, dates, cherries, Brazil nuts, and sunflower seeds in a large bowl and mix.

2 Place the unsweetened coconut in a frying pan and dry fry gently for a few minutes until golden, stirring it around the pan so it doesn't burn.

3 Divide the muesli between 6 individual serving bowls, then sprinkle with the coconut. Pour over enough milk for serving and top with Greek yogurt and fresh fruit, if desired.

Cook's Tip

The quantities can easily be scaled up and the muesli stored in an airtight container for up to 3 weeks. If storing, allow the coconut to cool before stirring it into the mix.

DRIED SOUR CHERRIES
These have a marvelously tart, yet fruity flavor. As well as in muesli, try them on their own as a snack or use in baking. Store in an airtight container for up to 6 months.

OATMEAL WITH FRUIT COMPOTE

Classic oatmeal, served with aniseed-infused fruits, is a real treat for breakfast. For a less indulgent porridge, replace the cream with more milk.

SERVES	6
PREP	10 mins
COOK	20 mins

2¼ cups rolled oats
2½ cups milk, plus extra
  if needed
1⅛ cups half-and-half

FOR THE COMPOTE
7oz (200g) soft pitted prunes
2½oz (75g) sour cherries
1¼ cups fresh orange juice
1 star anise

GUIDELINES PER SERVING

● ● ●   Calories

● ● ●   Saturated fat

● ● ○   Salt

STATISTICS PER SERVING

Energy 403kcals/1692kJ

Protein 11g

Fat 16g
Saturated fat 8g

Carbohydrate 54g
Sugar 31g

Fiber 7g

Salt 0.3g

1 First prepare the compote. Place the prunes and cherries in a pan and pour over the orange juice, add the star anise, bring to a boil, then reduce the heat and simmer gently for 15 minutes. Set aside to steep.

2 Meanwhile, place the oats in a pan. Add two-thirds of the milk and stir well so it is all incorporated. Bring slowly to a boil, stirring continuously, until the milk has been absorbed by the oats. Gradually stir in the remaining milk and the half-and-half, bring back to a boil, and simmer gently, stirring, for 10–15 minutes or until thick and creamy. Add more milk, if needed.

3 Drain the dried fruit, reserving the liquid, and remove the star anise. Ladle the oatmeal into deep bowls and top with the drained fruit and a little of the reserved juice.

Variation
Flavor the oatmeal with cinnamon spice: add 1 cinnamon stick and 2 teaspoons ground cinnamon to the oats along with the milk. When it's ready, remove the stick and serve with a sprinkle of cinnamon and a bit of half-and-half. The spice gives the porridge a sweet flavor, so there is no need to add sugar. You can also swap the fruits with dried apricots and golden raisins or figs and cranberries.

Cook's Tip
You can store the fruit compote in an airtight container in the fridge for up to 1 week.

GREAT FOR KIDS

NUTRIENT BOOST
Prunes are rich in fiber, good for digestion and controlling blood cholesterol.

GRANOLA WITH APPLE CRISPS

SERVES 8
PREP 20 mins
COOK 1½–2 hours

This granola is on the right side of sweetness and will give you lots of energy at the start of the day.

GUIDELINES PER SERVING

● ● ●   Calories

● ● ○   Saturated fat

● ○ ○   Salt

STATISTICS PER SERVING

Energy 446kcals/1868kJ

Protein 8.5g

Fat 12.4g
Saturated fat 1.1g

Carbohydrate 64.2g
Sugar 27g

Fiber 7.4g

Salt trace

4–6 sweet apples, cored
  and very thinly sliced into rings
juice of 1 lemon
1 tsp coarse sugar
1 tbsp ground cinnamon
3 cups buckwheat flakes
3 cups rice flakes

drizzle of honey or maple syrup
3 tbsp sunflower or vegetable oil
7oz (200g) blanched almonds
10oz (300g) dried apricots,
  roughly chopped
3½oz (100g) dried cranberries
milk and yogurt, to serve

1 For the apple crisps, preheat the oven to 300°F (150°C). Toss the apples in lemon juice and arrange them in a single layer on baking sheets lined with parchment paper. Sprinkle with the sugar and 1 teaspoon of the cinnamon and put in the oven. Leave for about 1–1½ hours, keeping an eye on them and turning them halfway through. Turn the oven down to 275°F (140°C) if they begin to color too much. Remove and spread on clean parchment paper to dry out. If you have time, leave them in the oven overnight, after switching off the heat, to crisp up some more.

2 Set the oven temperature to 350°F (180°C). Place the buckwheat flakes, rice flakes, and the remaining cinnamon in a large bowl (you can substitute other gluten-free grains, such as quinoa flakes or puffs, millet flakes, or soy flakes). Mix the honey or maple syrup with the oil, pour it over the grain mixture, and toss until all the flakes are well coated. Spread out onto a baking sheet and bake for 10 minutes or until golden. Stir well, add the almonds, and cook for a further 20 minutes or until the nuts are lightly toasted. Remove from the oven, stir in the fruit, and leave to cool. Serve with the apple crisps, milk, and a dollop of yogurt.

Cook's Tip
You can also double up the quantities for the granola and apple crisps and store them in separate airtight containers for up to 3 weeks.

AUTUMN FRUIT COMPOTE

When the temperature is cooler, try this seasonal fruit salad for breakfast or dessert, served hot or cold.

SERVES 4
PREP 10 mins
PLUS SOAKING
COOK 15 mins

GUIDELINES PER SERVING

● ● ●   Calories

● ● ●   Saturated fat

● ● ●   Salt

STATISTICS PER SERVING

Energy 165kcals/703kJ

Protein 2.6g

Fat trace
Saturated fat trace

Carbohydrate 38g
Sugar 38g

Fiber 8g

Salt trace

3½oz (100g) dried apples
3½oz (100g) dried figs
3½oz (100g) dried prunes
1 cinnamon stick
½ vanilla bean, halved lengthwise

finely grated zest and juice of
  1 orange
1 tbsp brown sugar
Greek yogurt to serve

1 Place all the dried fruits in a mixing bowl. Add the cinnamon, vanilla bean, and orange zest and juice. Pour in ¾ cup of boiling water. Cover the bowl and set aside overnight.

2 In the morning, transfer the contents of the bowl to a saucepan. Add the sugar and ⅔ cup of cold water and bring to a boil.

3 Reduce the heat and simmer very gently, uncovered, for 15 minutes. Remove the vanilla bean and cinnamon stick. Serve with a dollop of Greek-style yogurt.

Variation
Any combination of dried fruits works well—try using apricots, peaches, or dates, or a mixture of dried berries. For a warming winter compote, add 2 finely chopped balls of stem ginger in syrup, plus 2 tbsp of the syrup.

CRUMPETS

Warm, toasted crumpets spread with butter and honey or jam make a quintessentially British breakfast treat.

SERVES 4
PREP 15 mins
PLUS RISING
COOK 20–25 mins
FREEZE 6 months

GUIDELINES PER SERVING

● ● ○ Calories
● ○ ○ Saturated fat
● ○ ○ Salt

STATISTICS PER SERVING

Energy 300kcals/1264kJ

Protein 8g

Fat 8g
Saturated fat 2g

Carbohydrate 48g
Sugar 8g

Fiber 2g

Salt 0.6g

1½ cups gluten-free bread flour mix
  (see page 38)
1 tsp xanthan gum
1 tbsp granulated sugar
1 tsp fast-acting dried yeast
½ tsp salt

1⅛ cup milk
vegetable oil, for greasing and frying

SPECIAL EQUIPMENT
3¼in (4 x 8cm) metal crumpet rings

1 Sift together the flour, xanthan, sugar, yeast, and salt. Heat the milk with 1⅛ cup water until lukewarm and stir into the flour. Whisk well with a hand whisk, then cover with lightly oiled plastic wrap and leave to rise for 1 hour.

2 Heat a heavy frying pan, lightly oil the crumpet rings and place them in the pan to heat up. Lightly stir the batter and ladle enough into each ring to fill halfway. Cook over low heat for 15–20 minutes; holes will appear on the surface and the batter will dry out.

3 Carefully remove the rings and turn the crumpets over to cook for another 5–10 minutes on the other side. Transfer to a wire rack to cool and repeat until the batter is used up. Serve lightly toasted.

CORNMEAL DROP SCONES

Cornmeal gives these drop scones a savory, nutty flavor and texture. Let the batter sit for 30 minutes or overnight so that the flour can fully absorb the liquid.

SERVES	4
PREP	10 mins
COOK	20 mins
FREEZE	1 month

1½ cups cornmeal or polenta
1¾ cups gluten-free all-purpose flour
2 tbsp sugar
pinch of salt
2 tsp gluten-free baking powder

½ tsp gluten-free baking soda
2 cups buttermilk
1 large egg
4 tbsp butter, melted
sunflower oil, for frying

GUIDELINES PER SERVING

●●● Calories
●●● Saturated fat
●●● Salt

STATISTICS PER SERVING

Energy 686kcals/2865kJ

Protein 15g

Fat 21g
Saturated fat 8g

Carbohydrate 104g
Sugar 14g

Fiber 2g

Salt 2g

1 Place the cornmeal, flour, sugar, salt, baking powder, and baking soda into a bowl and mix. Make a well in the center.

2 Mix the buttermilk, egg, and melted butter in a measuring cup until well combined. Gradually pour this into the flour mixture and stir, spooning a little flour from the edge of the bowl as you go. Add and stir until incorporated, but don't overwork the batter or you will have dense scones.

3 Heat a little oil in a large, nonstick frying pan over high heat until hot, swirl it around the pan to coat, then pour out any excess into a measuring cup (to reuse). Reduce the heat to medium-low and add 3–4 separate ladlefuls of batter to the pan to form individual drop scones. Cook for 2 minutes, until the edges start to cook and the underside turns golden, then flip with a spatula and cook the other side. Repeat for the remaining scones. Serve with a sweet or savory accompaniment (see below).

Choose Your Accompaniment
Sweet Try one or more of the following: orange juice, sugar, sliced banana, honey, yogurt, or blueberries.
Savory Best with crispy bacon and scrambled eggs.

Cook's Tip
To freeze, layer the cooled drop scones between wax paper and seal in a freezer bag. To reheat, defrost and heat through in a frying pan or microwave.

BUTTERMILK PANCAKES

A stack of pancakes served with maple syrup and fresh fruit is hard to beat for a special family breakfast. Heat the pancakes slowly so that they cook in the middle.

SERVES   4
PREP   5 mins
COOK   10 mins
FREEZE   6 months

GUIDELINES PER SERVING

● ● ○   Calories

● ○ ○   Saturated fat

● ○ ○   Salt

STATISTICS PER SERVING

Energy 218kcals/912kJ

Protein 8g

Fat 10g
Saturated fat 2g

Carbohydrate 22g
Sugar 6g

Fiber 0.6g

Salt 1g

½ cup rice flour
1 tsp xanthan gum
1 tbsp granulated sugar
1½ tsp gluten-free baking powder
pinch of salt
⅔ cup buttermilk

2 fl oz milk
2 large eggs, separated
a few drops of pure vanilla extract
vegetable oil, for frying
maple syrup and fresh berries,
   to serve

1 Sift the flour, xanthan gum, sugar, baking powder, and salt together into a bowl. Add the buttermilk, milk, egg yolks, and vanilla, and beat well.

2 In a clean bowl, whisk the egg whites with an electric whisk until they are stiff. Stir a good spoonful of egg white into the batter mix to loosen it, then gently fold in the remainder.

3 Heat a large, heavy frying pan over medium-high heat, add a couple of drops of oil, and wipe it around the pan with a piece of paper towel. Drop 4 separate heaped tablespoons of batter into the hot pan to make 4 pancakes, leaving plenty of space between them, they should spread to be about 3¼in (8cm) wide. Cook them over low heat for about 2–3 minutes until the base is golden, then flip them over and cook for a further 2 minutes.

4 Once cooked, wrap the pancakes in a clean paper towel to keep them warm. Repeat to make 8 pancakes in total. Serve warm, drizzled with maple syrup and with a handful of fresh berries scattered on top.

GREAT FOR KIDS

CHESTNUT PANCAKES WITH CHOCOLATE AND PRUNES

Chestnut flour is available from Italian delis or online and is well worth seeking out to make these rich, nutty pancakes.

SERVES 4
PREP 20 mins
PLUS RESTING
COOK 20 mins
FREEZE 1 month

GUIDELINES PER SERVING

● ● ● Calories
● ● ● Saturated fat
● ● ● Salt

STATISTICS PER SERVING

Energy 422kcals/1766kJ

Protein 9g

Fat 18g
Saturated fat 7.2g

Carbohydrate 68g
Sugar 44g

Fiber 8g

Salt 1.4g

$^2/_3$ cup chestnut flour
$^1/_2$ cup gluten-free flour
pinch of salt
1 tsp sugar
1 tsp gluten-free baking soda
1$^1/_4$ cups milk, extra if needed
1 large egg

sunflower or vegetable oil, for frying

FOR THE FILLING
9oz (250g) soft pitted prunes
3$^1/_2$oz (100g) chocolate (70% cocoa solids), broken into even-sized pieces

1 For the batter, place the flours in a large bowl with the salt, sugar, and baking soda and mix. In a measuring cup, gently whisk together the milk and egg, then slowly pour into the flour, whisking continuously until well incorporated. If the batter is too thick, add a little more milk. For best results, allow the batter to sit for 30 minutes or overnight in the fridge.

2 For the filling, place the prunes in a small pan and just cover with water. Simmer gently for about 10 minutes to soften the prunes, then remove with a slotted spoon and chop each prune in half. Set aside.

3 Place the chocolate in a heatproof bowl over a pan of barely simmering water, stir occasionally until it melts, remove the bowl, and set aside.

4 Heat a nonstick frying pan or crêpe pan over high heat until hot. Add a drizzle of oil, swirl it around the pan, and tip out into a measuring cup (to reuse). Reduce the heat to low-medium, add a ladleful of batter, and tip the pan so it spreads. Cook for 2 minutes until it starts to come away from the sides. Flip over with a spatula and cook the other side until it begins to crisp. Turn out on to a plate; top with a few prunes and a drizzle of melted chocolate, then fold or roll. Drizzle with more chocolate and serve. Repeat using up all the batter and filling.

BUCKWHEAT PANCAKES WITH ORANGE

The slightly nutty flavor of buckwheat flour combines well with oranges. The secret is to treat the batter gently.

1 cup buckwheat flour
⅛ cup rice flour
salt
1 tsp sugar
1 large egg, beaten
¾ cup milk

3 oranges, peeled and thinly sliced,
  any juice reserved
1½ tbsp maple syrup, plus extra
  sunflower oil, for frying

SERVES 4
PREP 15 mins
PLUS RESTING
COOK 30 mins
FREEZE 1 month

GUIDELINES PER SERVING

● ● ○ Calories

● ● ○ Saturated fat

● ● ○ Salt

STATISTICS PER SERVING

Energy 258kcals/1078kJ

Protein 6g

Fat 8g
Saturated fat 2g

Carbohydrate 40g
Sugar 16g

Fiber 3.4g

Salt trace

1 To make the batter, place the flours in a bowl along with a pinch of salt and the sugar and mix. Make a well in the middle and add the egg. Stir well. Mix the milk and ⅔ cup water in a measuring cup and gradually pour it into the flour, whisking with a balloon whisk until the batter is smooth and not lumpy. Set aside for 30 minutes to rest or overnight in the fridge.

2 For the oranges, heat a grill pan over high heat until hot. Mix any reserved orange juice with the maple syrup and brush over the orange slices to coat both sides. Place a few slices at a time on the grill pan and cook each side for 2 minutes until they take on a little color. Set aside.

3 Stir the batter. Heat 1 tablespoon oil in a nonstick frying pan or a crêpe pan over high heat until hot. Swirl it around the pan so it coats, and pour most of it into a measuring cup (to reuse). Reduce the heat to medium-low and add a ladleful of batter. Tilt the pan so it spreads; the mixture will be thick so it won't cover the pan completely. Cook for 2 minutes or until the underside is pale golden, then flip it and cook for 2 more minutes. To serve, top with orange slices and maple syrup. Repeat to use up all the batter.

Cook's Tip

If freezing, layer the pancakes between wax paper and seal in a freezer bag. To serve, defrost overnight and reheat in a frying pan or microwave.

NUTRIENT BOOST
This dish is rich in vitamin C.

BRITISH BREAKFAST FRITTATA

An all-in-one breakfast treat, which is easier to make and serve than cooking a fried breakfast for the whole family.

SERVES 4
PREP 20 mins
COOK 30–35 mins
PLUS RESTING

GUIDELINES PER SERVING

● ● ○ Calories

● ● ● Saturated fat

● ● ● Salt

STATISTICS PER SERVING

Energy 299kcals/1234kJ

Protein 15.5g

Fat 23g
Saturated fat 8g

Carbohydrate 7g
Sugar 1g

Fiber 1.2g

Salt 1.5g

1 tbsp olive oil
5$\frac{1}{2}$oz (150g) thick-cut bacon, chopped
2$\frac{1}{2}$oz (75g) button mushrooms, quartered
5$\frac{1}{2}$oz (150g) cooked, cold potatoes, cut
  into $\frac{1}{2}$in (1cm) cubes
4 large eggs
1 tbsp heavy cream
salt and freshly ground black pepper

2$\frac{1}{2}$oz (75g) cherry tomatoes, halved
butter, for greasing
1oz (30g) grated cheese,
  such as Cheddar

SPECIAL EQUIPMENT
8in (20cm) non-stick cake pan

1 Preheat the oven to 375°F (190°C). Heat the oil in a heavy-bottomed frying pan and cook the bacon gently for 3 minutes until it starts to brown. Add the mushrooms and cook over high heat for another 5 minutes until browned all over. Add the potatoes and cook for a final 2 minutes.

2 Whisk together the eggs and cream in a large bowl and season well. Add the cooked mushroom mixture and the cherry tomatoes, and mix well.

3 Grease an 8in (20cm) non-stick cake pan with the butter and pour in the egg mixture. Make sure all the bits are distributed evenly and the egg just covers the filling. Sprinkle with the cheese and bake for 20–25 minutes, until just set, golden brown on top, and puffed up at the sides.

4 Remove from the oven and rest for at least 5 minutes. Cut into wedges and serve warm or at room temperature.

Variation
Use slices of cooked sausage instead of bacon. Cook them in the same way so they crisp up a little.

SWEET POTATO CAKES WITH ONION SEEDS

Onion seeds add a subtle spice to the mixture and cut through the richness of sweet potato. These make a lower carb option from regular potato pancakes.

SERVES 6
PREP 30 mins
COOK 20–30 mins
FREEZE 1 month

GUIDELINES PER SERVING

● ● ○ ○ Calories

● ● ○ ○ Saturated fat

● ● ● ○ Salt

STATISTICS PER SERVING

Energy 210kcals/880kJ

Protein 6g

Fat 5g
Saturated fat 1.6g

Carbohydrate 36g
Sugar 4g

Fiber 2g

Salt 0.8g

NUTRIENT BOOST
Sweet potatoes are rich in the antioxidant betacarotene.

2 medium sweet potatoes, skin on
2 large eggs, lightly beaten
1 cup rice flour
3 tsp gluten-free baking powder
½ tsp freshly ground nutmeg

1 tbsp black onion (nigella) seeds
salt and freshly ground pepper
knob of butter, for frying
bacon and fried tomatoes, to serve

1 Cook the whole potatoes in a pan of salted water for about 15–20 minutes or until soft, then drain. When cool enough to handle, peel and mash until smooth. Add the eggs and mix until well incorporated. Set aside.

2 Sift the flour and baking powder into a bowl, add the nutmeg, and mix. Add to the sweet potato and stir gently to mix. Don't overwork the mixture or it will get sloppy. Stir in the onion seeds and season with salt and pepper.

3 In a nonstick frying pan, heat a little butter over medium heat until it is foaming, then add 1 heaped tablespoon of the potato mixture and flatten slightly with a palette knife. Cook for 4–5 minutes until the underside becomes golden, then flip, and cook the other side for the same time or until browned. Repeat to use up the batter. Serve with bacon and fried tomatoes.

Variation
Add 1 finely chopped jalapeño chile or, for a sweeter version, omit the onion seeds and seasoning, add 1 tsp of cinnamon, and serve with a bit of maple syrup.

Cook's Tip
To reheat from frozen, defrost in the fridge overnight and reheat in a frying pan or microwave on medium heat for 2 minutes, or in the oven at 350°F (180°C) for 10–15 minutes.

POTATO FARLS

These Irish potato cakes can be fried or griddled—they are wonderfully creamy on the inside and crisp on the outside.

1½lb (675g) floury potatoes, such as
  Russet or Yukon Gold, skin on
salt and freshly ground pepper
4 tbsp butter
1 cup gluten-free all-purpose flour, plus
  extra to dust

3 tbsp olive oil or a knob of butter,
  for cooking
crispy bacon and eggs, to serve

1 Cook the potatoes in a large pan of boiling salted water for 20–25 minutes or until tender when poked with a sharp knife. Drain and, when cool enough to handle, peel and mash. Add butter and mash until there are no lumps.

2 Sift the flour into the mixture, season well, and mix with a spoon. With your hands, bring the dough together. Turn it out onto a lightly floured board and either roll or use the back of your hand to flatten it, so it is about ¼in (5mm) thick. Cut the dough out to make 1½ x 2½in (4 x 6cm) rectangles, then slice these into triangles.

3 To fry, heat a large, nonstick frying pan over medium heat with half the oil or half the butter. Add half the potato cakes and fry for 2 minutes on each side until golden. Sit them on paper towels to drain. Repeat for the remaining farls and drain. To griddle, brush the griddle pan with a little oil, heat it to hot, add the farls a few at a time, and griddle for 2–3 minutes. Turn and cook the other side. Sit them on paper towels to drain. Repeat to cook the remaining farls. Serve for breakfast with bacon and eggs.

Cook's Tip
Cooking the potatoes with their skin on helps keep them dry. You can also use leftover mashed potato, but warm it slightly first. To reheat the farls from frozen, defrost in the fridge overnight and reheat in a frying pan or microwave on medium heat for 2 minutes, or in the oven at 350°F (180°C) for 10–15 minutes.

SERVES	4
PREP	15 mins
COOK	40 mins
FREEZE	1 month

GUIDELINES PER SERVING

●●● Calories

●●● Saturated fat

●○○ Salt

STATISTICS PER SERVING

Energy 422kcals/1765kJ

Protein 7g

Fat 19g
Saturated fat 8g

Carbohydrate 55g
Sugar 1.5g

Fiber 4.5g

Salt 0.2g

GREAT FOR KIDS

EGGS BENEDICT

For white muffins, use the gluten-free white bread flour blend on page 38 and add 2 tablespoons granulated sugar.

SERVES 4
PREP 20 mins
PLUS RISING
COOK 35 mins
FREEZE 3 months

GUIDELINES PER SERVING

● ● ● Calories

● ● ● Saturated fat

● ● ○ Salt

STATISTICS PER SERVING

Energy 753kcals/3167kJ

Protein 28g

Fat 38g
Saturated fat 19g

Carbohydrate 75g
Sugar 11g

Fiber 13.5g

Salt 0.8g

3 cups gluten-free brown bread flour blend (see page 38), plus extra for dusting
2 tsp fast-acting dried yeast
1 tsp xanthan gum
salt and freshly ground black pepper
1½ cups milk

6 tbsp unsalted butter, plus extra to serve
2 tbsp molasses
5 large eggs, plus 2 large egg yolks
3 tbsp white wine vinegar

1 Sift the flour, yeast, xanthan, and a pinch of salt into a large bowl and stir to combine. Warm the milk to lukewarm, add 1 tbsp butter, the molasses, and 1 egg, and whisk with a fork. Make a well in the center of the dry ingredients, add the wet ingredients, and mix. Turn onto a board and knead for 5 minutes, until smooth. Roll out the dough to a thickness of ¾in (2cm) and use a 3in (7.5cm) round cookie cutter to cut out 8 rounds. Transfer to a floured baking sheet, cover with oiled plastic wrap, and leave the muffins somewhere warm for 1 hour until doubled in size.

2 Heat a large, heavy frying pan or flat griddle pan. Add the muffins, making sure they don't touch each other, and cook over medium heat for 6–7 minutes, or until the bases are golden. Turn over, place a baking sheet on top of the pan to intensify the heat, and cook for 7–8 minutes, until golden.

3 To poach the eggs, place a frying pan over low heat and add boiling water to a depth of 1in (2.5cm). Carefully break 4 eggs, one at a time, into the water and let them barely simmer, for 1 minute. Remove the pan from the heat and set aside for 10 minutes to finish poaching.

4 For the hollandaise sauce, simmer the vinegar in a small pan until reduced by half. Pour into a heatproof bowl with the egg yolks and place over a pan of gently simmering water. Melt 5 tbsp butter, gradually add it to the bowl, and whisk continuously with a hand whisk until a smooth, thick sauce forms. Remove from the heat and season. Split and butter the muffins, top each half with an egg, and pour the sauce over the top.

BAKED BEANS

SERVES 4
PREP 10 mins
COOK 40 mins
FREEZE 3 months

Commercial baked beans often contain gluten, but making your own is surprisingly easy.

GUIDELINES PER SERVING

● ○ ○ Calories

● ○ ○ Saturated fat

● ○ ○ Salt

STATISTICS PER SERVING

Energy 210kcals/889kJ

Protein 10.5g

Fat 4g
Saturated fat 0.7g

Carbohydrate 34g
Sugar 5.3g

Fiber 12g

Salt 0.2g

1 tbsp olive oil
1 onion, finely chopped
salt and freshly ground pepper
2 garlic cloves, finely chopped
1 tsp ground allspice
1 tsp paprika
1 tbsp tomato paste
1 tsp Dijon mustard

1 tbsp molasses
2 cups tomato sauce
2 x 14oz (400g) cans navy beans,
  drained and rinsed
gluten-free toast (see pages 38
  or 216) or browned bacon,
  to serve

1 Heat the oil in a large pan, add the onion, season with salt and pepper, and cook gently for about 2–3 minutes until translucent; do not allow to brown. Stir in the garlic, allspice, paprika, tomato paste, and mustard and cook for a few seconds.

2 Now add the molasses and 2 tablespoons tomato sauce, stir well, cook for a few minutes, then add the remaining sauce and bring to a boil. Reduce to low heat and simmer for about 20–30 minutes.

3 Add in the beans, stir, and cook for a further 15 minutes or until thickened. Taste and season some more if required. Serve with toast or browned bacon.

GREAT FOR KIDS

Cook's Tip
You can also use cannellini beans or butter beans as an alternative.

NUTRIENT BOOST
The soluble fiber in beans balances blood sugar and controls cholesterol.

HASH BROWNS

These crispy, golden shredded potato cakes certainly shouldn't be reserved just for breakfast.

2lb (900g) waxy potatoes,
  such as Yukon Gold or red
1 large egg, lightly beaten
salt and freshly ground pepper

1–2 tbsp rice flour
vegetable oil, for frying
eggs, bacon, and baked beans
  (see opposite), to serve

1 Peel the potatoes, pat them dry, and grate into a large bowl. Transfer to a clean kitchen towel and squeeze to remove as much moisture as possible. Return the grated potato to the bowl.

2 Trickle in the egg, just enough to bind the mixture; you may not need it all. Stir well and season with salt and pepper. Sprinkle over the rice flour and turn with a spoon so it coats the potato.

3 Take a scoop of the mixture, form it into a ball, then flatten into a patty. Make 2–3 patties at a time, you should get about 12 in total. Heat 1 tablespoon oil in a large nonstick frying pan and add 2–3 patties at a time, giving them plenty of room. Cook for 4–5 minutes, undisturbed, so the underside gets really crispy and golden. Turn with a spatula and cook the other side for the same amount of time or until golden and cooked right through. Remove, drain on paper towels, and cover with foil to keep warm. Cook the remaining patties a few at a time. Serve as part of a breakfast with eggs, bacon, and some homemade baked beans.

Cook's Tip
The potatoes must be as dry as possible before adding the egg for the hash browns to properly crisp up. To reheat the hash browns from frozen, allow to defrost in the fridge overnight, then reheat in a frying pan or in the microwave on medium heat for 2 minutes, or in the oven at 350°F (180°C) for 10–15 minutes.

SERVES   4
PREP   20 mins
COOK   45 mins
FREEZE   3 months

GUIDELINES PER SERVING

● ● ○ Calories

● ● ○ Saturated fat

● ● ○ Salt

STATISTICS PER SERVING

Energy 303kcals/1270kJ

Protein 7g

Fat 13g
Saturated fat 1.7g

Carbohydrate 39g
Sugar 1.3g

Fiber 4g

Salt trace

GREAT FOR KIDS

TURKISH EGGS

SERVES 4
PREP 15 mins
COOK 40–45 mins

This dish, known as menemen *in Turkey, is spicy and utterly irresistible. Add more chile if you like it hot.*

GUIDELINES PER SERVING

● ● ● Calories
● ● ● Saturated fat
● ● ● Salt

STATISTICS PER SERVING

Energy 208 kcals/871kJ

Protein 12g

Fat 12g
Saturated fat 4g

Carbohydrate 13g
Sugar 13g

Fiber 4g

Salt 0.5g

1 tbsp olive oil
1 onion, sliced
1 green bell pepper, sliced
1 red bell pepper, sliced
1 orange pepper, sliced
²/₃ cup (6oz) Greek yogurt
3 tbsp chopped mint leaves

2 garlic cloves, crushed
1 red chile, seeded and finely chopped
1 x 14oz (400g) can of chopped tomatoes
pinch of granulated sugar
salt and freshly ground black pepper
4 large eggs
3 tbsp roughly chopped cilantro leaves

1 Heat the oil in a large, non-stick frying pan over medium heat and cook the onion for 5 minutes. Add the peppers to the pan and cook for 20 minutes, stirring occasionally.

2 Meanwhile, place the yogurt, mint, and garlic in a small serving bowl and stir together. Cover and set aside.

3 Add the chile, tomatoes, and sugar to the frying pan, season well, and cook for 10 minutes.

4 Make 4 hollows in the tomato mixture and crack an egg into each. Cover the pan and cook for 5–10 minutes, or until the eggs are cooked to your liking.

5 Sprinkle the dish with the cilantro and serve with the herb and garlic yogurt.

BLUEBERRY BREAKFAST MUFFINS

Start the day with a boost of fresh blueberries packed into muffins. Serve with a glass of milk—delicious!

SERVES 6
PREP 10 mins
COOK 25–30 mins
FREEZE 6 months

GUIDELINES PER SERVING

● ● ○ Calories

● ● ○ Saturated fat

● ○ ○ Salt

STATISTICS PER SERVING

Energy 390kcals/1640kJ

Protein 8g

Fat 17g
Saturated fat 3g

Carbohydrate 48g
Sugar 22g

Fiber 2g

Salt 0.6g

1½ cups gluten-free all-purpose flour
½ cup polenta or fine cornmeal
½ cup granulated sugar
1 tsp xanthan gum
1½ tsp gluten-free baking powder
½ tsp gluten-free baking soda
pinch of salt
5oz (140g) blueberries

zest of 1 lemon
½ cup vegetable oil
½ cup milk
3 large eggs

SPECIAL EQUIPMENT
deep 12-hole muffin pan lined with
  paper liners

1 Preheat the oven to 350°F (180°C). Mix together the flour, polenta, sugar, xanthan, baking powder, soda, and salt in a large bowl.

2 Stir in the blueberries and lemon zest. Mix together the oil, milk, and eggs, add to the dry ingredients, and mix briefly.

3 Spoon the mixture into the paper liners. Bake for 25–30 minutes or until risen and golden brown on top. Cool in the pan for 5 minutes before transferring to a wire rack. Best served slightly warm.

GREAT FOR KIDS

NUTRIENT BOOST
Blueberries are rich in antioxidants, linked to heart health and fighting cancer.

BLUEBERRIES
Blueberries have a mild flavor that is markedly enhanced by cooking, one reason why they are such a popular fruit for baking. Raspberries or chopped strawberries would also work in this recipe.

FRUIT AND NUT BREAKFAST BARS

These energy-packed oat bars are perfect for breakfast on the go and equally good as a mid-morning snack.

SERVES 8
PREP 15 mins
COOK 30–35 mins

vegetable oil, for greasing
4oz (115g) ready-to-eat dried apricots
3oz (85g) blanched hazelnuts
3oz (85g) raw almonds
3oz (85g) raisins or golden raisins
3oz (85g) dried cranberries
14oz (400g) can sweetened
  condensed milk

2¼ cups rolled oats
3oz (85g) crispy rice or puffed rice

SPECIAL EQUIPMENT
9 x 13in (23 x 33cm) baking pan

GUIDELINES PER SERVING

● ● ● Calories
● ● ○ Saturated fat
● ○ ○ Salt

STATISTICS PER SERVING

Energy 534kcals/2244kJ

Protein 12g

Fat 20g
Saturated fat 4g

Carbohydrate 66g
Sugar 40g

Fiber 6g

Salt 0.4g

1 Preheat the oven to 325°F (160°C). Lightly oil the pan and line with parchment paper. Use scissors to snip the apricots into small pieces and place in a bowl. Roughly chop the hazelnuts and almonds, keeping them fairly chunky. Add the nuts to the bowl with the raisins or golden raisins and cranberries.

2 Pour the condensed milk into a large, heavy pan and slowly bring to a boil over low heat. Stir constantly as it can stick to the bottom and burn. Remove once it is boiling, add the fruit, nuts, oats, and rice, and mix well with a wooden spoon. Pour into the prepared pan and level the surface with the back of a wet spoon. Bake for 30–35 minutes or until pale golden.

3 Remove from the oven, cool in the tray for 5 minutes, then transfer onto a cutting board. Cut into 16 bars and leave to cool completely. They will store in an airtight container for up to 1 week.

Variation
CHOCOLATE FRUIT AND NUT BARS Stir 2 tablespoons cocoa powder into the condensed milk before mixing in the remaining ingredients and add 2oz (60g) roughly chopped dark chocolate (70% cocoa solids).

NUTRIENT BOOST
Almonds are a source of calcium, also rich in vitamin E and heart-friendly fats.

GREAT FOR KIDS

BREAKFAST BERRY BARS

SERVES 8
PREP 10 mins
COOK 30–35 mins

So easy to make, these fruit-packed bars are ready to grab for a breakfast on the go!

GUIDELINES PER SERVING

● ● ● Calories
● ● ○ Saturated fat
● ○ ○ Salt

STATISTICS PER SERVING

Energy 476kcals/2000kJ

Protein 11g

Fat 12g
Saturated fat 4g

Carbohydrate 80g
Sugar 44g

Fiber 7g

Salt 0.3g

oil, for greasing
14oz (400g) can sweetened condensed
  milk
10oz (300g) mixed dried berries,
  such as cranberries, blueberries,
  and sour cherries
2¾ cup rolled oats

1¾oz (50g) crispy rice
1oz (30g) sunflower seeds
1oz (30g) pumpkin seeds

SPECIAL EQUIPMENT
9 x 13in (23 x 33cm) rectangular
  baking pan

1 Preheat the oven to 325°F (160°C). Lightly oil the baking pan.

2 Heat the condensed milk in a large, heavy saucepan and slowly bring to a boil. Remove it from the heat, then add in the fruit, oats, crispy rice, and seeds. Mix well with a wooden spoon.

3 Add into the prepared pan, then level the surface with the back of a wet spoon. Bake for 30–35 minutes or until pale, golden brown.

4 Remove from the oven, cool in the pan for 5 minutes, and cut into 16 bars. Transfer the bars to a wire rack to cool completely. Store in an airtight container for up to 1 week.

GREAT FOR KIDS

NUTRIENT BOOST
Oats provide low-GI carbohydrate energy.

Cook's Tip
Tailor these to suit your personal taste: chopped dried apricots, raisins, or golden raisins can be used instead of the berries, just keep the quantity the same; and try using the same quantity of chopped hazelnuts in place of the seeds.

APPETIZERS, PARTY FOOD, AND DIPS

BREADSTICKS WITH PEPPER DIP

These party nibbles come in three different flavors, but if preferred, simply dust with gluten-free polenta.

MAKES 18
PREP 15 mins
PLUS RISING
COOK 45–50 mins

GUIDELINES PER SERVING

● ● ○ Calories
● ● ● Saturated fat
● ● ○ Salt

STATISTICS PER SERVING

Energy 158kcals/662kJ

Protein 6g

Fat 9.5g
Saturated fat 2.5g

Carbohydrate 16g
Sugar 2.5g

Fiber 1.5g

Salt 0.4g

2 cups gluten-free white bread flour mix
(see page 38), plus extra for dusting
2 tsp fast-action dried yeast
2 tsp xanthan gum
2 tsp granulated sugar
1 tsp salt
2 eggs
2 tbsp olive oil
vegetable oil, for brushing
4 tbsp poppy seeds
4 tbsp sesame seeds
6 tbsp finely grated Parmesan cheese

FOR THE ROASTED PEPPER DIP

2 large red peppers
4 garlic cloves, unpeeled
3 tbsp olive oil
1 tsp smoked paprika
½ tsp granulated sugar
½ tsp ground cumin
½ tsp salt
dash of Tabasco sauce

1 Preheat the oven to 425°F (220°C). Sift the flour, yeast, xanthan, sugar, and salt into a large bowl. Lightly beat 1 egg with the olive oil and 1⅛ cup lukewarm water, add to the dry ingredients, and mix to form a dough. Knead for 5 minutes. Return to the bowl, cover with oiled plastic wrap, and leave to rise in a warm place for about 1 hour until doubled in size.

2 Meanwhile, roast the peppers on a baking sheet for 15–20 minutes until lightly charred. Add the garlic and cook for a further 10 minutes. Transfer the peppers and garlic to a plastic bag and leave to cool. Core and seed the peppers and peel off the skin. Pop the garlic from their skins. Combine with the remaining ingredients in a food processor and blend to a coarse dip.

3 Lightly oil 2 baking sheets. Roll out the dough into a fat sausage and cut into 18 equal-sized pieces. Roll each piece into a stick 5in (12cm) long. Scatter the seeds and grated Parmesan onto three separate plates. Beat the remaining egg. Brush the sticks with the beaten egg and roll a third of the sticks in each flavor. Place them a little apart on the baking sheets and bake for 15–20 minutes, or until crisp and golden. Allow to cool.

CHEESE STRAWS WITH TOMATO AND BASIL DIP

Shape the cheese straw trimmings into little biscuits—they still taste great, whatever the shape.

MAKES   18
PREP   15 mins
PLUS CHILLING
COOK   15–20 mins

2 cups gluten-free all-purpose flour,
  plus extra for dusting
7 tbsp butter, cubed
2 tsp mustard powder
1 tsp xanthan gum
½ tsp salt
3oz (85g) aged Cheddar cheese, grated, or
  blue cheese, crumbled
1 large egg, beaten
milk for brushing

3 tbsp finely grated Parmesan cheese
paprika, for sprinkling

FOR THE DIP
4 tomatoes
2 tbsp finely chopped basil
1 tbsp olive oil
1 tbsp tomato paste
½ tsp granulated sugar
salt and freshly ground black pepper

GUIDELINES PER SERVING

- ● ● ○   Calories
- ● ● ●   Saturated fat
- ● ● ○   Salt

STATISTICS PER SERVING

Energy 133kcals/554kJ

Protein 4g

Fat 8.5g
Saturated fat 5g

Carbohydrate 10g
Sugar 1g

Fiber 0.8g

Salt 0.4g

1 Place the flour, butter, mustard, xanthan, and salt in a food processor and pulse until the mixture looks like crumbs. Transfer to a bowl. Stir in the Cheddar cheese, then add the egg, along with 4 tablespoons cold water. Using a palette knife, mix to form a ball of dough. Lightly knead on a floured surface, wrap in plastic wrap, and chill for 30 minutes.

2 Preheat the oven to 400°F (200°C). Roll out the dough on a lightly floured surface to a rectangle measuring 9 x 14½in (23 x 36cm), and trim the edges. Brush with milk, then sprinkle over the Parmesan and paprika. Cut ¾in (2cm) wide strips from the dough and place them on baking sheets. Bake for 15–20 minutes, or until the strips are golden and puffy. Leave to cool.

3 For the dip, score the tomatoes and soak in boiling water for 30 seconds. Peel and discard the skin, then roughly chop the tomatoes on a board to make a pulp. Pour the flesh and all the juices into a small bowl. Add the remaining ingredients, stir well, and season to taste. Serve at room temperature with the cheese straws.

LAVOSH WITH EGGPLANT DIP

SERVES 8
PREP 20 mins
COOK 1 hour 10 mins

Iranian-style seeded crisp breads served with a sesame scented eggplant dip make a great snack or appetizer.

GUIDELINES PER SERVING

● ● ● Calories
● ● ● Saturated fat
● ● ○ Salt

STATISTICS PER SERVING

Energy 226kcals/994kJ

Protein 5.5g

Fat 17g
Saturated fat 3.5g

Carbohydrate 15.5g
Sugar 1.5g

Fiber 3g

Salt 0.6g

1 cup gluten-free all-purpose
  flour, plus extra to dust
2 tsp xanthan gum
½ tsp salt
2 large egg whites
1 tbsp butter, melted
2 tbsp sesame seeds
1 tbsp poppy seeds

FOR THE DIP
2 medium eggplants
2 garlic cloves, crushed
zest and juice of 1 lemon
3 tbsp tahini paste
½ tsp salt
⅓ cup olive oil
3 tbsp chopped fresh cilantro
¼ cup Greek yogurt
freshly ground pepper

1 Preheat the oven to 400°F (200°C). For the dip, bake the eggplants on a baking sheet for 30–40 minutes or until soft and lightly charred. Cool.

2 Meanwhile, make the lavosh. Sift the flour, xanthan, and salt into a large bowl. Beat 1 egg white with ⅓ cup water, stir into the flour with the melted butter, and mix well to form a dough. Lightly knead the dough on a flour-dusted surface, divide into 6 balls, and roll out each ball until paper thin, then place on baking sheets. Repeat with all the dough.

3 Brush the remaining egg white over the lavosh, sprinkle the seeds, and bake in 2 batches for 10–15 minutes or until crisp and golden.

4 Halve the eggplants and scoop the flesh into a food processor. Add the rest of the ingredients and blend to a chunky spread. Check the seasoning, spoon into a bowl, and serve with the crisp breads.

Cook's Tip
You can also store the lavosh, after it has cooled, in an airtight container for 2–3 days. Re-crisp in a warm oven. The dip can also be stored for 2–3 days in an airtight container, but needs to be kept in the fridge.

SESAME RICE CRACKERS

These fiery hot crackers are perfect for serving with dips or spicy relishes and pickles.

SERVES   6
PREP   20 mins
         PLUS DRYING
COOK   20 mins

GUIDELINES PER SERVING

● ● ●   Calories
● ● ○   Saturated fat
● ● ○   Salt

STATISTICS PER SERVING

Energy 363kcals/1514kJ

Protein 7g

Fat 7g
Saturated fat 1g

Carbohydrate 62g
Sugar 1g

Fiber 0.5g

Salt 0.6g

2¼ cups sticky rice (sushi rice), washed in cold running water, until the water runs clear
salt
2 tbsp sesame seeds
1 tsp wasabi paste
2 tsp tamari (gluten-free soy sauce)
sunflower or vegetable oil, for frying
hot carrot and onion seed pickle or spicy cauliflower pickle, to serve

1 Pour the washed rice into a large pan, add 2 cups cold water, cover with a lid, bring to a boil, and simmer for 10 minutes or until all the water has been absorbed; make sure it doesn't dry out or the rice will burn. Remove from the heat, but do not remove the lid. Leave covered for 15 minutes.

2 Season the cooked rice with salt, stir in the sesame seeds, wasabi, and tamari, and mix well until it is all combined.

3 Spread the mixture out onto a baking sheet lined with parchment paper. Press on the rice a little and top with another sheet of parchment. Use a rolling pin to roll over the paper and flatten the rice so it is about ¼in (5mm) thick. Remove the parchment paper and place in the fridge to dry overnight.

4 Remove the rice from the fridge 20 minutes before you are ready to cook. Pour the oil to a depth of 2in (5cm) in a deep frying pan. Slice the rice into squares, breaking pieces off (it will be irregular), and add to the hot oil a few at a time. Continue frying until they are all cooked. Drain on paper towels and serve with a hot carrot and onion seed or spicy cauliflower pickle.

VEGETABLE CHIPS

Deliciously sweet and healthier than regular chips, these make an ideal snack for children; omit the salt if you prefer.

SERVES 4
PREP   20 mins
COOK   30 mins

2 parsnips
1 sweet potato
2 beets

sunflower or vegetable oil, for deep-frying, enough to fill half the pan
sea salt (optional)

GUIDELINES PER SERVING

● ● ● Calories
● ● ○ Saturated fat
● ○ ○ Salt

1 Peel and trim the vegetables, then cut them into wafer-thin slices using a vegetable peeler or a mandolin, if you have one.

2 Heat the oil in a heavy, deep-sided pan over high heat until really hot. Don't leave the pan unattended, take off the heat when not using, and keep a fire blanket nearby in case of fire. Add the vegetable slices a few at a time. Fry each batch for 2–3 minutes or until crisp and golden, then remove with a slotted spoon and spread out over paper towels on a baking sheet. Repeat until all are cooked.

3 Sprinkle with sea salt (if using) and then place them piled high in bowls to serve with drinks, or serve alongside meat such as game.

STATISTICS PER SERVING

Energy 258kcals/1076kJ

Protein 3g

Fat 17.5g
Saturated fat 2g

Carbohydrate 22g
Sugar 10g

Fiber 7.5g

Salt 0.15g

Variations
Sprinkle with either paprika, pepper, or chili flakes for chips with more punch.

YELLOW BEETS
If you are wary of the staining juices from red beets, look out for Burpee's Golden, a bright yellow beet that does not bleed when cut.

NUTRIENT BOOST
Beets produce nitric oxide gas in the blood, which lowers blood pressure.

GREAT FOR KIDS

TZATZIKI

SERVES 4
PREP 10 mins

Traditionally served in Greece as an appetizer, this dip can also be served with lamb dishes.

GUIDELINES PER SERVING

● ● ○ Calories
● ○ ○ Saturated fat
● ○ ○ Salt

STATISTICS PER SERVING

Energy 49kcals/203kJ

Protein 2.5g

Fat 3g
Saturated fat 2g

Carbohydrate 3g
Sugar 3g

Fiber 0.2g

Salt 0.2g

4in (10cm) piece of cucumber, quartered lengthwise and seeded
¾ cup (7oz) Greek yogurt or thick plain yogurt
1 tbsp finely chopped mint leaves

1 tbsp finely chopped dill
1 small garlic clove, crushed
1 tbsp lemon juice
salt and freshly ground black pepper

1 Grate the lengths of cucumber into a sieve, pressing them down to remove most of the excess water.

2 Put the grated cucumber in a clean kitchen towel and squeeze it well to remove the last of the water. Place the squeezed ball of cucumber on a chopping board and chop it up to make it even finer.

3 Mix it together with the remaining ingredients and season to taste. Cover and chill until needed.

Cook's tip
Serve this delicious dip with a big pile of crudités appetizers including carrots, cucumber, and celery, to encourage children who are fussy eaters to eat more vegetables.

ZUCCHINI AND CHILE FRITTERS

SERVES 4
PREP 25 mins
      PLUS RESTING
COOK 10 mins

GUIDELINES PER SERVING

● ○ ○ ○   Calories

● ● ○ ○   Saturated fat

● ○ ○ ○   Salt

STATISTICS PER SERVING

Energy 370kcals/1574kJ

Protein 11g

Fat 20g
Saturated fat 4g

Carbohydrate 33g
Sugar 5.5g

Fiber 4g

Salt 0.2g

Perfect for a light supper, these fritters shouldn't be at all oily: use minimal oil and drain well.

2lb (900g) zucchini, ends removed
salt and freshly ground pepper
1 cup gluten-free rice flour
1 tbsp olive oil
2 large eggs, separated
⅔ cup milk

1 tsp dried chili flakes
sunflower or vegetable oil, for frying
fresh tomato salsa or homemade
  mayonnaise, to serve

1 Grate the zucchini into a colander, sprinkle over a little salt, and leave for 30 minutes. Tip them into a kitchen towel and squeeze out the excess water (see Cook's Tip).

2 For the batter, place the flour in a bowl, season, and add the olive oil, egg yolks, and milk. Mix well to combine. Leave to rest for 30 minutes, if time permits.

3 Meanwhile, whisk the egg whites until fairly stiff, then fold this into the batter mixture. Add the grated zucchini to the batter mixture along with the chili flakes and fold them in gently.

4 Heat a little sunflower oil in a nonstick frying pan and add dollops of the batter; they will spread so add only about 3 at a time. Cook for 1–2 minutes or until they begin to turn golden, then flip and cook the other side. Drain on paper towels and continue until all the batter is used up. Serve with fresh tomato salsa or some homemade mayonnaise.

Cook's Tip
It's essential that the zucchini are drained of all the excess water, so squeeze and pat them dry really well.

CORN AND FETA FRITTERS

A very easy, light supper dish that uses only a few ingredients from the fridge and pantry.

1 cup gluten-free all-purpose flour
2 tsp gluten-free baking powder
1 large egg
½ cup milk
7oz (195g) can corn, drained, or the
  kernels from 2 fresh cobs (see below)

freshly ground pepper
2½oz (75g) feta cheese, crumbled
2–3 tbsp sunflower or vegetable oil,
  for frying
fried or grilled bacon, to serve (optional)

1 Sift the flour and baking powder into a bowl and make a well. Add the egg and milk, and start to incorporate the flour, whisking until smooth. Add the corn, some pepper, and mix. Rest in the fridge for 15 minutes.

2 When ready to cook, stir in the feta, then heat a little oil in a nonstick frying pan over medium heat. Spoon in 2 tablespoons of the mixture and flatten together to form each fritter, leaving plenty of space between them; you will have to cook them in batches.

3 Fry for 1–2 minutes or until the underside is pale golden, then turn and cook the other side for a further 1–2 minutes. Remove and drain on paper towels. Serve alone or with bacon, as a main meal or breakfast.

Variations
Once you've mastered the batter mix, try varying it with grated Cheddar cheese and scallions, peas and chopped mint, or blue cheese and chopped red onion.

SERVES 4
PREP 15 mins
PLUS RESTING
COOK 15 mins
FREEZE 1 month

GUIDELINES PER SERVING

● ● ● Calories
● ● ● Saturated fat
● ● ● Salt

STATISTICS PER SERVING

Energy 294kcals/1230kJ

Protein 8g

Fat 13g
Saturated fat 4.5g

Carbohydrate 36g
Sugar 5.5g

Fiber 0.8g

Salt 1.9g

GREAT FOR KIDS

CORN ON THE COB
To prepare fresh corn, pull off the husk and silk, hold upright, and slice straight down the sides to cut off the kernels. Steam or boil for 2–3 minutes.

NUTRIENT BOOST
The phytochemicals in canned corn are more easily absorbed than in fresh.

BLINIS WITH SMOKED TROUT AND HOT AND SOUR CUCUMBER

SERVES 10
PREP 15 mins
PLUS STANDING
COOK 10–15 mins
FREEZE 6 months
BLINIS ONLY

GUIDELINES PER SERVING

● ● ○ Calories

● ● ● Saturated fat

● ● ○ Salt

STATISTICS PER SERVING

Energy 171kcals/714kJ

Protein 6.5g

Fat 8.5g
Saturated fat 4g

Carbohydrate 16g
Sugar 3.5g

Fiber 0.6g

Salt 0.9g

Serve these little pancakes as smart canapés daintily topped with the cucumber, trout, and sour cream.

½ cup buckwheat flour
½ cup gluten-free all-purpose white flour
½ tsp gluten-free baking powder
1 tsp fast-acting dried yeast
salt
¾ cup milk
1 large egg, separated
1 tbsp butter, melted
9oz (250g) cucumber, peeled, halved, seeded, and thinly sliced
½ tsp white mustard seeds
½ tsp Sichuan peppercorns
3 tbsp cider vinegar
1 tbsp chopped dill
1 tbsp superfine granulated sugar
½ tsp dried chili flakes
5oz (140g) smoked trout, chopped
⅔ cup sour cream
vegetable oil, for frying

1 Sift the flours, baking powder, yeast, and ½ teaspoon salt into a large bowl. Heat the milk until lukewarm, and pour into the flour with the egg yolk and melted butter. Mix well and cover. Leave to stand for 30 minutes.

2 Place the cucumber in a bowl. Lightly crush the mustard seeds and peppercorns with a mortar and pestle. Add to the cucumber with the vinegar, dill, sugar, ½ teaspoon salt, and chili flakes, and mix. Cover and marinate for 20 minutes.

3 Stir the batter. Whisk the egg white in a clean bowl until it forms stiff peaks, then fold it into the batter. Heat a heavy nonstick frying pan, add a couple of drops of oil, and wipe it around the pan with paper towels. Drop tablespoons of the batter into the hot pan; they should be 2in (5cm) wide. Cook over medium heat for 1–2 minutes until bubbles form and the base is golden brown. Flip and cook for 1 minute. Repeat to make 35–40 blinis. Serve warm with the cucumber, smoked trout, and sour cream.

SAUSAGE ROLLS

A real favorite with everyone—perfect for parties, snacks, or picnics.

SERVES 6
PREP 20 mins
COOK 30 mins
FREEZE 3 months

GUIDELINES PER SERVING

● ● ○ Calories

● ● ● Saturated fat

● ● ● Salt

STATISTICS PER SERVING

Energy 428kcals/1786kJ

Protein 14g

Fat 30g
Saturated fat 12g

Carbohydrate 26g
Sugar 2g

Fiber 0.6g

Salt 1.8g

GREAT FOR KIDS

14oz (400g) gluten-free sausages,
  removed from their casings
½ onion, very finely chopped
handful of flat-leaf parsley,
  finely chopped
salt and freshly ground pepper

14oz (400g) gluten-free rough puff pastry
  (see pages 46–7)
1 large egg, lightly beaten, or more
  if needed

1 Preheat the oven to 400°F (200°C). Add the sausage to a bowl and chop using a fork, stir in the onion and parsley, and season if required (the sausages may be salty enough already).

2 On a lightly floured surface, roll out the pastry to a large rectangle about 9½ x 12in (24 x 30cm) and ¼in (4mm) thick, then cut it lengthwise so you have two rectangles. Halve the sausage mixture, roll each half into a long sausage shape, and place down the middle of each piece of pastry.

3 Brush the edges of the pastry with the beaten egg and then fold the pastry over, so it wraps the sausage with the seam underneath. Press the edges together to seal. Repeat with the other rectangle of pastry. Now slice each roll into 6 pieces. Slash the tops so that steam escapes as they cook, then brush them with the remaining beaten egg. Set them on a lightly oiled baking sheet and cook in the oven for 25–30 minutes until evenly golden brown and the sausage is cooked through. Remove and serve hot or cold.

Variation

CHEESE ROLLS Follow the same recipe for a non-meat version, but replace the sausage with 7oz (200g) strong Cheddar cheese, grated, and 7oz (200g) gluten-free bread crumbs, mixed with the onion and parsley. Use your hands to squeeze the mixture together into a sausage shape, fill the pastry rectangles, and seal. Brush with beaten egg and bake for 20–25 minutes or until golden.

FISH STICKS

So much better than store-bought ones, and you have complete control over what goes into them and coats them.

SERVES 4
PREP 20 mins
COOK 20 mins
FREEZE 3 months

GUIDELINES PER SERVING

● ● ○ Calories
● ● ○ Saturated fat
● ○ ○ Salt

STATISTICS PER SERVING

Energy 406kcals/1700kJ

Protein 30g

Fat 13g
Saturated fat 4g

Carbohydrate 40g
Sugar 0.2g

Fiber 0.8g

Salt 0.6g

14oz (400g) white fish fillets or loin, such as haddock, skin and pinbones removed
1 cup polenta or fine cornmeal, plus extra if needed
1¾oz (50g) fresh Parmesan cheese, grated

5 tbsp gluten-free all-purpose flour or chickpea flour, plus extra if needed
salt and freshly ground pepper
1 large egg, lightly beaten
2–3 tbsp sunflower or vegetable oil
lemon wedges and gluten-free tartare sauce, to serve

1 Cut the fish into 12–16 lengths to form sticks and then trim to neaten. The number will depend on the size and shape of the fish.

2 Mix the polenta with the Parmesan, then season the all-purpose or chickpea flour with salt and pepper. Pour the flour out onto a plate, the beaten egg onto another plate, and the polenta mix onto a third.

3 Dip each fish stick into the flour and turn to cover so the egg will stick, then dip into the egg to coat, and roll in the polenta until completely covered. Place the sticks on a baking sheet and put in the fridge to firm up for 20 minutes. When ready to cook, heat a little oil in a nonstick frying pan and add a few at a time, frying on medium-high heat for 5–6 minutes on each side or until golden brown. Repeat with all the sticks, adding more oil to the pan as needed. Serve with lemon wedges and tartare sauce.

Cook's Tips
You could oven-bake these if you prefer: place them on a lightly oiled baking sheet and cook in the oven at 400°F (200°C) for 20 minutes, turning them halfway through. Excellent for children: serve sandwiched between slices of gluten-free bread for the perfect fish stick sandwich.

GREAT FOR KIDS

CHICKEN NUGGETS

SERVES 4
PREP 20 mins
COOK 20–30 mins
FREEZE 1 month

Processed nuggets are justly criticized for the poor quality of their meat; with these homemade versions, you know exactly what has gone into them.

GUIDELINES PER SERVING

● ● ○ Calories

● ○ ○ Saturated fat

● ○ ○ Salt

STATISTICS PER SERVING

Energy 424kcals/1785kJ

Protein 60g

Fat 5.5g
Saturated fat 1g

Carbohydrate 31g
Sugar 0.5g

Fiber 1g

Salt 0.5g

GREAT FOR KIDS

2lb (900g) chicken breast, boneless, skinless, and cut into cubes or bite-sized pieces
2–3 tbsp gluten-free all-purpose flour, rice flour, or cornstarch, plus extra if needed
salt and freshly ground pepper

1 large egg, lightly beaten, or more if needed
1-1½ cups polenta or fine cornmeal
2 tsp paprika
oil, for greasing
green salad and fresh tomato relish, to serve

1 Preheat the oven to 400°F (200°C). Toss the chicken pieces in the flour until they are evenly coated, then season well with salt and pepper. Pour the beaten egg out onto a plate. Mix the polenta with the paprika and pour this out onto a separate plate.

2 Dip the chicken pieces into the beaten egg, transfer them to the polenta, and toss to coat.

3 Place all the coated pieces on a lightly oiled baking sheet and bake in the oven for 20–30 minutes until golden, turning them halfway through cooking so they color evenly. Remove and serve with a lightly dressed green salad and a fresh tomato relish.

Cook's Tip
Prepare these ahead and freeze uncooked on a baking sheet, transfer to a plastic bag, and seal. To eat, defrost overnight and cook as per recipe.

CHICKEN SATAY KEBABS

The spicy cubes of chicken in these kebabs are charred on the outside but remain juicy and tender on the inside.

SERVES   4
PREP   15 mins
          PLUS MARINATING
COOK   35–50 mins

3 chicken breasts, boneless, skinless, and cut into bite-sized cubes
1 tbsp sunflower or vegetable oil
3 tbsp tamari (gluten-free soy sauce)
1 red or jalapeño chile, seeded and finely chopped
juice of ½ lemon
2 tsp palm or brown sugar
salt and freshly ground pepper

FOR THE SATAY SAUCE
14oz (400ml) can coconut milk
1–2 tbsp gluten-free red curry paste
1¼ cups hot gluten-free vegetable stock
1 tbsp tamari (gluten-free soy sauce)

1–2 tbsp palm or brown sugar
7oz (200g) unshelled peanuts, freshly shelled and ground, or 5 tbsp gluten-free peanut butter
salt
2 tsp tamarind paste or juice of 1 lemon or 1 lime

SPECIAL EQUIPMENT
8 wooden skewers, soaked in cold water
grill pan

GUIDELINES PER SERVING

⬤ ⬤ ⬤ Calories
⬤ ⬤ ⬤ Saturated fat
⬤ ⬤ ⬤ Salt

STATISTICS PER SERVING

Energy 647kcals/2703kJ

Protein 44g

Fat 45g
Saturated fat 20g

Carbohydrate 17g
Sugar 10g

Fiber 3g

Salt 3g

1 Put the chicken pieces in a bowl, add the oil, tamari, chile, lemon juice, and sugar, and season. Stir to combine and leave to marinate for 30 minutes.

2 For the sauce, place the coconut milk in a pan and bring to a boil. Reduce the heat, stir in the curry paste, stock, tamari, and sugar, and cook gently for 10 minutes, stirring occasionally. Add the peanuts, stir until they dissolve in the sauce, bring to a boil, and simmer for 10–15 minutes or until thickened. Season with salt and add the tamarind paste or lemon or lime juice to taste. Set aside to cool and for all the flavors to mingle. The sauce can be prepared ahead and kept in the fridge for up to 3 days.

3 Meanwhile, mix the marinade around a little, then thread the chicken pieces onto skewers, so they sit tightly. Heat a grill pan to hot. Cook 4 at a time for about 4–6 minutes until golden, then turn and cook the other side for about the same time or until the chicken begins to char at the edges. Repeat to cook the remaining kebabs and serve with the satay sauce.

VEGETABLE SPRING ROLLS

MAKES 10
PREP 30 mins
COOK 15–20 mins

Fry these ahead and crisp them in a hot oven just before serving. Look for spring roll wrappers in Asian markets.

GUIDELINES PER SERVING

●●○ Calories

●○○ Saturated fat

●●○ Salt

STATISTICS PER ROLL

Energy 105kcals/440kJ

Protein 1.1g

Fat 6g
Saturated fat 0.7g

Carbohydrate 12g
Sugar 8g

Fiber 1g

Salt 0.7g

½oz (15g) dried shiitake mushrooms, soaked in boiling water for 20 mins
1 small carrot, cut into matchsticks
3 scallions, cut into matchsticks
3oz (85g) green cabbage, shredded
2 garlic cloves, crushed
¾in (2cm) piece fresh ginger, peeled and grated
2 tbsp tamari (gluten-free soy sauce)
1 tbsp Chinese cooking wine
½ tsp Chinese 5 spice powder
1 tbsp vegetable oil
2oz (60g) bean sprouts

20 spring roll wrappers
vegetable oil, for deep frying

FOR THE CHILE DIPPING SAUCE
2 tbsp granulated sugar
⅓ cup rice wine vinegar
2 garlic cloves, chopped
2 red or jalapeño chiles, chopped

SPECIAL EQUIPMENT
Deep-fat fryer, or large pan
cooking thermometer

1 Drain and finely chop the mushrooms and mix together with the next five ingredients. In a small liquid measuring cup, mix the tamari, wine, and spice powder. Heat the oil in a frying pan or wok, add the vegetable mix, mushrooms, and bean sprouts, and stir-fry for 1 minute. Add the tamari mix and simmer for 30 seconds. Remove from the heat and leave to cool.

2 For the dipping sauce, place the ingredients in a medium pan with ¼ cup of water, boil, then simmer for 5 minutes. Remove and leave to cool.

3 Dip a wrapper in a bowl of warm water for 10–15 seconds or until soft. Lay it on a damp kitchen towel and blot until slightly sticky. Place a heaped tablespoon of filling in the center. Fold the bottom of the wrapper up over the filling, fold in the sides, rolling up the wrapper tightly. Soak a second wrapper, wrap it around the first layer, and set aside. Repeat until the filling is used up. Heat the oil in a deep-fat fryer or large pan until it reaches 350°F (180°C). Do not leave the fryer or pan unattended, switch off when not using, and keep a fire blanket nearby in case of fire. Cook the spring rolls in the hot oil, two at a time, for 3–4 minutes or until golden. Remove with a slotted spoon and drain on paper towels. Keep warm while you fry the remainder. Serve the rolls hot with the chile dipping sauce.

VEGETABLE TEMPURA

SERVES 6
PREP 25 mins
COOK 10 mins

Don't let the batter for these Japanese snacks sit: it needs to be used immediately, so prepare the vegetables ahead.

GUIDELINES PER SERVING

● ● ● Calories
● ● ○ Saturated fat
● ○ ○ Salt

STATISTICS PER SERVING

Energy 221kcals/918kJ

Protein 3g

Fat 13g
Saturated fat 2g

Carbohydrate 22g
Sugar 0.5g

Fiber 3g

Salt 0.3g

1 red bell pepper, seeded and cut into strips
1 small head of broccoli, broken into florets
1 medium onion, cut into eights
2 carrots, cut into batons
1 tbsp cornstarch
sunflower or vegetable oil, for frying

FOR THE DIPPING SAUCE
2 tbsp mirin
3 tbsp tamari (gluten-free soy sauce)

1–2 tsp sugar, or to taste
1 tbsp lime juice

FOR THE BATTER
1 large egg yolk
2 cups sparkling mineral water, ice cold
2 cups rice flour, sifted
salt and freshly ground pepper

SPECIAL EQUIPMENT
large, deep, nonstick frying pan or wok

1 To make the sauce, place the mirin, tamari, and sugar in a bowl and mix. Then add the lime juice and 3 tablespoons water to dilute it. Mix again, taste, and add more water if needed. Set aside.

2 For the batter, place the egg in a bowl and mix with a fork. Pour in the mineral water and mix. Add the rice flour and seasoning and mix lightly.

3 Toss the prepared vegetables in the cornstarch. Pour the oil into the pan or wok, to a depth of 3in (7.5cm). Heat on high until hot. Do not leave the fryer or pan unattended, switch off when not using, and keep a fire blanket nearby in case of fire. Dip the vegetables, one by one, into the batter until just coated, then place them in the oil. Don't overcrowd the pan. Remove with a slotted spoon as soon as the batter is crispy and golden, about 2–3 minutes, and drain on paper towels. Serve hot with the dipping sauce.

TAMARI
Most soy sauce is made by fermenting soya beans with roasted wheat. Tamari, however, is made only with beans and is naturally gluten-free.

SESAME SHRIMP TOASTS

Ready in minutes and great to serve as a canapé with drinks. If you omit the chile from the shrimp mixture, they make a delicious after-school snack for children.

MAKES   32
PREP   15 mins
COOK   15–20 mins

9oz (250g) ready-cooked shrimp
1 red chile, seeded and
  finely chopped
handful of fresh cilantro leaves,
  finely chopped
salt and freshly ground pepper
8 slices of gluten-free white bread
  (see page 38), lightly toasted

¼ cup sesame seeds, or more
  if needed
4–5 tbsp sunflower oil, or more
  if needed

GUIDELINES PER SERVING

● ● ○   Calories
● ● ○   Saturated fat
● ○ ○   Salt

STATISTICS PER TOAST

Energy 43kcals/182kJ

Protein 2g

Fat 3g
Saturated fat 0.5g

Carbohydrate 3g
Sugar 0.2g

Fiber 0.3g

Salt 0.2g

1 Add the shrimp to a food processor along with the chile, cilantro, salt, and pepper, then purée until really well minced. Slice the crusts off the bread and reserve (see Cook's Tip).

2 Spread the minced shrimp mixture over the toast slices and press down well to make sure it sticks. Cut the toasts into quarters and then triangles. Pour the sesame seeds out onto a plate and dip each toast, shrimp-side down, into them to cover.

3 Heat 1 tablespoon oil in a frying pan over medium heat. Add a few toasts at a time, plain-side down, and cook for 1–2 minutes, then turn and cook the topped side for 1–2 minutes or until golden brown. Remove and place on paper towels. Remove excess sesame seeds from the pan and continue until all the toasts are done, adding more oil as needed.

Cook's Tip
Use the bread crusts to make bread crumbs: purée in a food processor and keep sealed in the fridge for a few days or in the freezer for up to 3 months.

LEMONGRASS-MARINATED SHRIMP SKEWERS

SERVES 4
PREP 15 mins
PLUS MARINATING
COOK 10 mins

GUIDELINES PER SERVING

● ○ ○ Calories

● ○ ○ Saturated fat

● ● ● Salt

STATISTICS PER SERVING

Energy 128kcals/541kJ

Protein 17g

Fat 1g
Saturated fat 0.1g

Carbohydrate 3g
Sugar 3g

Fiber 0g

Salt 2g

Serve these alongside Chicken satay kebabs (see page 95) for an Asian-inspired family feast.

2 garlic cloves, roughly chopped
½ red chile, seeded and roughly chopped
2 lemongrass stalks, bottom (thickest) one-third only, peeled of hard layers and roughly chopped
1in (3cm) fresh ginger root, finely chopped
1 tbsp chopped cilantro roots or stalks
2 tbsp fish sauce

2 tsp light brown sugar
1 tbsp lime juice, plus lime wedges, to serve
40 raw, shelled, and deveined large shrimp

SPECIAL EQUIPMENT
blender or food processor
8 bamboo skewers

1 Prepare the grill for cooking. To make the marinade, simply put all the ingredients, except the shrimp, in a blender or food processor and pulse to a fine paste.

2 Toss the shrimp in the marinade, cover, and leave in the refrigerator to marinate for 1 hour. Meanwhile, soak 8 bamboo skewers in water, as this will help to keep them from burning on the grill.

3 Thread 5 shrimp onto each skewer, threading through the top and bottom of the shrimp to make a curved "C"-shape. Grill the shrimp on the barbecue for 2–3 minutes on each side, until pink and charred in places. Serve with a squeeze of lime.

Cook in the oven
Preheat the broiler to its highest setting and line the broiler pan with foil. Lay the shrimp skewers on the broiler pan and cook for 2–3 minutes on each side.

How to freeze
Wrap well and freeze the marinated, uncooked shrimp. Defrost thoroughly, covered, in the refrigerator before use.

MINI FISHCAKES WITH CILANTRO MAYONNAISE

SERVES 4
PREP 30 mins
PLUS CHILLING
COOK 30 mins
FREEZE 3 months
FISHCAKES ONLY

GUIDELINES PER SERVING

● ● ● Calories

● ● ● Saturated fat

● ● ○ Salt

STATISTICS PER SERVING

Energy 766kcals/2534kJ

Protein 32g

Fat 37g
Saturated fat 7.5g

Carbohydrate 37g
Sugar 7g

Fiber 2.5g

Salt 1g

GREAT
FOR KIDS

NUTRIENT
BOOST
Oily fish like salmon are rich in omega-3 fats that help keep your heart healthy.

Omit the mayonnaise if you are in a vulnerable health group as it contains raw eggs, which have a risk of salmonella.

2 large egg yolks
1 tsp Dijon mustard
salt and freshly ground pepper
1¼ cups sunflower or vegetable oil,
  plus extra for frying
1 tbsp white wine vinegar
handful of fresh cilantro,
  leaves only, finely chopped
1lb (450g) salmon fillet, skinned
1¼ cups milk

7oz (200g) mashed potato
small handful of dill, finely chopped
zest and juice of ½ lemon
¼–½ tsp cayenne pepper
½ green bell pepper, finely chopped
2–3 tbsp rice flour
1 large egg, lightly beaten
3½oz (100g) gluten-free white bread
  (see page 38), pulsed into
  fine bread crumbs

1 For the mayonnaise, place the egg yolks and mustard in a bowl, season, and whisk until creamy. Add a tiny drop of oil and whisk until incorporated. Keep adding the oil slowly, a drop at a time, whisking until the mixture emulsifies and thickens. Trickle in the oil faster and add the vinegar. Keep whisking until thick and creamy, taste, and add seasoning or vinegar if necessary. Stir in the cilantro, cover, and set aside.

2 For the fishcakes, add the salmon to a deep-sided frying pan and pour over the milk, season, bring to a boil, and simmer gently for 4–6 minutes until the fish starts to turn opaque. Transfer the salmon with a slotted spoon to a bowl. Flake the fish, add the mashed potato, dill, lemon zest and juice, cayenne, and green bell pepper, and season. Stir, then scoop out ½ tablespoon of mixture and flatten into a mini cake. Repeat to make about 20 cakes. Place on a baking sheet lined with wax paper.

3 Dredge the fishcakes in flour, dip in egg, and coat with bread crumbs. Chill for 30 minutes. Heat 1 tablespoon oil in a nonstick frying pan and cook a few cakes at a time, 3–4 minutes each side, until golden. Serve with the mayo.

SOUPS
AND
SALADS

FRENCH ONION SOUP

SERVES 6
PREP 25 mins
COOK 1 hour 25 mins–
1 hour 40 mins

An extremely satisfying soup and filling enough for a main meal when served with delicious cheese toasties on top.

GUIDELINES PER SERVING

● ● ●   Calories
● ● ●   Saturated fat
● ● ●   Salt

STATISTICS PER SERVING

Energy 298kcals/1249kJ

Protein 13g

Fat 13g
Saturated fat 6g

Carbohydrate 28g
Sugar 9g

Fiber 3g

Salt 0.9g

2 tbsp olive oil
6 onions, peeled, halved, and
  thinly sliced
salt and freshly ground black pepper
1 bay leaf
1 tbsp brown sugar
½ cup dry white wine
1 quart hot gluten-free
  beef or vegetable stock

FOR THE TOASTIES
4–6 slices of gluten-free white bread
  (see page 38), crusts removed and
  lightly toasted
5½oz (150g) Gruyère cheese, grated

1 Heat the oil in a flameproof casserole dish, add the onions, and stir. Season and add the bay leaf. Cook on low heat for about 15 minutes, until they begin to soften. Raise the heat a little, sprinkle in the sugar, and stir. Cook for another 35 minutes, until the onions are golden and caramelized. Stir them occasionally, watching that they don't burn; turn the heat down, if required.

2 Over medium-high heat, add the wine, and stir to get all the sticky pieces of onion off the bottom of the casserole dish. Cook for 1–2 minutes, then pour in the hot stock. Bring to a boil, then reduce to a simmer and cook uncovered for 20–30 minutes. Remove the bay leaf and season to taste.

3 Preheat the oven to 350°F (180°C). Sprinkle a handful of cheese into the soup and stir well. Place the slices of toast on the top of the soup and divide the remaining cheese over the toast. Cook in the oven until the cheese begins to bubble and turns golden. Divide between bowls, topped with a cheese toastie.

Cook's Tips
The trick for rich-tasting French onion soup is to let the onions caramelize. Use a wide, heavy flameproof casserole dish—cast iron is ideal—so there is little chance of it burning. This is a perfect recipe for using up any leftover bread.

MINESTRONE SOUP

This soup can use up a glut of seasonal vegetables, simply change them depending on the time of the year.

SERVES 8
PREP 40 mins
COOK 1¾–2¼ hours
FREEZE 3 months

GUIDELINES PER SERVING

● ● ○ Calories
● ● ○ Saturated fat
● ○ ○ Salt

STATISTICS PER SERVING

Energy 215kcals/910kJ

Protein 11g

Fat 4g
Saturated fat 0.5g

Carbohydrate 34g
Sugar 7g

Fiber 9.5g

Salt 0.8g

1 ham knuckle or "hock," or 1 package of bacon, roughly chopped
1 tbsp olive oil
1 onion, finely chopped
2 bay leaves
3 carrots, diced
1 fennel bulb, finely chopped
2 garlic cloves, finely chopped
freshly ground black pepper
4 large ripe tomatoes, chopped
handful of thyme sprigs, leaves only
pinch of freshly grated nutmeg
14oz (400g) can chickpeas, drained and rinsed

14oz (400g) can cannellini or butter beans, drained and rinsed
3½oz (100g) fava beans, fresh or defrosted, shelled weight
3½oz (100g) peas, fresh or defrosted, shelled weight
7oz (200g) small gluten-free pasta shapes (store-bought or see pages 42–3)
3½oz (100g) spinach
grated Parmesan or Pecorino cheese

1 Put the ham hock in a large pan and add enough cold water to nearly fill the pan. Bring to a boil, reduce to medium-low heat, partially cover the pan with a lid, and cook for 1–1½ hours, or until the ham begins to soften. Strain the stock, reserving the bones and meat. Strain the stock again, through a fine strainer into a measuring cup; you will need 1 quart, and add water if necessary. Set aside. Strip the meat from the bones, discard the bones, and set the meat aside.

2 Heat the oil in a large, heavy pan. Add the onion and bay leaves, and cook for 5–7 minutes, until soft. Add the carrots and fennel and cook for 8 more minutes, until soft. Stir in the garlic and season with pepper, add the tomatoes, and cook on low heat for 10 minutes. Ladle in a little stock if it starts to get dry. Add the thyme leaves, nutmeg, chickpeas, beans, and peas, and stir. Add enough stock to cover and simmer gently for 10 minutes. Add the pasta shapes, the reserved meat, and remaining stock. Bring to a boil, then simmer until the pasta is cooked. Add the spinach and stir. Taste and season again, if needed. Serve with the grated cheese.

GREAT FOR KIDS

NUTRIENT BOOST
Canned beans and peas are an excellent source of soluble fiber.

HARVEST VEGETABLE SOUP

Also known as "bottom-of-the-refrigerator soup," this is a great way to use up leftover vegetables.

SERVES 4–6
PREP 10 mins
COOK 30 mins

GUIDELINES PER SERVING

Calories

Saturated fat

Salt

STATISTICS PER SERVING

Energy 124–186kcals/519–778kJ

Protein 1–1.5g

Fat 6–9g
Saturated fat 0.8–1g

Carbohydrate 10–14g
Sugar 4.5–7g

Fiber 3–4.5g

Salt 0.4–0.6g

3 tbsp olive oil
1 onion, chopped
1 leek, white part only, chopped
1 celery stalk, chopped
1lb 2oz (500g) mixed root vegetables,
   peeled weight, such as carrots,
   potatoes, parsnips, and turnips,
   cut into even-sized cubes
salt and freshly ground black pepper

FOR THE STOCK
1 onion
2 cloves
1 carrot, cut into 4 pieces
1 celery stalk, cut into 4 pieces
2 bay leaves
2 leeks, trimmed and roughly chopped
pinch of salt
1 tsp black peppercorns

1 For the stock, stud the onion with the cloves and place in a large pan with the carrot, celery, bay leaves, leeks, salt, and peppercorns. Add 2½ pints (1.4 liters) water and bring to a boil. Reduce to a simmer; partially cover with a lid, and cook for 1 hour on low heat. Turn off the heat, cover, and leave for the flavors to infuse.

2 Heat the oil in a large, heavy-bottomed saucepan with a lid. Add the onion, leek, and celery and cook for 5 minutes until they soften, but do not brown.

3 Add the mixed root vegetables and 2½ cups of the stock, and season well.

4 Bring to a boil, then reduce the heat to a gentle simmer. Cover and cook for 20 minutes, until all the vegetables are soft.

5 Blend the soup, either in a blender or using a handheld blender, until it is completely smooth. Add more stock if you want a thinner soup. Check the seasoning and add a swirl of cream to serve.

BEET AND GINGER SOUP

SERVES   4
PREP   10 mins
COOK   55 mins

Earthy beets always make a colorful soup. Here, ginger adds a pleasant zing and the wasabi cream, swirled in at the last minute, gives a fiery kick.

GUIDELINES PER SERVING

● ● ●   Calories

● ● ●   Saturated fat

● ● ●   Salt

STATISTICS PER SERVING

Energy 113kcals/475kJ

Protein 4g

Fat 5.5g
Saturated fat 2g

Carbohydrate 12g
Sugar 12g

Fiber 4g

Salt 0.7g

NUTRIENT BOOST
Beets are rich in antioxidants and folate.

1lb 2oz (500g) raw beets,
   greens removed
salt
pinch of sugar
1 tbsp olive oil
bunch of scallions, trimmed and
   finely chopped
2in (5cm) piece of fresh ginger,
   peeled and grated

sea salt and freshly ground pepper
1½ cups hot gluten-free vegetable stock
   (see page 108)
3 tbsp sour cream
¼ tsp wasabi paste, or more
   if you like it hot

1 To cook the beets, place them in a pan of salted water, add the sugar, and bring to a boil. Cook on medium-low heat with the lid ajar for 40 minutes or until the beets are tender when poked with a sharp knife. Drain and, when cool enough to handle, peel and roughly chop the beets.

2 In a clean pan, heat the oil and add the scallions. Cook for 2–3 minutes on medium heat, just enough for them to soften, then add the ginger and cook for a further minute. Add the chopped beets and stir well to coat with the oil. Season, pour in the stock, and bring to a boil.

3 Reduce to a simmer and cook gently for about 10 minutes, then ladle into a blender and purée until smooth, or use an immersion blender. Taste and season some more, if needed. Mix the sour cream with the wasabi. Ladle the soup into bowls with a swirl of the wasabi cream.

Cook's Tip
If you don't have wasabi paste, use gluten-free hot horseradish sauce instead.

EGYPTIAN LENTIL SOUP

The gentle spice flavors of this hearty vegetarian soup are greatly enhanced by a squeeze of lemon before serving.

SERVES   6
PREP   15 mins
COOK   30 mins
FREEZE   3 months

GUIDELINES PER SERVING

● ● ●   Calories

● ● ●   Saturated fat

● ● ●   Salt

STATISTICS PER SERVING

Energy 245kcals/1028kJ

Protein 7g

Fat 9g
Saturated fat 5g

Carbohydrate 25g
Sugar 4g

Fiber 4g

Salt 0.6g

GREAT FOR KIDS

NUTRIENT BOOST
Lentils are an excellent source of fiber and count toward your 5-a-day.

1 tbsp olive oil
4 tbsp butter
1 onion, finely chopped
salt and freshly ground black pepper
1 tsp cumin seeds
1 tsp turmeric
1 tsp paprika
2 garlic cloves, finely chopped
2 carrots, diced
2 potatoes, diced

4½oz (125g) red lentils
3 cups hot gluten-free vegetable stock
  (see page 108)
lemon wedges and 2 warmed
  gluten-free pita breads (see page 232),
  to serve

1 Heat the oil and butter in a large pan, add the onion, and cook on low heat for 2–3 minutes, until soft. Season and stir in the cumin seeds, turmeric, and paprika. Add the garlic, carrots, and potatoes and cook, stirring occasionally, for 5 minutes.

2 Stir in the lentils, making sure they get coated with any buttery juices. Ladle in a little hot stock, bring to a boil, stir, and then add the rest of the stock. Boil again, reduce to a simmer, and cook gently for 15–20 minutes, or until the soup thickens and the potatoes are cooked. Add more hot water, if required.

3 Season to taste. Transfer to a food processor and blend until smooth, in batches, if necessary, or use a handheld blender. Pour the soup into a clean pan and top with hot water, if required. Heat through until piping hot and serve in shallow bowls with lemon wedges and warmed gluten-free pita breads.

Cook's Tips
You could top the soup with a sprinkling of dukkah, an Egyptian spice blend made with toasted nuts and herbs. For a sweeter version that will appeal to kids, add a 14oz (400g) can of chopped tomatoes with the stock.

INDIAN SPLIT PEA SOUP WITH PANEER CROUTONS

This rich, creamy soup is topped with spicy croutons made from Indian paneer. The ghee gives it an authentic touch.

1 tbsp ghee or 1 tbsp sunflower
  or vegetable oil
1 onion, finely chopped
1 tsp turmeric
seeds of 4 cardamom pods, crushed
2 garlic cloves, finely chopped
1–2 jalapeños, seeded and finely chopped
salt and freshly ground black pepper
5½oz (150g) yellow split peas, rinsed
  and drained
14oz (400g) can coconut milk
3 cups hot gluten-free vegetable stock

FOR THE CROUTONS
1 tbsp ghee or 1 tbsp sunflower or
  vegetable oil
1–2 pinches of dried chili flakes
½ tsp ground cumin
½ tsp ground cinnamon
3½oz (100g) paneer, cut
  into small cubes
fresh cilantro leaves, to garnish
2 warmed gluten-free pita breads
  (see page 232), to serve

SERVES 4
PREP 25 mins
COOK 50 mins

GUIDELINES PER SERVING

● ● ○ Calories
● ● ● Saturated fat
● ○ ○ Salt

STATISTICS PER SERVING

Energy 397kcals/1666kJ

Protein 16g

Fat 25g
Saturated fat 16g

Carbohydrate 27g
Sugar 3g

Fiber 4g

Salt 0.23g

1 Heat the ghee or oil in a large pan. Add the onion, turmeric, and crushed cardamom seeds. Cook on low heat for 2–3 minutes, until the onion softens. Stir in the garlic, chile, and seasoning and cook for another 1–2 minutes.

2 Stir in the split peas and turn, so they soak up any liquid and get coated with spices. Pour in a little coconut milk, increase the heat, and stir. Pour in the remaining coconut milk with half the stock and bring to a boil. Reduce to a simmer and cook uncovered for 30–35 minutes, until the peas are soft, adding more stock, if required. Season to taste and blend in a food processor until smooth, or use a handheld blender.

3 For the croutons, place the ghee or oil in a small frying pan along with the spices, season, and heat gently over low heat. Add the paneer, turn the heat up a little, and fry for 10 minutes, until golden on all sides.

4 Heat the soup through until piping hot and top with the paneer croutons and cilantro. Serve with warmed gluten-free pita breads.

SMOKED OYSTER SOUP

SERVES   4
PREP   10 mins
COOK   30 mins

This sophisticated soup is a perfect dinner-party appetizer. No one will realize it's actually quite simple to make.

GUIDELINES PER SERVING

● ● ○   Calories

● ● ●   Saturated fat

● ● ●   Salt

STATISTICS PER SERVING

Energy 209kcals/869kJ

Protein 4g

Fat 13g
Saturated fat 5g

Carbohydrate 17g
Sugar 2g

Fiber 2g

Salt 2.5g

2 tbsp olive oil
1 onion, finely chopped
2 large white potatoes, approx.
  12oz (350g) in total, peeled and
  roughly chopped
1 x 3oz (85g) can of smoked oysters in
  sunflower oil, drained and rinsed
3½ cups gluten-free fish stock

¼ cup whipping cream, plus extra
  to serve
salt and freshly ground black pepper
1 tbsp dry sherry (optional)

SPECIAL EQUIPMENT
blender

1 Heat the olive oil in a large, heavy-bottomed saucepan. Cook the onion over low heat, covered, for 5–7 minutes until it softens, but is not brown.

2 Add the potatoes, smoked oysters, fish stock, and cream, and season with a little salt and pepper. Bring the soup to a boil, then reduce to a simmer, partially cover, and cook for 20–25 minutes, until the potatoes are soft.

3 Purée the soup until smooth (if you are using a blender, you may have to do this in batches; it is important not to fill the blender more than one-third full with hot liquid). Now pass it through a sieve so that it is completely smooth.

4 Return the soup to the pan and heat it gently. Add the sherry (if using) and serve with a swirl of cream in the center of the bowls and a sprinkling of pepper.

SMOKED HADDOCK CHOWDER

SERVES 4
PREP 20 mins
COOK 30 mins

This hearty, creamy soup with delicate white fish and meaty shrimp is a meal in itself.

GUIDELINES PER SERVING

● ● ● Calories
● ● ● Saturated fat
● ● ● Salt

STATISTICS PER SERVING

Energy 693kcals/2908kJ

Protein 44g

Fat 33.5g
Saturated fat 17g

Carbohydrate 43g
Sugar 10g

Fiber 3.5g

Salt 3g

2 tbsp butter
1 onion, finely chopped
salt and freshly ground pepper
7oz (200g) smoked pancetta, chopped,
　or smoked bacon bits
1 bay leaf
3 medium waxy potatoes, such as
　Yukon gold or Red, peeled and cut
　into bite-sized pieces
2 tbsp rice flour

1 large glass of white wine
1¼ cup half-and-half
2 cups gluten-free vegetable or fish stock
14oz (400g) can corn, drained
12oz (350g) smoked, undyed haddock,
　skinned and roughly chopped
9oz (250g) raw, shelled shrimp

1 Heat the butter in a large pan, add the onion, and season. Cook on low heat for 2–3 minutes until softened, then increase the heat a little, add the pancetta and bay leaf, and cook for 4–5 minutes.

2 Turn the heat down, add the potatoes, and stir well to coat with the juices. Add the flour and mix thoroughly. Add the wine, increase the heat, and let the wine boil for 1–2 minutes, stirring occasionally. Stir in the half-and-half and stock, and bring to a boil.

3 Reduce the heat, add the corn, and simmer gently for about 15 minutes or until the potatoes are cooked. Add the haddock and shrimp, cover with a lid, and cook for 4–6 minutes until the fish is just turning opaque and the shrimp are pink. Taste and season if necessary.

Cook's Tip
The secret to a good chowder lies in not overcooking the fish. It will be ready in minutes and will continue cooking in the hot stock once taken off the stove.

ASIAN CRAB AND NOODLE SOUP

Prepare this soup a day in advance to allow the flavors to develop, then add the noodles and crab before serving.

SERVES 4
PREP 15 mins
PLUS CHILLING
COOK 30 mins

GUIDELINES PER SERVING

● ● ● Calories
● ● ● Saturated fat
● ● ● Salt

STATISTICS PER SERVING

Energy 369kcals/1550kJ

Protein 24g

Fat 9.5g
Saturated fat 1g

Carbohydrate 44g
Sugar 13g

Fiber 4g

Salt 3g

1 tbsp sunflower oil
1 bunch of scallions,
  diagonally sliced
1–2 red chiles or jalapeños, seeded
  and finely chopped
1–2 garlic cloves, finely chopped
3 carrots, diagonally sliced
14oz (400g) can corn, drained
salt and freshly ground black pepper

2 tbsp tamari (gluten-free soy sauce)
2½ cups hot gluten-free vegetable stock
3½oz (100g) fine dried rice noodles
14oz (400g) white crab meat
small bunch of chives, finely chopped
small bunch of fresh cilantro, roughly
  chopped (see Cook's Tip)

1 Heat the oil in a large pan and swirl it around. Add the scallions and cook over medium heat for 1 minute, until softened. Add the chile, garlic, carrots, and corn. Stir and season with salt and pepper.

2 Add the tamari and stir it around so everything gets coated, then add a little of the stock and bring to a boil. Add the rest of the stock, bring to a boil again, partially cover with a lid, reduce to simmer, and gently cook over low heat for 15–20 minutes, or until the carrots are soft. Set aside to cool, then chill overnight in the refrigerator to allow the flavors to develop.

3 Place the noodles in a large bowl and pour over enough boiling water to cover. Leave to soak according to package instructions, then drain.

4 Gently warm the soup, add the noodles, and stir in the crab meat and half the herbs until piping hot. Ladle the soup into bowls and sprinkle with the remaining herbs to serve.

Cook's Tip
Use the cilantro stalks as well as leaves, which are full of flavor and give a much more distinctive taste than the leaves alone.

CHINESE CHICKEN SOUP WITH SHRIMP DUMPLINGS

If you don't have time to make dumplings, simply chop the shrimp and stir them right into the soup.

SERVES 4
PREP 20 mins
COOK 50 mins

2 large boneless, skinless chicken breasts
salt and freshly ground black pepper
5 scallions, diagonally sliced
2in (5cm) piece of ginger, peeled and
  sliced into matchsticks
1–2 tbsp tamari (gluten-free soy sauce)
$^1\!/_2$–1 red chile or jalapeño, thinly sliced
  diagonally
5$^1\!/_2$oz (150g) shiitake mushrooms, sliced
4$^1\!/_2$oz (125g) cooked rice

FOR THE DUMPLINGS
12oz (350g) shrimp, cooked and peeled
2in (5cm) piece of ginger, peeled and
  roughly chopped
1 red chile, seeded, finely chopped
small handful of cilantro leaves,
  plus extra to garnish
2 tsp gluten-free nam pla (fish sauce)
2 tbsp cornstarch, plus extra for rolling

GUIDELINES PER SERVING

- Calories
- Saturated fat
- Salt

STATISTICS PER SERVING

Energy 250kcals/1047kJ

Protein 36g

Fat 2g
Saturated fat 0.5g

Carbohydrate 19g
Sugar 1g

Fiber 0.9g

Salt 2.5g

1 For the stock, pour 6 cups water into a large pan and add the chicken breasts and seasoning. Bring to a steady simmer and cook on low-medium heat, partially covered, for 15–20 minutes, until the chicken is cooked. Remove with a slotted spoon and set aside to cool. Strain the stock into a clean pan; you will need about 1 quart. Shred the chicken and set aside.

2 For the dumplings, put all ingredients in a food processor, season, and pulse until minced. Scoop up small handfuls and roll into balls; you may need more cornstarch. Place the dumplings on a plate; chill in the refrigerator.

3 Heat the stock over low-medium heat, add the scallions, ginger, tamari, chile, and the mushrooms, and cook for about 20 minutes. Taste and adjust the seasoning as needed.

4 Stir in the rice and shredded chicken and simmer gently for 2 minutes. Add the dumplings, cover, and cook for about 5–8 minutes. Ladle into bowls and top with cilantro leaves to serve.

MEXICAN CORN SOUP WITH TORTILLA CHIPS

SERVES 6
PREP 15 mins
COOK 25 mins

Make this easy-to-prepare soup as hot and spicy as you like, and use gluten-free chips as an alternative topping.

GUIDELINES PER SERVING

● ● ● Calories

● ● ● Saturated fat

● ● ● Salt

STATISTICS PER SERVING

Energy 330kcals/1384kJ

Protein 4g

Fat 11g
Saturated fat 5g

Carbohydrate 32g
Sugar 12g

Fiber 2.5g

Salt 1.4g

2 x 14oz (400g) cans corn
1 tbsp olive oil
4 tbsp butter
1 onion, finely chopped
2 garlic cloves, finely chopped
½ tsp cumin seeds
3–4 pickled red or green jalapeños, finely chopped
salt and freshly ground black pepper

pinch of cayenne pepper (optional)
a few sprigs of thyme, leaves only
1 tbsp gluten-free all-purpose flour
3¾ cups hot gluten-free vegetable or chicken stock
2 corn tortillas (see page 233)
handful of fresh cilantro leaves, roughly chopped
lime wedges, to serve

1 Pulse half the corn in a food processor until smooth. Heat the oil and butter in a large, heavy pan, add the onion, and cook over low heat for 2–3 minutes, until beginning to soften. Stir in the garlic, cumin, and jalapeños, cook for 1 minute, and season.

2 Add the cayenne and thyme and cook gently for 1 minute. Then remove from the heat, stir in the flour, and pour in the pulsed and whole corn. Pour in a little stock and return the pan to the heat. Heat until it bubbles, stirring, then add the remaining stock and bring to a boil. Reduce to a simmer and cook gently for 15 minutes, or until the soup begins to thicken.

3 Preheat the broiler to medium and lightly broil the tortillas for about 1 minute on each side, or until they start to crisp and bubble. Cut the tortillas into small triangles. Taste the soup and season again, if necessary. Divide between bowls, top with the tortilla triangles and cilantro, and serve with lime wedges.

Cook's Tip
If you don't have a food processor, substitute a can of creamed corn instead of pulsing.

NUTRIENT BOOST
Corn provides a useful amount of fiber, vitamin B6, and magnesium.

GREAT FOR KIDS

TOMATO PANZANELLA SOUP

This rustic soup is a great way to use up leftover bread. Make it in summer when fresh tomatoes are flavorful.

2 tbsp olive oil
1 onion, finely chopped
salt and freshly ground black pepper
2 garlic cloves, finely chopped
2lb (900g) tomatoes, skinned
  (see Cook's tip)
2½ cups hot gluten-free vegetable stock
  (see page 108)
4 chunky slices of stale gluten-free bread
  (see page 38), roughly torn

handful of basil leaves
fruity extra virgin olive oil,
  for drizzling

GUIDELINES PER SERVING

● ● ○   Calories
● ● ○   Saturated fat
● ○ ○   Salt

STATISTICS PER SERVING

Energy 225kcals/947kJ

Protein 6.5g

Fat 10g
Saturated fat 1.5g

Carbohydrate 27g
Sugar 9g

Fiber 4g

Salt 0.6g

1 Heat the olive oil in a large pan, add the onion, and cook over low heat for 5–6 minutes, until soft. Season with salt and pepper, stir in the garlic, and cook for another minute.

2 Roughly chop the tomatoes, add these with any juices to the pan, and cook on low heat for 5 minutes. Pour in the stock and add the bread, pushing it down with a spoon so it is completely immersed.

3 Partially cover the pan with a lid and cook gently for about 15 minutes. The soup should be fairly dense, so you could almost eat it with a fork, but add more hot water, if required. Season to taste. Stir in the basil, ladle into bowls, and drizzle with the olive oil to serve.

Cook's Tips
To skin the tomatoes, simply cross the top of each one with a sharp knife, place them in a bowl, and cover with boiling water. Count to 10, remove with a slotted spoon, and place them in a bowl of cold water: the skins should slip off easily.

GREAT FOR KIDS

NUTRIENT BOOST
Tomatoes are rich in lycopene, believed to protect against some cancers.

QUINOA SALAD WITH MANGO, LIME, AND TOASTED COCONUT

A healthy salad full of big, tropical flavors and bright colors. Try to get Alphonso mangoes, if possible, which are famed for their sweetness.

SERVES   4
PREP   15 mins
COOK   10 mins

GUIDELINES PER SERVING

● ● ○   Calories

● ● ●   Saturated fat

● ○ ○   Salt

STATISTICS PER SERVING

Energy   460kcals/1935kJ

Protein   15g

Fat   20g
Saturated fat   8g

Carbohydrate   54g
Sugar   12.5g

Fiber   7.5g

Salt   0.8g

NUTRIENT BOOST
Mango is an excellent source of betacarotene.

1¾oz (50g) unsweetened or flaked coconut
10oz (300g) quinoa
14oz (400g) can butter beans, drained and rinsed
½ red onion, finely chopped
1 large mango, peeled, pitted, and cut into bite-sized pieces
1 lime, peeled, segmented, and segments halved
handful of mint, finely chopped
handful of flat-leaf parsley, finely chopped

FOR THE DRESSING
3 tbsp olive oil
1 tbsp white wine vinegar
pinch of sugar
salt and freshly ground pepper

1 Toast the coconut by dry frying it in a pan over medium heat for 2–3 minutes until golden, stirring so that it doesn't burn. Set aside and cool.

2 To make the dressing, place all the ingredients in a small bowl or liquid measuring cup and whisk. Taste and adjust the seasoning as needed.

3 Cook the quinoa according to the instructions on the package. Drain well and place into a large serving bowl. While the quinoa is still warm, stir in the butter beans, onion, mango, lime, mint, and parsley, and season.

4 Pour over the dressing and stir well. Sprinkle the toasted coconut on top and serve immediately.

QUINOA, FAVA BEAN, AND DILL SALAD

SERVES 4
PREP 15 mins
COOK 20 mins

If possible, prepare this salad at least an hour in advance so that the flavors have time to develop.

GUIDELINES PER SERVING

● ○ ○   Calories

● ○ ○   Saturated fat

● ○ ○   Salt

STATISTICS PER SERVING

Energy 290kcals/1215kJ

Protein 12g

Fat 9g
Saturated fat 1g

Carbohydrate 40g
Sugar 13g

Fiber 6g

Salt trace

7oz (200g) quinoa
9oz (250g) fava beans, fresh
  or frozen, shelled weight
salt and freshly ground black pepper
1 tbsp olive oil
3 small zucchini, trimmed, halved
  lengthwise, and chopped

2 garlic cloves, finely chopped
a pinch of dried chili flakes
zest and juice of 1 lemon
handful of golden raisins (optional)
bunch of dill, finely chopped
1 tbsp fruity extra virgin olive oil
gluten-free bread, to serve

1 Put the quinoa in a pan, cover with water, bring to a boil, and cook according to package instructions. Drain well, rinse under cold running water, and transfer to a large serving dish.

2 Cook the fava beans in a pan of boiling salted water for 2 minutes, until tender. Drain and rinse under cold water. If using fresh beans, peel the outer skin of any larger than your thumbnail. Add to the quinoa in the serving dish.

3 Heat the olive oil in a large frying pan, add the zucchini, and season well. Stir in the garlic, chili flakes, and lemon zest, and cook on medium heat for 5–6 minutes, until golden. Stir the zucchini into the quinoa and beans. Add the golden raisins (if using) and dill, and mix well. Add the lemon juice and extra virgin olive oil. Taste and season, if necessary. Serve with some gluten-free bread.

PANZANELLA

This classic Italian salad combines torn bread tossed with fresh tomatoes and basil.

SERVES   4
PREP   10 mins

8 slices of gluten-free white bread, preferably homemade (see page 38), crusts removed
handful of basil leaves, torn
extra virgin olive oil, for drizzling
1–2 tbsp balsamic vinegar

sea salt and freshly ground black pepper
5 tomatoes, skinned and roughly chopped (see Cook's Tip)
handful of pitted black olives

GUIDELINES PER SERVING

- Calories
- Saturated fat
- Salt

STATISTICS PER SERVING

Energy 225kcals/953kJ

Protein 7g

Fat 6g
Saturated fat 1g

Carbohydrate 37g
Sugar 6g

Fiber 3.5g

Salt 1g

1 Tear the bread into chunky pieces and place them in a bowl. Cover with a little cold water and leave to soak for 2 minutes. Remove and squeeze out any excess water, then place in a serving bowl.

2 Add the basil leaves and a drizzle of olive oil. Sprinkle balsamic vinegar to taste, and season well.

3 When ready to serve, add the tomatoes and olives, and toss together well. Season to taste and drizzle over more oil, if required.

Cook's Tip
Use firm tomatoes for this salad. It's best made in the summer when full-flavored tomatoes are plentiful.

GOLDEN QUEEN TOMATOES
To add extra visual appeal, choose colorful varieties of tomatoes, such as Golden Queen. Yellow tomatoes tend to have a milder flavor, however, so mix with the stronger-tasting red varieties.

GREAT FOR KIDS

CANNELLINI BEAN, TUNA, AND RED ONION SALAD

SERVES 4
PREP 10 mins

GUIDELINES PER SERVING

● ● ○ Calories

● ● ○ Saturated fat

● ● ○ Salt

STATISTICS PER SERVING

Energy 231kcals/965kJ

Protein 18g

Fat 13g
Saturated fat 2g

Carbohydrate 13g
Sugar 3.5g

Fiber 6g

Salt 1.5g

This classic Italian salad is a great dish to take on a picnic because it is quite robust and easy to transport.

3 tbsp olive oil
1 tbsp red wine vinegar
salt and freshly ground black pepper
7oz can of tuna in olive oil, drained
1 red onion, quartered and very
  finely sliced

2 tbsp capers, drained or rinsed, and
  roughly chopped
14oz (410g) can of cannellini beans,
  drained and rinsed
handful of flat-leaf parsley leaves,
  finely chopped

1 In a bowl, whisk together the olive oil and vinegar, and season well. Pour the tuna into the bowl and mash it gently with a fork to break it up a little, leaving some chunks.

2 Add the remaining ingredients and toss the salad well until everything has a good coating of dressing. Serve, or pack into a container for transportation.

Variation
If serving at home, simply add a bag of salad leaves and some halved cherry tomatoes to make a complete meal.

Cook's tip
This salad is also great served with leftover cold mackerel instead of tuna, or with any canned beans instead of the cannellini used here.

SOBA NOODLE AND SHRIMP SALAD

SERVES 4
PREP 15 mins
COOK 25 mins

Here, nutty-flavored soba noodles are teamed with jumbo shrimp and drizzled with an orange and ginger dressing.

7oz (200g) soba noodles
salt and freshly ground black pepper
1 tbsp sunflower oil
9oz (250g) raw jumbo shrimp, shelled and
  tails removed
10oz (300g) frozen soybeans or edamame
4 scallions, finely chopped
1 red chile, seeded and finely sliced
handful of fresh cilantro leaves,
  roughly chopped

handful of mint leaves, roughly
  chopped

FOR THE DRESSING
juice of 1 orange
2in (5cm) piece ginger, peeled and grated
1 tbsp tamari (gluten-free soy sauce)
2 garlic cloves, grated
pinch of sugar

GUIDELINES PER SERVING

⬤ ⬤ ◯ Calories

⬤ ⬤ ◯ Saturated fat

⬤ ⬤ ◯ Salt

STATISTICS PER SERVING

Energy 396kcals/1670kJ

Protein 27g

Fat 12g
Saturated fat 1.5g

Carbohydrate 45g
Sugar 2g

Fiber 4g

Salt 1.2g

1 Add the noodles to a large pan of boiling salted water and cook according to package instructions. Drain well and place in a serving dish. In a bowl, whisk all the dressing ingredients together. Season, taste, and adjust as needed. Set aside.

2 Heat the oil in a frying pan, add the shrimp, and season. Cook on medium-high heat for 3–4 minutes, or until the shrimp are pink. Remove with a slotted spoon and leave to cool slightly. Slice them in half lengthwise and add to the noodles.

3 Add the soybeans to a pan of boiling salted water and cook for 3–5 minutes, until tender. Drain and refresh in cold water. Add the beans, scallions, and chile to the serving bowl along with half the herbs. Drizzle over the dressing and toss, so everything gets coated. Sprinkle over the remaining herbs and serve.

 Cook's Tip
Soba noodles are a naturally gluten-free Japanese noodle made from buckwheat.

GREAT FOR KIDS

NUTRIENT BOOST
Soybeans provide fiber, protein, and useful amounts of iron and folate.

SPINACH AND PINE NUT SALAD

Crispy bread crumbs and toasted nuts top this leafy salad. Good on its own or as a side dish to accompany broiled lamb cutlets.

SERVES   4
PREP   15 mins
COOK   10 mins

9oz (250g) baby spinach leaves
handful of juicy raisins (optional)
3½oz (100g) sun-dried tomatoes, roughly chopped
1¾oz (50g) pine nuts, toasted

FOR THE DRESSING
3 tbsp extra virgin olive oil

1 tbsp orange juice
pinch of sugar
salt and freshly ground black pepper

FOR THE BREAD CRUMB TOPPING
2–3 slices of gluten-free bread (see page 38), torn
pinch of dried chili flakes

1 For the dressing, mix the ingredients together in a bowl, taste, and adjust the seasoning as needed. Set aside. Preheat the oven to 400°F (200°C).

2 For the bread crumb topping, put the bread in a food processor and pulse to form crumbs. Pour the crumbs into a roasting pan and bake for 5–10 minutes, or until golden. Don't let them brown. Stir the chili flakes and salt and pepper into the crumbs. Set aside.

3 To assemble the salad, pour the dressing into a large salad bowl and swirl it around. Add the spinach leaves and shake so they get coated. Add the raisins (if using) and sun-dried tomatoes and toss gently. Top with the pine nuts, sprinkle the bread crumbs over the top, and serve.

Cook's Tip
For a more substantial salad, add some cheese: Parmesan shavings, crumbled feta, or torn buffalo mozzarella all work well.

GUIDELINES PER SERVING

●	○	○	Calories
●	○	○	Saturated fat
●	○	○	Salt

STATISTICS PER SERVING

Energy 270kcals/1124kJ

Protein 6g

Fat 19g
Saturated fat 2g

Carbohydrate 17.5g
Sugar 9.5g

Fiber 4g

Salt 0.8g

NUTRIENT BOOST
Spinach is rich in betacarotene, which the body converts into vitamin A.

CHICKPEA, RED RICE, AND ARTICHOKE SALAD

A substantial main meal salad, it's also good as a side dish to accompany grilled or broiled salmon or chicken.

SERVES 4
PREP 10 mins
COOK 35 mins

GUIDELINES PER SERVING

● ● ○ Calories

● ● ○ Saturated fat

● ○ ○ Salt

STATISTICS PER SERVING

Energy 710kcals/2958kJ

Protein 17g

Fat 28g
Saturated fat 5.5g

Carbohydrate 90g
Sugar 7g

Fiber 5g

Salt 1.3g

NUTRIENT BOOST
Soluble fiber in chickpeas helps balance blood sugar and reduce cholesterol.

14oz (400g) Camargue red rice
14oz (400g) can chickpeas, drained and rinsed
8–10 jar artichokes, drained
1 red chile, seeded and finely chopped
handful of fresh cilantro, finely chopped
handful of flat-leaf parsley, finely chopped
2 tbsp pine nuts, toasted
2½oz (75g) feta cheese, crumbled

FOR THE CORIANDER AND ORANGE DRESSING
6 tbsp extra virgin olive oil
2 tbsp white wine vinegar
juice of 1 large orange
1½ tsp coriander seeds, lightly crushed
1 tsp Dijon mustard
pinch of sugar
salt and freshly ground pepper

1 For the dressing, place all the ingredients in a small bowl or measuring cup and mix well. Taste and adjust the seasoning as required.

2 Place the rice in a pan of salted water and cook according to package instructions until tender. Drain well and transfer to a serving bowl.

3 While the rice is still warm, stir in the chickpeas, artichokes, chile, and herbs, and mix well. Pour the dressing over the rice mixture and toss together. Taste and adjust the seasoning. Top with the pine nuts and feta cheese and serve.

Cook's Tip
Camargue red rice has a slightly nutty taste. You can also use half Camargue rice and half basmati rice.

BEETS AND HAZELNUT SALAD WITH BLUE CHEESE

SERVES	4
PREP	15 mins
COOK	1 hour

GUIDELINES PER SERVING

● ○ ○   Calories

● ● ●   Saturated fat

● ● ○   Salt

STATISTICS PER SERVING

Energy 370kcals/1525kJ

Protein 10g

Fat 30g
Saturated fat 8g

Carbohydrate 14g
Sugar 12g

Fiber 6g

Salt 1.2g

NUTRIENT BOOST

Beets helps produce nitric oxide in the body, which can lower blood pressure.

A mix of earthy flavors and a classic combination of blue cheese and nuts makes this a substantial salad.

1lb 2oz (500g) beets, trimmed
few sprigs of thyme
2 tbsp olive oil
2 red onions, thickly sliced into rings
5½oz (150g) salad leaves, such as lamb's
   lettuce, watercress, or arugula
sea salt and freshly ground
   black pepper
1¾oz (50g) hazelnuts, toasted
   and roughly chopped

3½oz (100g) Gorgonzola
   cheese, crumbled
gluten-free bread, to serve

FOR THE DRESSING
3 tbsp extra virgin olive oil
1 tbsp white wine vinegar

1 Preheat the oven to 400°F (200°C). Line a roasting pan with foil, then add the beets, thyme, and half the oil. Mix with your hands, so that the beets are coated. Bring the ends of the foil together to form a sealed package, and roast for 40 minutes until the beets are tender when pierced with a knife. Unwrap the beets, add the onions and the remaining oil, seal the foil again, and cook for another 20 minutes. Remove, leave to cool, then peel away the skin from the beets, and slice into quarters.

2 For the dressing, whisk together the oil and vinegar, and season.

3 Place the salad leaves on a serving plate or large shallow bowl and top with the beets and onion mix. Sprinkle with salt and pepper, then scatter the hazelnuts and cheese on top. Spoon over a little dressing, leaving some on the side for people to help themselves, and serve with gluten-free bread.

Cook's Tip
Try swapping the Gorgonzola for a mild Stilton or some slightly warmed slices of goat cheese.

CHORIZO AND WATERCRESS SALAD

This warm salad makes a light main meal or hearty lunch, with lots of gutsy flavors on a bed of fresh leaves.

SERVES   4
PREP   20 mins
COOK   15–20 mins

14oz (400g) baby new potatoes
9oz (250g) gluten-free cooking chorizo
  sausages, roughly chopped
few sprigs of thyme, leaves only
6oz (175g) watercress, thick
  stalks removed
½ red onion, finely diced

FOR THE DRESSING
3 tbsp olive oil
1 tbsp white wine vinegar
juice of 1 orange
few sprigs of thyme, leaves only
pinch of sugar
salt and freshly ground black pepper

GUIDELINES PER SERVING

● ● ● Calories
● ● ● Saturated fat
● ● ● Salt

STATISTICS PER SERVING

Energy 352kcals/1468kJ

Protein 14.5g

Fat 23g
Saturated fat 7.5g

Carbohydrate 20.5g
Sugar 6.5g

Fiber 2.5g

Salt 0.9g

1 Place all the dressing ingredients in a liquid measuring cup, whisk well to combine, and set aside.

2 Cook the baby potatoes in a pan of boiling salted water for about 15–20 minutes, until tender when poked with a knife. Drain well, and halve any large ones. Set aside.

3 Meanwhile, place the chorizo in a large frying pan and cook over medium heat for 5–6 minutes, or until just turning golden brown on both sides. Sprinkle the thyme leaves over the top and fry for 1 minute. Remove with a slotted spoon and drain on paper towels.

4 Pour the watercress into a large shallow bowl, add the potatoes and chorizo, toss them together, sprinkle over the onion, and spoon the dressing over to serve. Leave some dressing on the side for people to help themselves.

NUTRIENT BOOST
"Superfood" watercress is full of vitamins B and C, iron, and phytochemicals.

CHORIZO SAUSAGE
This Spanish delicacy is usually made with pork and always generously seasoned with paprika. Look for the uncured cooking chorizo, or *chorizo fresco*, for this recipe.

PASTA, NOODLES, AND RICE

LEMON AND ASPARAGUS PASTA

SERVES 4
PREP 5 mins
COOK 10–12 mins

Try to get the freshest new season asparagus for this simple supper dish.

GUIDELINES PER SERVING

● ● ● Calories

● ● ● Saturated fat

● ● ● Salt

STATISTICS PER SERVING

Energy 420kcals/1770kJ

Protein 12g

Fat 13g
Saturated fat 2g

Carbohydrate 63g
Sugar 3g

Fiber 5g

Salt trace

9oz (250g) asparagus, trimmed
  and halved
1/3 cup olive oil
salt and freshly ground black pepper
12oz (350g) gluten-free tagliatelle
  (store-bought or see pages 42–3)
2 garlic cloves, crushed

zest and juice of 1 large lemon
1 red chile or jalapeño, seeded and
  finely chopped
1/2 tsp grated nutmeg
3 tbsp flat-leaf parsley, chopped
grated Parmesan cheese, to serve

1 Bring a small pan of salted water to a boil. Blanch the asparagus in the boiling water for 2 minutes. Drain and refresh in cold water.

2 Place a grill pan on the stove to heat up. Drizzle the blanched asparagus with a little of the olive oil and season well with salt and pepper. Cook the asparagus on the hot pan for 5–6 minutes, turning it occasionally until charbroiled. Set aside.

3 Bring a large pan of salted water to a boil. Add the pasta to the pan and cook according to instructions, stirring it at the beginning to prevent it from sticking together.

4 Heat the remaining olive oil in a large frying pan and add the garlic, lemon zest, and chile. Sauté for 30 seconds, then add the lemon juice, plenty of black pepper, and the nutmeg. Remove from the heat.

5 Drain the pasta and add it to the frying pan along with the asparagus and parsley. Toss well to mix. Divide between plates and serve sprinkled with Parmesan cheese.

PASTA GENOVESE

A quick homemade pesto is tossed with linguine for this timeless classic from the Italian city of Genoa.

SERVES   4
PREP   10 mins
COOK   up to 12 mins

2 garlic cloves, roughly chopped
large handful of basil leaves
3½oz (100g) Parmesan cheese,
   finely grated
3½oz (100g) Pecorino cheese,
   finely grated
3oz (85g) pine nuts, toasted
salt and freshly ground black pepper

about ¾ cup extra virgin
   olive oil
12oz (350g) gluten-free linguine
   (store-bought or see pages 42–3)
tomato salad, to serve

GUIDELINES PER SERVING

●●○   Calories

●●●   Saturated fat

●●○   Salt

STATISTICS PER SERVING

Energy   658kcals/2766kJ

Protein   32g

Fat   31g
Saturated fat   11g

Carbohydrate   63g
Sugar   3g

Fiber   4g

Salt   1g

1   To prepare the pesto, add the garlic to a food processor and pulse until minced. Then add the basil leaves, Parmesan, Pecorino, pine nuts, and seasoning, and pulse a few times until it reaches your preferred texture.

2   Slowly trickle in the olive oil, pressing the pulse button as you go, adding as much or little to get the correct consistency—avoid a sloppy pesto. Taste and season if required. Set aside. Alternatively, make the pesto in a mortar and pestle for a coarser texture.

3   Put the pasta in a large pan of boiling salted water and cook according to instructions, stirring at the beginning to prevent it from sticking together. Drain well and return to the pan with a little of the cooking water. Add enough pesto just to coat the pasta and toss well. Serve with a fresh tomato salad.

Cook's Tip

For a more substantial meal, add some cooked, chopped green beans and cooked, diced potatoes.

RICOTTA AND SQUASH RAVIOLI WITH SAGE BUTTER

Make the ravioli a day in advance. Dust them with polenta, place them on a tray covered with plastic wrap, and chill.

SERVES 4
PREP 30 mins
PLUS COOLING
COOK 50–55 mins
FREEZE 1 month

GUIDELINES PER SERVING

● ● ○ Calories
● ● ● Saturated fat
● ○ ○ Salt

STATISTICS PER SERVING

Energy 640kcals/2670kJ

Protein 16g

Fat 40g
Saturated fat 15g

Carbohydrate 53g
Sugar 3g

Fiber 3g

Salt 1.2g

6oz (175g) butternut squash, peeled, seeded, and cut into 2in (5cm) cubes
1 tbsp olive oil
salt and freshly ground black pepper
3oz (85g) ricotta cheese
1oz (30g) Parmesan cheese, grated
1 garlic clove, crushed
½ tsp freshly grated nutmeg
12oz (350g) gluten-free pasta dough (see pages 42–3)
polenta or fine cornmeal, for dusting

FOR THE SAGE BUTTER

3 tbsp olive oil
4 tbsp butter
zest of ½ lemon
2 tsp roughly chopped sage leaves
grated Parmesan cheese, to serve

SPECIAL EQUIPMENT

2½in (6cm) round cookie cutter

1 For the filling, preheat the oven to 400°F (200°C). Place the butternut cubes in a roasting pan and drizzle over the oil, 3 tablespoons water, and seasoning. Cover with foil and roast for 30–35 minutes, or until tender. Transfer to a food processor and pulse until smooth. Spread in the roasting pan and leave until cold. Place the ricotta, Parmesan cheese, garlic, and nutmeg in a bowl. Stir in the butternut squash and season to taste. Chill.

2 Roll out the pasta dough onto a flour-dusted surface to a thickness of ⅛in (3mm). Cut out 64 rounds using a cookie cutter. Top half the rounds with ½ teaspoon filling. Brush water around the filling and place a plain pasta round on top. Pinch the edges to seal. This will make 32 ravioli. Dust with polenta to keep them from sticking together. Cover and chill until needed.

3 Bring a large pan of salted water to a boil. Add the pasta and cook for 4–5 minutes, or until al dente. For the sage butter, heat a large frying pan, add the olive oil, butter, lemon zest, and sage, and sauté for 30 seconds. Remove and add plenty of pepper. Drain the pasta in a colander, add to the frying pan, and toss well to mix. Serve sprinkled with Parmesan cheese.

PASTA PRIMAVERA

Serve this light and fresh vegetarian dish in the spring, when young, tender vegetables are easily available.

SERVES 4
PREP 15 mins
COOK 30 mins

GUIDELINES PER SERVING

● ○ ○ Calories
● ○ ○ Saturated fat
● ○ ○ Salt

STATISTICS PER SERVING

Energy 384kcals/1629kJ

Protein 15g

Fat 5g
Saturated fat 1g

Carbohydrate 68g
Sugar 6g

Fiber 8g

Salt 0.1g

7oz (200g) green beans, trimmed
1 bunch of fine asparagus, trimmed
12oz (350g) gluten-free linguine
  or other pasta shapes (store-bought
  or see pages 42–3)
1 tbsp olive oil
3 zucchini, halved lengthwise
  and chopped

salt and freshly ground black pepper
pinch of saffron threads (optional)
4 tomatoes, roughly chopped
grated Parmesan or Pecorino cheese,
  to serve

1 Add the beans to a pan of boiling salted water and cook for 4–5 minutes, until tender but still with some bite. Remove with a slotted spoon (reserve the water in the pan), refresh in cold water, and roughly chop. Add the asparagus to the reserved boiling water and cook for 6–8 minutes, until almost tender. Drain, refresh, and roughly chop.

2 Put the pasta in a large pan of boiling salted water and cook according to instructions. Stir at the beginning of cooking to prevent it from sticking together. Drain well, return to the pan with a little of the cooking water, and toss together to combine.

3 Meanwhile, heat the oil in a large frying pan, add the zucchini, and season. Add the saffron threads (if using) and cook on medium-low heat for about 10 minutes, until the zucchini turn golden.

4 Add the beans, asparagus, and tomatoes to the frying pan. Stir and cook over low heat for 5 minutes. Add the vegetables to the pasta and toss to combine. Serve with the Parmesan or Pecorino and more freshly ground black pepper, if you wish.

Cook's Tip
Swap the asparagus for frozen peas, if asparagus
is not in season.

CRAB AND TOMATO PASTA

Pasta absorbs wonderfully the sweet flavor of crab. This is an easy dish for last-minute entertaining.

1 tbsp olive oil
1 onion, very finely chopped
1 celery stalk, very finely chopped
1 bay leaf
salt and freshly ground black pepper
2 garlic cloves, finely chopped
1 red chile, seeded and
　finely chopped

½ cup dry white wine
⅔ cup tomato sauce
12oz (350g) gluten-free linguine
　or other pasta shapes (store-bought
　or see pages 42–3)
9oz (250g) fresh white crab meat
handful of flat-leaf parsley,
　finely chopped

GUIDELINES PER SERVING

● ● ○ 　Calories

● ● ○ 　Saturated fat

● ○ ○ 　Salt

STATISTICS PER SERVING

Energy 446kcals/1888kJ

Protein 23g

Fat 8g
Saturated fat 1g

Carbohydrate 66g
Sugar 3.5g

Fiber 4.5g

Salt 0.7g

1 Heat the oil in a large pan, add the onion, and cook over low heat for 5–6 minutes, until soft. Add the celery, bay leaf, and salt and pepper, and cook on low heat, stirring, for about 10 minutes, making sure the vegetables don't brown. Stir in the garlic and chile, and cook for another minute.

2 Raise the heat, add the wine, and let it bubble for 1 minute. Add the tomato sauce and let this bubble for 2–3 minutes. Reduce to low heat and simmer for about 15 minutes.

3 Put the pasta in a large pan of boiling salted water and cook according to instructions. Stir well at the beginning of cooking to prevent it from sticking together. Drain and return to the pan with a little of the cooking water. Stir the crab meat into the tomato sauce and warm through. Pour the sauce over the linguine and toss to combine. Sprinkle over the parsley and serve right away.

FRESH CRAB
If buying whole crab or cooking your own crab, the white meat can be found in the central body, legs, and claws. Use a lobster or nut cracker to break the shell and extract the flesh with a lobster pick or skewer.

SMOKED SALMON PASTA

Cream cheese makes an instant and cheap pasta sauce for this easy midweek supper dish.

SERVES 4
PREP 10 mins
COOK 15 mins

GUIDELINES PER SERVING

● ● ○ Calories
● ● ● Saturated fat
● ● ● Salt

STATISTICS PER SERVING

Energy 636kcals/2669kJ

Protein 26g

Fat 31g
Saturated fat 16g

Carbohydrate 62g
Sugar 2g

Fiber 3.5g

Salt 2.5g

12oz (350g) gluten-free linguine or
  other pasta shapes (store-bought
  or see pages 42–3)
7oz (200g) cream cheese
9oz (250g) smoked salmon
  trimmings, chopped

2–3 sprigs of dill, chopped
salt and freshly ground black pepper
arugula leaves dressed with olive oil and
  lemon juice, to serve

1 Put the pasta in a large pan of boiling salted water and cook according to the instructions. Stir it well at the beginning of cooking to prevent it from sticking together. Drain and return to the pan with a little of the cooking water.

2 Stir the cream cheese into the pasta, so it melts to form a sauce. Add the salmon and stir again.

3 Sprinkle over the dill and season. Serve with a lightly dressed, lemony wild arugula salad.

Cook's Tip
For a more sophisticated version, swap the cream cheese for fresh ricotta.

MUSHROOM AND HAM PASTA

This is flavor-packed comfort food at its best, perfect for the whole family.

SERVES 4
PREP   15 mins
COOK   40 mins

10oz (300g) button mushrooms
2 tbsp olive oil
1 onion, finely chopped
salt and freshly ground black pepper
2 garlic cloves, grated
3 sage leaves, finely chopped
½ cup dry white wine
⅔ cup heavy cream

handful of grated Parmesan cheese, plus extra for serving
7oz (200g) good-quality, gluten-free ham, cut into bite-sized chunks
12oz (350g) gluten-free linguine or other pasta shapes (store-bought or see pages 42–3)

GUIDELINES PER SERVING

● ● ○ Calories
● ● ● Saturated fat
● ● ○ Salt

STATISTICS PER SERVING

Energy 681kcals/2855kJ

Protein 26g

Fat 33g
Saturated fat 17g

Carbohydrate 65g
Sugar 4.5g

Fiber 5g

Salt 1.8g

1 Chop 7oz (200g) of the mushrooms into quarters and grate the remainder (see Cook's Tip). Heat half the oil in a large frying pan, add the onion, and cook on low heat for 5–6 minutes, until soft. Season with salt and pepper, stir in the garlic and chopped sage, and cook for 1 minute more.

2 Add the quartered and grated mushrooms and the remaining oil, and cook over medium–low heat, stirring occasionally. Let the mushrooms warm gently in the pan for about 10 minutes, until they begin to release their juices.

3 Raise the heat, add the wine, and bubble for 2–3 minutes. Reduce the heat a little and stir in the cream. Cook for 1–2 minutes, add the Parmesan, and stir. Season to taste again, if necessary. Stir in the ham and heat.

4 Put the pasta in a large pan of boiling salted water and cook according to instructions. Stir it well at the beginning of cooking to prevent it from sticking together. Drain well and return to the pan with a little of the cooking water. Add the sauce to the pasta and toss gently to coat. Serve with grated Parmesan cheese.

GREAT FOR KIDS

Cook's Tip
Grating the mushrooms really enriches the sauce—you can always add some soaked dried porcini for added depth and richness.

PASTA AND MEATBALLS

Anchovies add richness to the meatballs without giving them a "fishy" flavor. Replace the red wine with ²/₃ cup gluten-free beef stock for a child-friendly version.

SERVES	4
PREP	20 mins
	PLUS CHILLING
COOK	40 mins

GUIDELINES PER SERVING

● ● ○ Calories

● ● ○ Saturated fat

● ○ ○ Salt

STATISTICS PER SERVING

Energy 601kcals/2521kJ

Protein 28g

Fat 24g
Saturated fat 7.5g

Carbohydrate 61g
Sugar 8g

Fiber 5g

Salt 0.7g

NUTRIENT BOOST
Lean red meat is an excellent source of iron.

GREAT FOR KIDS

1 red onion, finely chopped
10oz (300g) ground beef
pinch of dried chili flakes
handful of flat-leaf parsley, finely chopped
3 anchovy fillets, chopped (optional)
rice flour, for dusting
2–3 tbsp olive oil
10oz (300g) gluten-free spaghetti or tagliatelle (see pages 42–3)

FOR THE SAUCE
1 tbsp olive oil
1 onion, finely chopped
salt and freshly ground pepper
1 small glass red wine
14oz (400g) can chopped tomatoes
pinch of dried oregano
freshly grated Parmesan cheese, to serve

1 Place the onion, beef, chili flakes, parsley, and anchovies (if using) in a large bowl, and mix well with your hands, so that the mixture is tightly packed. With floured hands, scoop out golf-ball sized portions and roll until neat. It should make about 12. Sit them on a baking sheet lined with parchment paper and chill in the fridge to firm up.

2 Heat a little oil in a large nonstick frying pan with a lid and add the meatballs a few at a time. Cook on medium-high heat until browned on all sides, about 6–8 minutes. Repeat with all the meatballs, adding more oil as needed. Transfer to a plate with paper towels to drain.

3 For the sauce, use the same frying pan to heat the oil, add the onion, season, and cook over low heat for 3–4 minutes until soft. Pour in the wine, raise the heat, and let it boil for 2–3 minutes. Reduce to a simmer. Add the tomatoes and oregano and cook gently for 5 minutes. Add the meatballs to the sauce and cook on low heat with the lid ajar for 20 minutes, turning occasionally and adding hot water, if it appears to be drying out.

4 Cook the pasta according to instructions. Season the sauce as needed. Serve with the pasta, topped with grated Parmesan cheese.

MACARONI CHEESE

A cheese sauce made with gluten-free flour bubbles away with pasta until golden. Raw onion is added to the mix to cut through the richness of the sauce.

SERVES 4
PREP 15 mins
COOK 50 mins
FREEZE 1 month

GUIDELINES PER SERVING

● ● ○ Calories
● ● ○ Saturated fat
● ○ ○ Salt

STATISTICS PER SERVING

Energy 631kcals/2651kJ

Protein 23g

Fat 28g
Saturated fat 17g

Carbohydrate 70g
Sugar 8g

Fiber 4g

Salt 1.3g

GREAT FOR KIDS

12oz (350g) gluten-free macaroni
  or penne pasta
½ red onion, very finely chopped

FOR THE CHEESE SAUCE
4 tbsp butter
1 tbsp gluten-free all-purpose flour
  or rice flour

1²⁄₃ cups milk
salt and freshly ground pepper
1 tsp Dijon mustard (optional)
4½oz (125g) sharp Cheddar cheese,
  grated, plus an extra handful to top

1 Preheat the oven to 375°F (190°C). For the cheese sauce, melt the butter in a pan, remove it from the heat, and stir in the flour. When combined, add a drop of the milk and stir, then put the pan back on the heat and add more milk, a little at a time. Cook on low heat, stirring constantly with a wooden spoon. When it starts to thicken slightly, switch to a balloon whisk and stir until smooth and lump-free; the sauce will not thicken as much as with regular flour. Season well, then stir in the mustard (if using) and the cheese until it melts. Remove from the heat and set aside.

2 Add the macaroni or pasta to a pan of boiling salted water, stir, and cook for 12 minutes or as per package instructions. Drain and return to the pan with a little of the cooking water.

3 Transfer the macaroni to a baking dish, add the onion, mix, and season to taste with pepper. Pour over the cheese sauce and turn to coat, then sprinkle more cheese over the top. Bake for 25–30 minutes until golden and bubbling.

Cook's Tip
To freeze, cook as per recipe and cool completely. To reheat, defrost overnight in the fridge, then reheat as portions in the microwave on high for 3 minutes, or return to room temperature, cover with foil, and bake at 350°F (180°C) until piping hot.

PUMPKIN, SPINACH, AND GORGONZOLA LASAGNE

A vegetarian lasagne that is rich and satisfying, with fresh sage and nutmeg bringing the flavors alive.

about 1¾lb (800g) small pumpkin
  or butternut squash, peeled, seeded,
  and chopped into bite-sized pieces
1 tbsp olive oil
salt and freshly ground pepper
8 sage leaves, roughly chopped
pinch of freshly grated nutmeg
pinch of dried chili flakes (optional)
pinch of allspice
7oz (200g) spinach
10 gluten-free pre-cooked lasagne sheets
  (store-bought or see pages 42–3)

4½oz (125g) Gorgonzola
  cheese, chopped
lightly dressed green salad, to serve

FOR THE SAUCE
7 tbsp butter
2 tbsp gluten-free all-purpose flour
  or rice flour
3 cups milk

SPECIAL EQUIPMENT
9 x 13in (23 x 33cm) ovenproof dish

SERVES 4
PREP 25–30 mins
COOK 1–1¼ hours
FREEZE 1 month

GUIDELINES PER SERVING

● ● ● Calories
● ● ● Saturated fat
● ● ● Salt

STATISTICS PER SERVING

Energy 531kcals/2221kJ

Protein 19g

Fat 30g
Saturated fat 16g

Carbohydrate 47g
Sugar 10g

Fiber 6g

Salt 1.8g

1 Preheat the oven to 400°F (200°C). Place the pumpkin in a large roasting pan, add the oil and plenty of seasoning, and stir to coat; the pan must be large or the pumpkin will steam rather than roast. Sprinkle over the sage, nutmeg, chili (if using), and allspice and stir. Roast for 20–30 minutes, stirring halfway, until golden, then remove. Stir in the spinach, which will wilt in a few minutes. Set aside. Reduce the oven temperature to 375°F (190°C).

2 For the sauce, melt the butter in a medium pan. Remove, add the flour, and stir. Add a little milk, stir, and return to the heat. Cook over low heat, adding the milk and stirring with a wooden spoon. As it thickens, switch to a balloon whisk and stir to remove any lumps. Season well and set aside.

3 For the lasagne, spoon half the pumpkin mixture into the ovenproof dish. Seasoning well between each layer, add half the lasagne sheets, half the sauce, and half the Gorgonzola. Repeat to use up all the ingredients. Place on a baking sheet and bake for 30–40 minutes until golden and bubbling. Serve with a lightly dressed green salad.

NUTRIENT BOOST
Spinach is a good source of vitamin K, which is important for healthy bones.

PAD THAI

Homemade versions of your favorite dishes mean that you can be sure of eating a gluten-free version.

SERVES 8
PREP 15 mins
COOK 15 mins

GUIDELINES PER SERVING

● ● ○ Calories

● ● ○ Saturated fat

● ● ○ Salt

STATISTICS PER SERVING

Energy 681kcals/2847kJ

Protein 40g

Fat 26g
Saturated fat 5g

Carbohydrate 51g
Sugar 7g

Fiber 0.5g

Salt 0.6g

1¼lb (550g) medium or thick
  dried rice noodles
3 tbsp sunflower or vegetable oil
4 large eggs, lightly beaten
1 tsp shrimp paste (optional)
4 hot red chiles, seeded and
  finely chopped
6 boneless, skinless chicken breasts,
  cut into ¼in (5mm) slices

2 bunches of scallions, finely chopped
splash of gluten-free nam pla (Thai
  fish sauce)
juice of 2 limes
2 tbsp brown sugar
salt and freshly ground black pepper
10oz (300g) unsalted peanuts
handful of cilantro leaves,
  finely chopped
lime wedges, to serve

1 Put the noodles in a large bowl, cover with boiling water, and leave for 8 minutes or until soft. Drain and set aside. Meanwhile, put 1 tablespoon of the oil in a large wok over high heat and swirl around the pan. Add the beaten egg and swirl it around the wok for about a minute, or until it begins to set—don't let it set completely—then remove, chop, and set aside.

2 Add the remaining 2 tablespoons of oil to the pan, then add the shrimp paste (if using) and chiles, and stir. With the heat still high, add the chicken and stir vigorously for 5 minutes, or until it is no longer pink. Stir in the green onions, fish sauce, lime juice, and sugar, and toss together well. Cook for a few minutes until the sugar has dissolved, then season well with salt and pepper. Return the egg to the pan.

3 Add the noodles to the pan and toss together to coat with the sauce, then add half the peanuts and half the cilantro, and toss again. Transfer to a large, shallow, warmed serving bowl and scatter over the rest of the peanuts and cilantro. Garnish with lime wedges to serve.

MEE GORENG

This classic Malaysian dish is traditionally made with wheat egg noodles but works just as well with rice noodles.

SERVES   4
PREP   25–30 mins
COOK   20 mins

GUIDELINES PER SERVING

● ● ○   Calories

● ○ ○   Saturated fat

● ● ○   Salt

STATISTICS PER SERVING

Energy   534kcals/2226kJ

Protein   20g

Fat   20g
Saturated fat   4g

Carbohydrate   62g
Sugar   4.5g

Fiber   2.5g

Salt   2.2g

GREAT FOR KIDS

4 garlic cloves, roughly chopped
10 black peppercorns
1 red or jalapeño chile, seeded and roughly chopped
3 tbsp sunflower oil
8oz (225g) firm tofu, cut into cubes or strips
3 tbsp tamari (gluten-free soy sauce)
1¼ cups hot gluten-free vegetable stock (see page 108)

10oz (300g) vermicelli dried rice noodles
½ small, firm white cabbage, finely shredded
handful of bean sprouts
4 scallions, sliced
4 large eggs, fried, to serve (optional)

SPECIAL EQUIPMENT
large, deep, nonstick frying pan or wok

1 Grind the garlic, pepper, and chile to a paste in a pestle and mortar, or put in a small food processor and purée until minced. Heat the oil in a wok on medium-high heat, add the garlic mixture, and cook for a few seconds. Add the tofu and cook for 5–8 minutes until it starts to turn golden brown. Add the tamari and stir carefully, then let it boil for 2–3 minutes. Add the stock, boil again, and cook until the mixture has reduced by half.

2 Meanwhile, place the noodles in a bowl, cover with boiling water, and leave for 5 minutes until beginning to soften, then drain.

3 Add the cabbage to the mixture and mix quickly, then add the noodles and mix well. Add the bean sprouts and scallions, toss together, and remove from the heat. Serve hot, topped with a fried egg and more tamari, if needed.

Cook's Tips
Make this with chicken and shrimp if you're not a fan of tofu. If making for kids, add more vegetables, such as green beans or broccoli, to increase their intake.

SWEET SHRIMP AND ZUCCHINI NOODLES

Succulent shrimp with zucchini and a little spice are all that this easy dish requires.

SERVES   4
PREP   20 mins
COOK   25 mins

7oz (200g) dried rice noodles
14oz (400g) raw Tiger shrimp,
  shells removed and tails on
2 tbsp olive oil
2 zucchini, sliced lengthwise, diced
sea salt and freshly ground pepper
pinch of chili flakes
3 garlic cloves, finely chopped
handful of bean sprouts
handful of fresh cilantro
  leaves, chopped
sesame seeds (optional)

FOR THE MARINADE
1 tbsp honey
1 tbsp tamari (gluten-free soy sauce)
juice of 1 lime
1 red or jalapeño chile, seeded and
  finely chopped
splash of gluten-free nam pla
  (fish sauce)

GUIDELINES PER SERVING

● ● ● Calories
● ● ● Saturated fat
● ● ● Salt

STATISTICS PER SERVING

Energy 327kcals/1366kJ

Protein 22g

Fat 6.5g
Saturated fat 1g

Carbohydrate 41g
Sugar 3g

Fiber 0.7g

Salt 1.9g

1 Place the rice noodles in a bowl, cover with boiling water, and leave for 10 minutes or as per instructions. Drain, separate the strands, and set aside.

2 Mix together the marinade ingredients, season to taste, and add the shrimp. Stir until combined, then set aside while you cook the zucchini.

3 Heat half the oil in a large frying pan, add the zucchini, season with salt and pepper, and add the chili flakes. Cook on low heat for 5–6 minutes until lightly golden, then add the garlic and cook for another minute. Stir in the bean sprouts, remove from pan, and set aside.

4 Heat the remaining oil in the pan, add the shrimp and the marinade, and cook on medium-high heat for about 5–6 minutes or until pink. Turn them occasionally and make sure that the honey doesn't burn. Place the noodles on a platter, spoon over the zucchini, and top with the shrimp. Sprinkle over the cilantro and sesame seeds (if using), before serving.

SPICED NOODLES WITH AROMATIC RED SNAPPER

SERVES 4

PREP 15 mins
PLUS MARINATING

COOK 25–30 mins

Sambal oelek, an Indonesian hot chili condiment, is the perfect partner for this delicate fish.

GUIDELINES PER SERVING

● ● ●   Calories

● ● ●   Saturated fat

● ● ●   Salt

STATISTICS PER SERVING

Energy 473kcals/1982kJ

Protein 35g

Fat 8g
Saturated fat 1g

Carbohydrate 59g
Sugar 11g

Fiber 4g

Salt 1g

1 red snapper, filleted, skinned, and
chopped into large chunks
9oz (250g) fine rice noodles
1 tbsp sunflower or vegetable oil
1 bunch of scallions, finely chopped
10oz (300g) French beans, trimmed
and chopped
1 red bell pepper, seeded and
finely chopped
2 garlic cloves, finely chopped
1–2 tsp sambal oelek, or 1 chopped red or
jalapeño chile, or ½–1 tsp chili flakes
mixed with 1 tsp vegetable oil
1 tbsp tamari (gluten-free soy sauce)

handful of fresh cilantro, leaves only
1 orange, peeled and cut
into segments

FOR THE MARINADE
zest and juice of 1 orange
a few sprigs of thyme, leaves only,
finely chopped
1 red or jalapeño chile, seeded
and finely chopped
2 garlic cloves, finely chopped
1 tbsp olive oil
salt and freshly ground pepper

1 Place the fish in a shallow dish. Combine all the marinade ingredients in a liquid measuring cup, stir well, and pour over the fish, turning the pieces to coat. Set aside to marinate for up to 1 hour. Preheat the oven to 350°F (180°C). Remove the fish using a slotted spoon and place in a roasting pan. Roast for 20–25 minutes or until the fish is cooked through and turning opaque. Set aside.

2 Cover the noodles with boiling water and rehydrate according to the package instructions. Drain. Add the oil to a wok and swirl it around the pan. Add the scallions and cook on medium-high heat for 2–3 minutes until soft. Add the beans and stir. Cook for about 5 minutes until they begin to soften. Stir in the pepper and garlic and cook for 2–3 minutes.

3 Add the sambal oelek and tamari. Add the noodles and toss. Cook for 3–5 minutes and transfer to a serving dish. Top with the fish and cilantro. Serve with the orange segments.

CHICKEN, CASHEW, AND CILANTRO NOODLE STIR-FRY

A simple stir-fry, zinging with fresh flavors. Use the best-quality chicken you can find—it will make all the difference.

SERVES 4
PREP 20 mins
COOK 20 mins

GUIDELINES PER SERVING

●●○ Calories

●●○ Saturated fat

●●○ Salt

STATISTICS PER SERVING

Energy 543kcals/2268kJ

Protein 35g

Fat 19g
Saturated fat 3.5g

Carbohydrate 51g
Sugar 7g

Fiber 3g

Salt 1.5g

GREAT FOR KIDS

NUTRIENT BOOST
Cashew nuts are rich in essential fatty acids and a good source of protein.

7oz (200g) dried rice noodles
3 chicken breasts, skinless, cut into
  bite-size pieces
salt and freshly ground pepper
1 tbsp cornstarch
2 tbsp sunflower or vegetable oil
2 red bell peppers, seeded and
  sliced into strips
bunch of scallions, diagonally sliced
3 garlic cloves, grated
2in (5cm) fresh ginger, peeled
  and grated

2 tbsp tamari (gluten-free soy sauce)
1 tbsp gluten-free mirin (Chinese rice
  wine) or dry sherry
3½oz (100g) unsalted cashew nuts,
  toasted and roughly chopped
large bunch of fresh cilantro,
  finely chopped

SPECIAL EQUIPMENT
large, deep nonstick frying pan or wok

1 Put the rice noodles in a bowl and cover with boiling water. Leave for 10 minutes or as per instructions. Drain, separate the strands, and set aside.

2 Season the chicken pieces and toss in the cornstarch. Heat half the oil in a wok on medium-high heat and add the chicken. Fry for 8–10 minutes or until the chicken is cooked through. Remove and set aside. Add the remaining oil and the peppers and fry for 2–3 minutes. Add the onions and toss the ingredients around the pan on fairly high heat. Add the garlic and ginger and cook for another 2–3 minutes. Add the tamari and mirin or sherry and bubble for 1 minute. Add a splash of water to loosen the sauce if necessary.

3 Return the chicken to the wok, add the cashews and cilantro, and stir to coat. Remove from the heat and serve with the rice noodles.

Cook's Tip
Stir-fries require a little speed so that everything remains crisp. Have the ingredients prepped and chopped, ready to throw in.

CHICKEN CHILE NOODLES

*The simplicity of ingredients works well in this dish.
If you would like more greenery on the plate, add 7oz
(200g) sugar snap peas or snow peas at the same time
as the chiles.*

SERVES   4
PREP   15 mins
COOK   20 mins

3 chicken breasts, skinless, cut into strips
salt and freshly ground pepper
1 tbsp cornstarch
pinch of chili flakes
4 tbsp sunflower or vegetable oil
4 nests of dried vermicelli
  rice noodles
2 red or jalapeño chiles, seeded and
  sliced into fine strips

3 garlic cloves, grated
2 tbsp tamari (gluten-free soy sauce)
handful of basil leaves, torn

SPECIAL EQUIPMENT
large, deep nonstick frying pan or wok

GUIDELINES PER SERVING

●●○   Calories
●○○   Saturated fat
●●○   Salt

STATISTICS PER SERVING

Energy 487kcals/2036kJ

Protein 31g

Fat 12g
Saturated fat 2g

Carbohydrate 57g
Sugar 0.5g

Fiber 0g

Salt 1.5g

1 Toss the chicken in the salt and pepper, cornstarch, and chili flakes. Heat
1 tablespoon oil in a wok and swirl it around. Add the coated chicken
pieces and fry on medium-high heat for 10 minutes or until the chicken
is cooked through. Remove and set aside.

2 Add the remaining oil, sit the rice noodle nests in the wok, and fry on
medium-high heat for 1–2 minutes on each side until pale golden brown.
Remove from the wok with a slotted spatula and drain on paper towels.

3 Add the chiles to the wok and cook for 2–3 minutes, then add the garlic
and stir. Add the tamari, bubble for a minute, return the noodles and
chicken to the wok, and simmer gently for 5 minutes or until the noodles
have softened. Stir in the basil and serve.

GROUND PORK AND NOODLES WITH CARROT PICKLE

Fresh carrot pickle cuts through the richness of the pork. Omit the chile if making this dish for children.

SERVES   4
PREP   15 mins
COOK   30 mins

GUIDELINES PER SERVING

● ● ●   Calories

● ● ●   Saturated fat

● ● ●   Salt

STATISTICS PER SERVING

Energy   396kcals/1653kJ

Protein   20g

Fat   12g
Saturated fat   4g

Carbohydrate   48g
Sugar   9g

Fiber   3g

Salt   0.9g

GREAT FOR KIDS

7oz (200g) dried rice noodles
1 tbsp olive oil
1 onion, finely chopped
salt and freshly ground pepper
3 garlic cloves, finely chopped
2 jalapeño chiles, seeded and
   finely chopped
pinch of dried mint
pinch of allspice
12oz (350g) ground pork meat
1 tbsp tamari (gluten-free soy sauce)

1 tsp granulated sugar
green beans, lightly steamed, to serve

FOR THE PICKLE
3 medium carrots
1 tbsp white wine vinegar
1–2 tsp granulated sugar
handful of fresh mint leaves, finely
   chopped, plus extra to garnish
   (optional)

1 Place the noodles in a bowl, cover with boiling water, and leave for 10 minutes or as per package instructions. Drain and set aside.

2 For the carrot pickle, peel the carrots and finely slice on the diagonal using a mandolin to make thin rounds. In a separate bowl, whisk together the vinegar and sugar and pour the mixture over the carrots. Stir in the mint leaves, season to taste, and set aside.

3 Heat the oil in a large, heavy frying pan. Add the onion and some seasoning. Fry for 2–3 minutes on low heat, stir through the garlic, chile, dried mint, and allspice, and cook for 1 minute.

4 Add the ground pork, increase the heat a little, and cook for 8–10 minutes, stirring occasionally, until the pork is cooked through. Stir in the tamari and sugar and cook for 1–2 minutes more. Taste and add more seasoning and tamari if needed. Spoon the pork over a bed of noodles with some carrot pickle on the side. Scatter over more chopped mint leaves for color, if desired, and serve with steamed green beans.

SALT-AND-PEPPER BEEF NOODLES

Succulent strips of beef are stir-fried in a Chinese-style sauce with crisp snow peas.

SERVES   4
PREP   15 mins
COOK   20 mins

7oz (200g) dried rice noodles
1lb 5oz (600g) sirloin steak,
  thinly sliced
salt and freshly ground pepper
1 tsp Sichuan pepper
1 tbsp sunflower oil
3 garlic cloves, finely sliced
2in (5cm) fresh ginger, peeled
  and finely sliced
1 jalapeño chile, seeded and sliced into
  fine strips
7oz (200g) snow peas or sugar snap peas,
  sliced (optional)
3 scallions, finely diced, to garnish

FOR THE SAUCE
2 tbsp tamari (gluten-free soy sauce)
1 tbsp gluten-free nam pla (fish sauce)
1 tbsp cornstarch
1 tsp granulated sugar

SPECIAL EQUIPMENT
large, deep nonstick frying pan or wok

GUIDELINES PER SERVING

● ● ●   Calories
● ● ●   Saturated fat
● ● ●   Salt

STATISTICS PER SERVING

Energy 450kcals/1884kJ

Protein 40g

Fat 10g
Saturated fat 3g

Carbohydrate 46g
Sugar 4g

Fiber 1.2g

Salt 1.9g

1 Place the noodles in a bowl, cover with boiling water, and leave for 10 minutes or as per package instructions. Drain and set aside.

2 For the sauce, mix together the tamari, nam pla, cornstarch, and sugar and set aside.

3 Toss the beef with the salt and pepper and Sichuan pepper. Heat the oil in a wok, add the beef, and stir-fry on medium-high heat for 3–4 minutes or until browned all over, then remove.

4 Add the garlic, ginger, chile, and snow peas or sugar snap peas (if using) to the wok, adding a little more oil if needed, and stir-fry for 2 minutes on medium-high heat. Pour in the sauce and let it bubble. Add 2–3 tablespoons water—more if it is still too thick—and let it cook for 2 more minutes. Return the beef to the wok and stir to coat, then add the noodles and stir again. Spoon out into a serving dish and top with the scallions.

HOT SPICED RICE WITH CHICKEN AND POMEGRANATE

The heady spice mix elevates this easy chicken dish—plus it's a real feast for the eyes!

SERVES 4
PREP 15 mins
PLUS MARINATING
COOK 35–40 mins

GUIDELINES PER SERVING

● ● ○ Calories
● ○ ○ Saturated fat
● ○ ○ Salt

STATISTICS PER SERVING

Energy 518kcals/2174kJ

Protein 38g

Fat 8g
Saturated fat 2g

Carbohydrate 68g
Sugar 13g

Fiber 2g

Salt 0.35g

½ tsp ground cinnamon
½ tsp ground allspice
½ tsp ground cloves
½ tsp ground coriander
salt and freshly ground pepper
juice of 1 orange
⅔ cup pomegranate juice
  (see Cook's Tip)

2 garlic cloves, finely chopped
8 chicken thighs, skin on
3 zucchini, thickly sliced
10oz (300g) basmati rice
1–2 Scotch bonnet chiles, left whole
5½oz (150g) pomegranate seeds,
  or seeds from 1 pomegranate

1 Preheat the oven to 400°F (200°C). Mix all the spices with the salt and pepper, orange juice, pomegranate juice, and garlic. Place the chicken pieces in a roasting pan and pour over half the mixture to coat. Cover and marinate for 30 minutes, then roast in the oven for 20–25 minutes. Add the zucchini to the roasting pan and cook for another 15 minutes or until the chicken is golden and the skin begins to char slightly.

2 Place the rice and chiles in a pan, and add water so it just covers the rice. Season with salt and add in the remaining spice mix. Cook on medium heat with the lid ajar for 15 minutes until the rice has absorbed all the water and is just cooked. Turn off the heat, sit the lid on top, and leave for 10 minutes to steam.

3 Transfer to a serving dish, top with the chicken pieces and any juices and the zucchini, and sprinkle with the pomegranate seeds to serve. Use Scotch bonnets for garnish, or chop and scatter over the dish for some real heat.

Cook's Tip
Make fresh pomegranate juice by pressing seeds from 3 pomegranates through a sieve. Alternatively, try pomegranate molasses for a more intense flavor.

BRAZILIAN-STYLE RICE, BLACK BEANS, AND CHORIZO

Rice absorbs beautifully the flavors of cured chorizo sausage, whose smokiness deepens the fresh taste of jalapeño chile and cilantro leaves.

SERVES 4
PREP 25–30 mins
PLUS SOAKING
COOK 2 hours

GUIDELINES PER SERVING

●●○ Calories

●●○ Saturated fat

●●○ Salt

STATISTICS PER SERVING

Energy 543kcals/2274kJ

Protein 25g

Fat 18g
Saturated fat 5.5g

Carbohydrate 59g
Sugar 3.5g

Fiber 7g

Salt 1.6g

NUTRIENT BOOST
Beans contain soluble fiber, which can help control blood cholesterol.

8oz (225g) black turtle beans or black-eyed peas, soaked overnight and refreshed with clean water
2 cups hot gluten-free beef stock
¾ cup basmati rice
2 tbsp olive oil
1 onion, finely chopped
salt and freshly ground pepper
2 jalapeño chiles, seeded and finely chopped
1 bay leaf
3½oz (100g) gluten-free cured Spanish chorizo sausage, roughly chopped
3½oz (100g) pancetta, cubed
handful of fresh cilantro leaves, finely chopped
orange slices, to serve

1 Drain the beans and add them to a large pan, then add the beef stock and more hot water to cover if needed. Cover with a lid, bring to a boil, and cook for 10 minutes, then reduce to a simmer and cook partly covered for 1–1½ hours until the beans are soft. Take off the heat and set aside.

2 Meanwhile, cook the rice in a pan of boiling salted water for 10–15 minutes or as per package instructions, drain, and set aside. Heat the oil in a large frying pan, add the onion, and season with a little salt and pepper. Cook on low heat for 6–8 minutes, stirring so they don't burn. Cook until soft, then add the chile and the bay leaf and stir. Increase the heat a bit, add the chorizo and pancetta, and cook for 10 minutes more or until golden brown.

3 Ladle in the beans, taking in a little of the stock too, and simmer gently for 5 minutes, then stir in the rice and the cilantro. Remove the bay leaf and serve with some fresh orange slices.

HADDOCK AND TURMERIC RICE

Children will love this kedgeree-style dish, just go easy on the garam masala—a pinch will suffice.

1½ cups basmati rice
salt and freshly ground pepper
12oz (350g) undyed smoked
  haddock fillet
1¼ cups milk
1 tbsp olive oil
knob of butter
1 onion, finely chopped

2 tsp turmeric
2 tsp garam masala or mild
  curry powder
2½oz (75g) frozen peas, defrosted
4 large eggs, hardboiled and halved
handful of fresh cilantro or parsley leaves,
  roughly chopped, lemon wedges, and
  mango chutney, to serve

SERVES 4
PREP 20 mins
COOK 25 mins

GUIDELINES PER SERVING

● ● ○ Calories
● ● ○ Saturated fat
● ● ○ Salt

STATISTICS PER SERVING

Energy 545kcals/2281kJ

Protein 34g

Fat 15g
Saturated fat 5g

Carbohydrate 64g
Sugar 6g

Fiber 1.6g

Salt 2g

1 Put the rice in a pan and pour in enough water to cover. Season with salt and simmer gently with the lid ajar for 10–15 minutes until tender and cooked. Drain and set aside.

2 Lay the fish in a frying pan, skin-side down, and cover with milk or 1¼ cups water. Cover the pan and cook on low heat for 4–5 minutes until the fish just begins to flake. Remove with a slotted spoon, discard the skin, and set aside, keeping warm.

3 Heat the oil and butter in a large frying pan and add the onion. Cook on low heat for 2–3 minutes. Season to taste. Stir in the turmeric and garam masala and cook for 1–2 minutes. Stir in the rice and add the peas. On very low heat, stir to combine and warm the peas through, then flake the fish into chunky pieces and add to the pan. Top with the eggs and season to taste. Sprinkle over cilantro or parsley and add a squeeze of lemon. Serve with mango chutney on the side.

GROUND TURMERIC
Turmeric imparts a slightly sweet, warm, and musky flavor, and is often used as the base spice in a curry as it binds and harmonizes the other spices.

GREAT FOR KIDS

NUTRIENT BOOST
Peas contain protein and good amounts of soluble and insoluble fiber.

SALMON KEDGEREE

SERVES 4
PREP 20 mins
COOK 20 mins

This Anglo-Indian dish is traditionally made with haddock, but here the addition of salmon adds a touch of class.

GUIDELINES PER SERVING

● ● Calories

● ● ● Saturated fat

● ● ● Salt

STATISTICS PER SERVING

Energy 574 kcals/2395kJ

Protein 41g

Fat 28g
Saturated fat 11g

Carbohydrate 37g
Sugar 1g

Fiber trace

Salt 1.9g

10oz (300g) undyed smoked
  haddock fillets
10oz (300g) salmon fillets
7oz (200g) basmati rice
salt and freshly ground black pepper
pinch of saffron threads

4 tbsp butter
4 hard-boiled eggs
2 tbsp chopped parsley leaves,
  plus extra to serve
lemon wedges and buttered, gluten-free
  toast, to serve

1 Place the fish in a single layer in a large frying pan. Pour in enough water to cover and heat gently to simmering point. Simmer for 5 minutes, then drain.

2 Meanwhile, cook the rice in boiling salted water with the saffron for 10–12 minutes, or according to the packet instructions. When it is cooked, drain, and stir in the butter.

3 Flake the fish into large chunks and add them to the rice, removing any tiny pin bones you find as you do so. Discard the skin.

4 Remove the yolks from the hard-boiled eggs and reserve. Chop the egg whites and stir into the rice. Add the parsley and season to taste with salt and pepper.

5 Divide the mixture between warmed plates and crumble the reserved egg yolks across the top with more chopped parsley. Serve with lemon wedges and triangles of buttered gluten-free toast.

MEAT
AND FISH

SALMON EN CROÛTE

This classic summer dinner party dish looks impressive and is surprisingly easy to make.

SERVES 6
PREP 30 mins
PLUS CHILLING
COOK 30 mins
FREEZE 1 month
UNCOOKED

GUIDELINES PER SERVING

● ● ○ Calories

● ● ● Saturated fat

● ○ ○ Salt

STATISTICS PER SERVING

Energy 516kcals/2151kJ

Protein 32g

Fat 32g
Saturated fat 10g

Carbohydrate 23g
Sugar 1.5g

Fiber 0.5g

Salt 0.8g

NUTRIENT BOOST
Try to eat at least one serving of oily fish each week.

3½oz (100g) spinach leaves
salt and freshly ground pepper
1¾lb (800g) salmon fillet, skinned
1–2 tbsp gluten-free hot horseradish
  sauce (optional)
bunch of dill, finely chopped
zest of 1 lemon

oil, for greasing
gluten-free all-purpose flour, to dust
14oz (400g) gluten-free rough puff pastry
  (see pages 46–7)
1 large egg, lightly beaten
green beans and new potatoes

1 Place the spinach in a pan and sprinkle over a few drops of water, sit the pan on low heat, cover, and cook for 2 minutes until the spinach wilts. Drain and, when cool enough to handle, squeeze out as much water from the leaves as possible. Set aside.

2 Season the salmon, place it between large sheets of plastic wrap and gently pound to flatten it to about ½in (1cm) thick. Remove the top layer of the plastic wrap and spread the horseradish over the salmon (if using), and then the spinach. Mix the dill with the lemon zest and sprinkle evenly.

3 Using the plastic wrap to pull the salmon toward you, carefully roll it into a thick roll (approximately 10 x 4in/25 x 10cm). Tighten the plastic wrap at the edges to form a secure roll. Chill in the fridge for about 1 hour.

4 Lightly oil a baking sheet. On a floured board, roll out the pastry into a 14in (35cm) square, about ⅛in (3mm) thick. Remove the plastic wrap and place the salmon in the middle of the pastry, seam up (the pastry and salmon seam should be aligned). Fold in and seal the edges with water to form a closed parcel. Sit it on the baking sheet, sealed side down. Brush with half the beaten egg and chill for 30 minutes. Preheat the oven to 400°F (200°C). Brush with the remaining beaten egg and bake until the pastry is cooked and golden, about 25–30 minutes. Slice and serve with green beans and new potatoes.

POLENTA FISH CAKES

Polenta makes a crunchy, gluten-free alternative to bread crumbs for coating fish cakes.

SERVES 4
PREP 20 mins
COOK 50 mins
FREEZE 1 month

GUIDELINES PER SERVING

● ● ●　Calories
● ● ●　Saturated fat
● ● ●　Salt

STATISTICS PER SERVING

Energy 409kcals/1715kJ

Protein 28g

Fat 14.5g
Saturated fat 3g

Carbohydrate 40g
Sugar 4g

Fiber 3g

Salt 0.5g

GREAT FOR KIDS

14oz (400g) potatoes, such as Russet
14oz (400g) white fish, skin on
¾ cup milk
1 bay leaf
knob of butter
1 onion, finely chopped
salt and freshly ground pepper
handful of flat-leaf parsley,
   finely chopped
2 tsp capers, rinsed and chopped

2 dill pickles, roughly chopped
⅔ cup polenta or fine cornmeal,
   to coat
leaves from a few sprigs of thyme,
   finely chopped
2 tbsp gluten-free all-purpose flour
1 large egg, lightly beaten
3–4 tbsp vegetable oil, for frying
gluten-free tartare sauce and salad,
   to serve

1 Cook the potatoes still in their skins, in boiling water for 20–30 minutes or until soft. Drain and leave to cool, then remove the skins and mash well. Set aside. Sit the fish in a frying pan, add the milk and the bay leaf, then cover and simmer on gentle heat for 5 minutes until the fish begins to flake. Remove from the heat and discard the bay leaf and most of the milk; keep some back for the potato mix. Discard the skin and bones. When cool enough to handle, pull apart into chunky flakes and set aside.

2 Melt the butter in a frying pan, add the onion, season, and cook on low heat for 5 minutes until softened but not browned. Leave to cool. In a large bowl, add the potatoes, fish, onions, parsley, capers, and pickles, and stir gently until combined; if the mixture is stiff, add 1–2 tablespoons of the cooking milk to help bind it. Season to taste, divide the mixture into 8 balls, and flatten into cakes.

3 Take three plates. Mix the polenta and the thyme and add to one plate, the flour to another, and the egg to a third. Dip the cakes into the flour for a light dusting, then dip in the egg, and coat in the polenta. Put on a baking sheet and chill in the fridge for 20 minutes; if freezing, do so at this point. To cook, heat a little oil in a nonstick frying pan, add the cakes a few at a time, and cook on medium heat for 3–4 minutes on each side until golden all over. Add oil as needed. Serve with tartare sauce and a lightly dressed mixed salad.

CHEESE-CRUSTED SALMON

The cheesy coating adds real flavor to the salmon; it's a bit like a rarebit mixture roasted with the fish and is a great way to get children to eat fish.

SERVES   4
PREP   10 mins
COOK   20 mins

4 large salmon fillets, about
   5½oz (150g) each, skin on
oil, for greasing
salt and freshly ground pepper
4½oz (125g) Cheddar cheese, grated
scant 1oz (25g) Parmesan cheese, grated

splash of gluten-free Worcestershire sauce
   or tamari (gluten-free soy sauce)
2 slices of gluten-free bread, pureed into
   bread crumbs
beet salad, to serve

GUIDELINES PER SERVING

- ⬤⬤◯   Calories
- ⬤⬤⬤   Saturated fat
- ⬤◯◯   Salt

STATISTICS PER SERVING

Energy   490kcals/2046kJ

Protein   42g

Fat   30g
Saturated fat   11g

Carbohydrate   13g
Sugar   1g

Fiber   2g

Salt   1.3g

1 Preheat the oven to 400°F (200°C). Place the fish in a large, lightly oiled roasting pan, and season with salt and pepper.

2 Mix together the cheeses, Worcestershire sauce or tamari, and bread crumbs, then spoon equal amounts onto each salmon fillet.

3 Press the mixture evenly onto the fillets to coat and bake in the oven for 20 minutes, or until the top begins to turn golden brown and the fish is flaky and cooked through. Cover with foil if it starts to brown too much. Remove and serve with a chopped beet salad.

Variation
Substitute the salmon for white fish, such as cod.

SALMON FILLETS
Try to get large loin fillets for this dish, which are thicker than the tail. If using tail fillets you may need to reduce the baking time.

GREAT FOR KIDS

NUTRIENT BOOST
Aim to eat 2 portions of fish a week, including an oil-rich fish like salmon.

BEER-BATTERED FISH AND CHIPS

SERVES 4
PREP 15 mins
COOK 40 mins

A favorite classic—the batter serves as a protective casing while the fish cooks, leaving it flaky and delicate.

1¾lb (800g) potatoes, peeled and cut into thickish fingers
2 tbsp olive oil
pinch of sea salt
4 haddock or cod fillets, skin on
salt and freshly ground pepper
juice of ½ lemon
1½ cups gluten-free all-purpose flour, sifted, plus extra to dust

1¼ cups gluten-free beer
vegetable oil, for frying
lemon wedges, to serve

SPECIAL EQUIPMENT
deep-fat fryer (optional)

GUIDELINES PER SERVING

● ● ○ Calories
● ○ ○ Saturated fat
● ○ ○ Salt

STATISTICS PER SERVING

Energy 703kcals/2955kJ

Protein 37g

Fat 26g
Saturated fat 3.5g

Carbohydrate 73g
Sugar 3.5g

Fiber 5.8g

Salt 1.3g

GREAT FOR KIDS

1 For the chips, preheat the oven to 400°F (200°C). Place the potatoes in a large roasting pan, add the olive oil, and coat them well. Spread them out so they roast rather than steam, and sprinkle with sea salt. Cook in the oven for 30–40 minutes until golden, turning them halfway through cooking.

2 Meanwhile, season the fish, squeeze a little lemon juice over each fillet, and dust with a little flour. Add the remaining flour along with a pinch of salt to a bowl and slowly pour in the beer, whisking as you go. You may not need all the beer, as the mixture should be thick. If it is too runny, it won't stick to the fish, so stop when you reach the required consistency.

3 Fill a fryer with the vegetable oil, or pour it into a large pan so that it is one-third full, and heat to 375°F (190°C); maintain this temperature throughout. Do not leave the pan or fryer unattended, switch off when not using, and keep a fire blanket nearby in case of fire. Hold the fish by the tail and pass it through the batter so that it's completely coated, then add it to the oil. Cook 2 fillets at a time for 2–3 minutes, turn over, and cook for a further 2–3 minutes until crisp and golden. Transfer to paper towels to drain and repeat with the remaining fish, keeping the finished pieces warm in a low oven. Serve with the chips and lemon wedges.

MONKFISH CATAPLANA

Quick and impressive, this Portuguese dish is named after the special pan used to prepare it—you can also use an ordinary, large lidded pan. Good-quality fresh fish is key.

3 tbsp olive oil

2 onions, finely chopped

4 tomatoes, chopped, or 7oz (200g) canned chopped tomatoes

1lb 2oz (500g) monkfish tail fillets, cut into chunky bite-sized pieces

7oz (200g) clams, well washed, (see below)

7oz (200g) raw shelled shrimp

4 garlic cloves, finely chopped

½ cup dry white wine

1 tsp thyme leaves

1 bay leaf

2 tsp paprika

4 chunky slices of gluten-free bread

lemon wedges and rice, to serve

SPECIAL EQUIPMENT

cataplana dish (optional)

SERVES 4
PREP 15 mins
COOK 15 mins

GUIDELINES PER SERVING

● ● ○ Calories

● ● ○ Saturated fat

● ● ○ Salt

STATISTICS PER SERVING

Energy 393kcals/1661kJ

Protein 44.5g

Fat 11g
Saturated fat 1.5g

Carbohydrate 25g
Sugar 5g

Fiber 2.2g

Salt 1.1g

1 In a large lidded pan or cataplana dish, heat the oil on medium heat, add the onion, and cook for 2–3 minutes until beginning to soften.

2 Now add the next 9 ingredients and combine well. Cover tightly and simmer over medium heat for 10–15 minutes until the shrimp are pink, the clams have opened, and the monkfish is cooked. Taste and season if needed and carefully remove the bay leaf.

3 To serve, roughly tear 1 slice of bread into each bowl (ideally rustic-style shallow bowls), then ladle over the fish and plenty of sauce. Serve with a lemon wedge and some rice.

CLAM SAFETY
Clams must be alive before cooking or they can be unsafe to eat. Tap any that are slightly open; throw away those clams that don't close. Also discard any that remain shut after cooking.

ASIAN-STYLE CRISPY FISH

A medley of vegetables topped with pan-fried red mullet and seasoned with a Vietnamese-style dressing.

SERVES 4
PREP 20 mins
COOK 15 mins

GUIDELINES PER SERVING

● ○ ○ Calories

● ● ○ Saturated fat

● ○ ○ Salt

STATISTICS PER SERVING

Energy 488kcals/2043kJ

Protein 34g

Fat 11g
Saturated fat 1g

Carbohydrate 56g
Sugar 5g

Fiber 4g

Salt 0.6g

4 red mullet fillets, skinned
1 tbsp rice flour
1 tbsp sunflower oil

FOR THE NOODLES AND VEGETABLES
9oz (250g) dried vermicelli rice noodles
7oz (200g) bok choy, trimmed
  and shredded
2 carrots, grated
handful of bean sprouts
4 scallions, finely sliced
handful of mint leaves, torn

handful of Thai basil leaves
  or regular basil, torn
handful of fresh cilantro leaves
1 tbsp sesame seeds, to garnish

FOR THE DRESSING
juice of 2 limes
2 tbsp rice wine vinegar
gluten-free nam pla (fish sauce)

1 For the dressing, mix together the lime juice and rice wine vinegar. Add the nam pla to taste, and set aside.

2 Toss the fish fillets in the rice flour, heat the oil in a wok or frying pan, and add them to the hot oil. Cook two at a time on medium-high heat for about 4–6 minutes turning halfway until golden and crispy. Remove with a fish slice and set aside on a plate layered with paper towels, to drain. Repeat to cook the remaining fillets.

3 Sit the noodles in a bowl, pour over boiling water to cover, and leave for 3–4 minutes, or follow the package instructions. Drain well, separate the strands if needed, and set aside to cool. In a large bowl, place the bok choy, grated carrot, and half the dressing and toss. Add the bean sprouts, scallions, and cooled noodles and toss again with the remaining dressing. Add half the herbs, toss, and transfer to a serving dish. Top with the fish fillets and sprinkle over the remaining herbs and sesame seeds.

EASY CHICKEN TIKKA SKEWERS WITH CUCUMBER AND MINT RAITA

Raita is an easy-to-make Indian dipping sauce that can be used as an accompaniment to many grilled dishes.

SERVES 4
PREP 20 mins
PLUS MARINATING
COOK 10 mins

GUIDELINES PER SERVING

● ● ○ Calories
● ● ○ Saturated fat
● ○ ○ Salt

STATISTICS PER SERVING

Energy 242kcals/1019kJ

Protein 40g

Fat 7g
Saturated fat 4g

Carbohydrate 4.5g
Sugar 4g

Fiber 0.5g

Salt 0.8g

FOR THE MARINADE
6 tbsp plain low-fat yogurt
1 tbsp lemon juice
1 tsp ground cumin
1 tsp ground coriander
½ tsp turmeric
2 tsp cayenne pepper or
  chili powder
½ tsp salt
1 garlic clove, crushed
1in (3cm) fresh ginger, grated
1lb 5oz (600g) boneless, skinless
  chicken breast or thigh, cut into
  1in (3cm) cubes

FOR THE RAITA
4in (10cm) piece of cucumber,
  seeded and grated
¾ cup Greek-style yogurt
handful of mint leaves,
  finely chopped
1 small garlic clove, crushed
salt and freshly ground black pepper

SPECIAL EQUIPMENT
8 bamboo skewers

1 Mix the marinade ingredients, except the chicken, in a bowl. Add the chicken, turning to coat. Cover and refrigerate for 1 hour.

2 Meanwhile, place 8 bamboo skewers to soak in water, to keep them from burning on the broiler.

3 Put the cucumber in a clean kitchen towel and squeeze well. Mix with the remaining raita ingredients and season to taste. Cover and chill.

4 Thread the chicken onto the soaked, drained skewers, distributing it evenly.

5 Preheat the broiler and broil the chicken for 3–5 minutes on each side, or until starting to char. Serve with the raita.

Variation
For an even easier recipe, mix 2 tbsp of store-bought, gluten-free tikka paste with the yogurt and use that as the marinade.

CHINESE-COATED CHICKEN WINGS

Chicken wings have plenty of succulent meat on them and are an economical cut.

SERVES   4
PREP   15 mins
          PLUS MARINATING
COOK   40–45 mins

GUIDELINES PER SERVING

● ○ ○   Calories

● ○ ○   Saturated fat

● ● ●   Salt

STATISTICS PER SERVING

Energy 446kcals/1856kJ

Protein 22.5g

Fat 29g
Saturated fat 4.5g

Carbohydrate 23g
Sugar 1.5g

Fiber 1.5g

Salt 2.4g

GREAT FOR KIDS

24 chicken wings
juice of 1 lemon
1/2 cup gluten-free all-purpose
   flour or rice flour
2 tsp salt
1 1/2 tsp five-spice powder
1 1/2 tsp freshly ground pepper
1/2 cup sunflower or vegetable oil
3 chiles, seeded and finely sliced at
   an angle (omit if making for kids)

5 garlic cloves, sliced
6 scallions, trimmed and cut into
   1in (2.5cm) lengths at an angle
tamari (gluten-free soy sauce)
   and rice, to serve

SPECIAL EQUIPMENT
large, deep nonstick frying pan or wok

1 Put the chicken wings in a large bowl, add the lemon juice, combine well, and allow to stand for 20 minutes. Mix the flour, salt, five-spice, and pepper together in a large bowl and add the chicken wings and juice. Combine well and marinate in the flour mixture for 5 minutes, turning over occasionally.

2 Heat the oil in the wok. Add the wings, 4 at a time, and cook them on medium–high heat for 8–10 minutes until golden and crisp, then transfer to a paper towel. Cook the remainder in the same way.

3 Leave about 3 tablespoons oil in the wok and drain the rest. Heat again on low-medium heat, then add the chile, garlic, and scallions, and cook for 2–3 minutes, being careful not to burn them. Return the chicken wings to the wok, toss together, then serve piled up on a plate with tamari and some rice on the side.

SWEET AND SOUR CHICKEN

Unlike most take-out versions, this sweet and sour dish is delicate, refreshing, and guaranteed gluten-free.

SERVES 4
PREP 15 mins
COOK 20 mins

10oz (300g) green beans, trimmed and cut in half at an angle
3 tbsp gluten-free all-purpose flour
½ tsp salt
6 tbsp sparkling mineral water, ice cold
14oz (400g) chicken breast, skinless, cut into strips
sunflower or vegetable oil, for frying
1 red bell pepper and 1 yellow bell pepper, seeded and cut into strips
1 onion, finely chopped
2 tbsp fresh cilantro leaves, finely chopped, to serve
rice, to serve

FOR THE SAUCE
3 tbsp gluten-free rice wine or medium-sweet sherry
½ tsp chili flakes
2 garlic cloves, grated
1 tbsp gluten-free nam pla (fish sauce)
3 tsp granulated sugar
juice of 1 lime

SPECIAL EQUIPMENT
large, deep nonstick frying pan or wok

GUIDELINES PER SERVING

Calories

Saturated fat

Salt

STATISTICS PER SERVING

Energy 245kcals/1028kJ

Protein 27.5g

Fat 7.5g
Saturated fat 1.1g

Carbohydrate 16.7g
Sugar 7.5g

Fiber 4.7g

Salt 0.7g

1 Blanch the beans in a pan of boiling water for 3 minutes, then drain and refresh in cold water to halt the cooking process.

2 For the sauce, place all the ingredients in a bowl, mix well, and set aside.

3 In a large bowl, add the flour, salt, and mineral water, then beat with a hand whisk to make a smooth batter. Add the chicken pieces and combine well to coat. Pour the oil into the wok to a depth of 1in (2.5cm) and heat until hot. Add the battered chicken pieces, several pieces at a time, and cook for 4–5 minutes on medium-high heat until golden. Remove and drain on paper towels. Repeat to cook all the chicken.

4 Leave about 3 tablespoons oil in the wok and drain the rest. On low–medium heat, add the peppers and beans and stir-fry for 2 minutes. Add the onion and cook for 1 minute. Add the sauce and cook for 1 minute to let it thicken slightly. Add the chicken pieces and turn to coat well. Scatter over the cilantro and serve with rice.

RICOTTA-STUFFED CHICKEN BREASTS

SERVES	4
PREP	20 mins
COOK	20–25 mins

A modest effort for an impressive midweek meal, or a weekend treat to impress your friends.

GUIDELINES PER SERVING

● ● Calories

● ● Saturated fat

● ● Salt

STATISTICS PER SERVING

Energy 281kcals/1181kJ

Protein 46g

Fat 11g
Saturated fat 4g

Carbohydrate 0.3g
Sugar 0.3g

Fiber 0g

Salt 1.4g

¼ cup ricotta cheese
2 tbsp finely grated Parmesan cheese
2 tbsp finely chopped basil leaves
1 tbsp finely chopped flat-leaf
  parsley leaves
finely grated zest of 1 lemon
salt and freshly ground black pepper
4 boneless, skinless chicken breasts
1 tbsp olive oil
8 prosciutto slices

1 Preheat the oven to 400°F (200°C). In a bowl, mash the ricotta cheese with the Parmesan cheese, herbs, and lemon zest. Season well.

2 Take the chicken breasts and cut a pocket into the thickest side. Stuff each one with one-quarter of the ricotta mixture, then rub with a little oil. Lay 2 prosciutto slices on a chopping board, overlapping slightly, and place the chicken on top. Carefully wrap the prosciutto around the breasts, making sure that it meets on top. (If necessary, use a toothpick to secure.)

3 Flip the breasts over and place seam-side down on a baking sheet. Cook at the top of the oven for 20–25 minutes, until golden brown. When pressed with a finger, the meat should bounce back. Remove the toothpicks, if you used them, before serving.

CREAMY CHICKEN CRUMBLE

SERVES   4
PREP   20 mins
COOK   1 hour
FREEZE   1 month

GUIDELINES PER SERVING

●●○ Calories

●●● Saturated fat

●●○ Salt

STATISTICS PER SERVING

Energy 712kcals/2960kJ

Protein 33g

Fat 45g
Saturated fat 27g

Carbohydrate 34g
Sugar 3g

Fiber 1.5g

Salt 1.6g

GREAT
FOR KIDS

If serving this for children, replace the wine with gluten-free stock. You could also stir in sweet corn kernels and replace the chicken with cooked ham.

2 large chicken breasts, skin on
1 tbsp olive oil
salt and freshly ground pepper
steamed leeks or peas, to serve

FOR THE CRUMBLE TOPPING
1 cup rice flour
pinch of salt
5 tbsp butter, cubed
3 tbsp grated Parmesan cheese
1³⁄₄oz (50g) Cheddar cheese, grated
1 tsp mustard seeds, crushed

FOR THE SAUCE
4 tbsp butter
7oz (200g) baby button mushrooms,
   left whole
1 tbsp rice flour or cornstarch
¹⁄₂ cup dry white wine or gluten-free
   chicken or vegetable stock
²⁄₃ cup milk
²⁄₃ cup half-and-half
1 tbsp Dijon mustard
a few tarragon leaves, chopped

1 Preheat the oven to 400°F (200°C). Place the chicken in a roasting pan, drizzle with the oil, and season. Roast in the oven for 25–35 minutes until golden and cooked through. Don't overcook or it will be dry. Leave to cool slightly, remove the skin, and shred into chunky pieces.

2 For the crumble topping, place the rice flour and salt in a bowl. Add the butter and rub it in with your fingers until it resembles bread crumbs. Stir in the cheeses and mustard seeds. Set aside.

3 For the sauce, melt the butter in a medium pan, add the mushrooms, and cook on low-medium heat for 5 minutes until golden. Remove the pan, stir in the rice flour, add the wine, and stir. Return it to the heat and cook for 2–3 minutes, stirring continuously. Add the milk and half-and-half and bring to a gentle boil. Reduce to a simmer, stirring continuously to remove any lumps. As it thickens, stir in the mustard and tarragon leaves, and season.

4 Remove the pan and add the shredded chicken. Stir to coat, spoon into a shallow 1 quart ovenproof dish, and top with the crumble mixture. Bake in the oven for 20–25 minutes until golden. Serve with steamed leeks or peas.

ROAST TURKEY

SERVES 8
PREP 20 mins
COOK approx. 3½ hours

Whip up this traditional juicy roast filled with delectable stuffing for a perfect gluten-free Thanksgiving or Christmas. Serve with popovers (see opposite) and roast potatoes.

GUIDELINES PER SERVING

● ● ○   Calories

● ● ●   Saturated fat

● ● ○   Salt

STATISTICS PER SERVING

Energy 570kcals/2375kJ

Protein 46g

Fat 32g
Saturated fat 14g

Carbohydrate 19g
Sugar 6g

Fiber 2g

Salt 2g

NUTRIENT BOOST
High-protein, low-fat turkey is a source of selenium, good for immune health.

1 turkey, weighing about 11lb (5kg)

FOR THE HERB BUTTER
4 tbsp salted butter
2 garlic cloves, grated
1 tsp dried oregano
1 tbsp finely chopped flat-leaf parsley
1 tsp finely chopped sage leaves

FOR THE STUFFING
1 tbsp olive oil
2 celery sticks, finely chopped
1 onion, finely chopped

1lb 2oz (500g) gluten-free pork sausages, casings removed
1 cup gluten-free bread crumbs
5 sage leaves, finely chopped
1 tsp thyme leaves
1 crisp sweet apple, chopped
¼ cup dried cranberries
2 tbsp chopped dried apricots
½ cup hot gluten-free chicken stock
5 tbsp butter, melted

1 Preheat the oven to 400°F (200°C). For the herb butter, mix all the ingredients and set aside. To make the turkey stuffing, heat the oil in a large frying pan, add the celery, and cook for 3 minutes. Add the onion and cook for 3 more minutes until soft, then add the sausage. Cook for 8 minutes until the pork is no longer pink, stirring well to break up the meat. Remove and cool, transfer to a large bowl, add the remaining ingredients, and combine well. If the mixture is too wet, add some more bread crumbs.

2 Stuff the turkey with as much mixture as you can; make a note of the bird's weight at this point. Spread the herb butter over the turkey, transfer to a large roasting pan, and roast in the oven for 15 minutes.

3 Reduce the temperature to 375°F (190°C) and cook for 20 minutes per 2¼lb (1kg) plus 90 minutes, or until the juices run clear when the thigh is pierced with a skewer. A 11lb (5kg) turkey would take 3¼ hours to cook; the cooking time depends on the weight of the turkey after stuffing. Baste with the juices as it cooks. If it starts looking too brown, cover loosely with foil. Leave the turkey to rest for 30 minutes before slicing to serve.

POPOVERS

Popovers are the US equivalent of Yorkshire puddings: savory baked puff pancakes to accompany roast meats.

SERVES   8
PREP   15 mins
COOK   20 mins

2 large eggs
1⅛ cups milk
1¾ cups gluten-free all-purpose flour
2 tsp gluten-free baking powder
salt and freshly ground pepper
4 tbsp melted butter

SPECIAL EQUIPMENT
8-hole muffin pan

GUIDELINES PER SERVING

● ● ○   Calories

● ● ●   Saturated fat

● ● ○   Salt

STATISTICS PER POPOVER

Energy 200kcals/819kJ

Protein 4g

Fat 8.5g
Saturated fat 4.5g

Carbohydrate 26g
Sugar 1.5g

Fiber 2g

Salt 0.7g

1 Preheat the oven to 400°F (200°C) and place the muffin pan in the oven to heat up. In a bowl, beat the eggs until foamy and whisk in the milk. Add the flour, baking powder, salt and pepper, and beat to a smooth batter.

2 Take the muffin pan out of the oven and add the butter evenly to each hole; be careful not to burn the butter. Pour in the batter mixture, return to the oven, and bake for 15–20 minutes until the popovers are golden brown. Serve immediately with roast turkey or other roast meats.

ROAST CHICKEN WITH ORANGE AND TAMARI

A simple sweet-and-spicy dish. Chicken drumsticks and wings would also work well.

SERVES 4
PREP   15 mins
        PLUS MARINATING
COOK   40 mins

GUIDELINES PER SERVING

- ● ○ ○ Calories
- ● ○ ○ Saturated fat
- ● ● ○ Salt

STATISTICS PER SERVING

Energy 205kcals/865kJ

Protein 33g

Fat 4g
Saturated fat 1g

Carbohydrate 9g
Sugar 9g

Fiber 0.5g

Salt 2.3g

8 chicken thighs on the bone
½ tsp ground ginger
1 tsp ground dried mint
¼ tsp ground allspice
salt and freshly ground pepper
2 tbsp pomegranate seeds
handful of fresh cilantro leaves,
  roughly chopped

steamed rice or baby roast potatoes,
  to serve

FOR THE MARINADE
3 tbsp tamari (gluten-free soy sauce)
juice of 3 oranges or 4 tangerines

1 Mix together the marinade ingredients in a large bowl, then add the chicken pieces and stir to coat thoroughly. Cover and put in the fridge for 30 minutes or 2 hours if time permits.

2 Preheat the oven to 400°F (200°C). Mix together the ginger, mint, and allspice. Set the chicken pieces and marinade in a roasting pan, sprinkle over the spice mixture, season, and bake in the oven for 40 minutes.

3 Remove from the oven, transfer to a serving plate, and sprinkle over the pomegranate seeds and cilantro. Serve the chicken with steamed rice or baby roast potatoes.

PREPARING POMEGRANATE
To get at the juicy seeds, cut off the spiky top of the pomegranate and score the skin into quarters. Break the fruit apart with your hands and use a spoon to remove the seeds from the membrane.

TOAD IN THE HOLE

If making for kids, halve the sausages and stand them on end in the pan so they stick up, and omit the wine in the gravy.

SERVES   4
PREP   15 mins
COOK   45 mins

2 tbsp olive oil
8 gluten-free sausages, pork or beef
1¼ cups gluten-free all-purpose flour
pinch of salt
2 large eggs
1⅛ cups milk
1 tbsp Dijon mustard (optional)

FOR THE GRAVY
½ cup red wine
1 tbsp cornstarch
1¼ cups hot gluten-free pork
  or beef stock
salt and freshly ground pepper
few sprigs of rosemary

GUIDELINES PER SERVING

● ● ○   Calories
● ● ●   Saturated fat
● ● ●   Salt

STATISTICS PER SERVING

Energy 577kcals/2401kJ

Protein 23g

Fat 34g
Saturated fat 11g

Carbohydrate 36g
Sugar 5g

Fiber 0g

Salt 3.5g

1 Preheat the oven to 425°F (220°C). Heat half the oil in a large frying pan, add the sausages, and cook on medium-high heat for 10–15 minutes, until golden all over. Transfer to a metal or ceramic baking pan and set aside.

2 For the batter, add the flour and salt to a bowl. Make a well in the center, add the eggs and a little milk, and stir, bringing in a little flour as you go. Slowly add the milk and continue stirring, pulling in more flour from the edges until you have a smooth batter. Use a balloon whisk at the end to avoid lumps. Stir in the mustard (if using). Add the remaining oil to the baking pan with the sausages and heat it on the stove top on medium. When hot, pour in the batter and bake in the oven for 30–35 minutes until golden.

3 For the gravy, heat the frying pan containing the leftover oil; pour off any excess oil. Add the wine and boil, scraping up any bits from the bottom of the pan. Reduce the heat, mix the cornstarch with a little water to form a paste, and add to the pan, stirring constantly. Gradually pour in the stock, season to taste, and add the rosemary. Bring to a boil, then simmer, stirring, for 10 minutes. Season to taste if needed. Strain to remove any lumps and the rosemary, pour into a pitcher, and serve with the toad in the hole.

Variations

Add roasted shallots or red onions to the sausages and stir your favorite flavor into the batter mix: horseradish, fresh herbs, or dried oregano all work well.

PORK ENCHILADAS

A rich mix of fabulous flavors: tortillas filled with smoky pork and tomato salsa, baked with sour cream and cheese.

SERVES 4

PREP 20–25 mins
PLUS MARINATING

COOK 1 hour

GUIDELINES PER SERVING

● ● ○ Calories

● ● ● Saturated fat

● ○ ○ Salt

STATISTICS PER SERVING

Energy 567kcals/2382kJ

Protein 32g

Fat 24g
Saturated fat 9.5g

Carbohydrate 55g
Sugar 6.5g

Fiber 5g

Salt 1.2g

12oz (350g) pork tenderloin
6 corn tortillas (see page 233)
6 tbsp sour cream, to top
2½oz (75g) sharp Cheddar
   cheese, grated, to top

FOR THE MARINADE

2 tbsp olive oil
1 chipotle chile, finely chopped
   (or dried jalapeño chile) or 1 tbsp
   adobo sauce or a generous splash
   of smoked chipotle Tabasco sauce
2 tsp coriander seeds
pinch of ground cinnamon
salt and freshly ground pepper
pinch of sugar

FOR THE TOMATO SALSA

1lb 2oz (500g) small vine-ripened
   tomatoes
1 red or jalapeño chile, halved and seeded
1 tbsp olive oil
2 scallions, finely chopped
juice of 1 lime
salt and freshly ground pepper
handful of fresh cilantro leaves,
   finely chopped

1 Put the pork in a shallow dish, mix the marinade ingredients, and pour over the pork to cover. Leave for 20 minutes or longer if time permits. Preheat the oven to 400°F (200°C). Transfer the pork (with the marinade) to a roasting pan and cook for 40 minutes, basting occasionally so the pork doesn't dry out. Remove and set aside.

2 For the salsa, heat a grill pan to hot. Toss the tomatoes and chile with the oil and add to the pan. Cook over medium-high heat for 5–6 minutes, turning halfway, until lightly charred. Remove and pulse with the scallions and lime juice in a food processor until chopped. Season to taste, transfer to a bowl, and stir in the cilantro.

3 Shred the pork, retaining any of the juices. Lay out the tortillas and spoon the pork into the center of each. Spoon over the salsa and roll the tortillas. Set them in an ovenproof dish, spoon the sour cream on top, and sprinkle the cheese. Bake for 15–20 minutes until the cheese has melted. Serve with the remaining salsa and a splash of smoked Tabasco sauce if you prefer.

LAMB TAGINE WITH CAULIFLOWER "COUSCOUS"

Nutty roasted cauliflower, processed until just grainy, makes a tasty gluten-free substitute for couscous.

SERVES   4
PREP   15 mins
COOK   1¾ hours

2lb (900g) lamb shoulder,
  cut into chunks
2 garlic cloves, finely chopped
2in (5cm) piece of fresh ginger, peeled
  and grated
salt and freshly ground pepper
½ tsp ground cinnamon
½ tsp turmeric
1 onion, grated
1 tbsp olive oil
1lb (450g) carrots, peeled or scrubbed
  and roughly chopped
3 cups hot gluten-free vegetable stock

2 preserved lemons, halved, flesh
  discarded and skin finely sliced, or the
  zest and juice of 1 fresh lemon
handful of flat-leaf parsley,
  finely chopped

FOR THE "COUSCOUS"
1 cauliflower, broken into large florets
1 tbsp olive oil
1–2 tsp ground cumin
salt and freshly ground pepper

GUIDELINES PER SERVING

● ● ●   Calories

● ● ●   Saturated fat

● ● ●   Salt

STATISTICS PER SERVING

Energy 555kcals/2316kJ

Protein 53g

Fat 26g
Saturated fat 9g

Carbohydrate 15g
Sugar 14g

Fiber 9g

Salt 1.1g

1 Toss the lamb with the garlic, ginger, salt and pepper, cinnamon, turmeric, and onion. Heat the oil in a large, heavy pan, add the lamb mixture, and cook on medium heat for 10 minutes until the lamb is sealed. Stir in the carrots so they get coated. Pour over the stock, bring to a boil, cover, and simmer on low heat for 1–1½ hours, until the lamb is tender, adding more hot water as needed; alternatively transfer to a casserole dish and bake in an oven preheated to 350°F (180°C) for 1½ hours.

2 Preheat the oven to 400°F (200°C). Toss the cauliflower with the oil and cumin and season. Transfer to a roasting pan and bake for 10 minutes or until just turning golden. Remove the cauliflower from the oven and leave to cool completely. Transfer to a food processor and pulse until it resembles grains; don't overwork or it will become mushy. Season to taste.

3 Stir the preserved lemons or zest and juice into the lamb for the last 15 minutes of cooking, then stir in the parsley when ready to serve.

SPICED LAMB AND HUMMUS WRAPS

A superb mix of textures and punchy flavors make up this Lebanese-inspired meal. If you would like an extra side dish, mix some Greek yogurt with chopped fresh mint.

SERVES 4
PREP 30 mins
PLUS MARINATING
COOK 4 hours

GUIDELINES PER SERVING

● ● ● Calories

● ● ● Saturated fat

● ● ● Salt

STATISTICS PER SERVING

Energy 900kcals/3769kJ

Protein 58g

Fat 44g
Saturated fat 11g

Carbohydrate 65g
Sugar 2g

Fiber 7.5g

Salt 1.4g

3lb 3oz (1.5kg) lamb shoulder
8 corn tortillas (see page 233), lemon wedges, and mixed salad, to serve

FOR THE SPICE RUB
½ tsp ground cinnamon
½ tsp ground coriander
¼ tsp ground cumin
1 tsp dried mint
salt and freshly ground black pepper
2 tbsp olive oil

FOR THE HUMMUS
14oz can chickpeas, drained and rinsed
3 garlic cloves, grated
2 tbsp gluten-free tahini
juice of ½–1 lemon to taste
4–5 tbsp olive oil, plus extra to drizzle
1 tsp paprika, plus extra to sprinkle

1 Mix together the spices, herbs, and seasoning and stir into 1 tablespoon of the oil. Rub into the lamb and leave for at least 30 minutes, or covered in the refrigerator overnight. Preheat the oven to 325°F (160°C). In a large, heavy frying pan, heat the remaining olive oil, add the lamb, and cook on medium-high heat for 5–10 minutes or until browned all over.

2 Place the lamb in a large roasting pan, cover it with foil, and cook for 4 hours, removing the foil for the last 15 minutes of cooking. Remove from the oven, cover, and leave to rest for at least 20 minutes.

3 For the hummus, pulse the chickpeas, garlic, and tahini in a food processor, until combined. Trickle in the lemon juice and olive oil, pulsing and tasting as you go. Season to taste, add the paprika, and pulse again. Transfer to a bowl, drizzle a little olive oil over the top, and add a dusting of paprika. Heat the wraps in the oven according to package instructions. Shred the lamb and transfer to a serving plate. Divide the salad and lamb between the wraps, top with hummus, add a squeeze of lemon, and roll or fold to serve.

LAMB AND BEANS SIMMERED IN WINE

An easy one-pan dish that can be served straight to the table with some gluten-free bread and steamed greens.

SERVES 4
PREP 10 mins
COOK 1 hour

GUIDELINES PER SERVING

● ● ●   Calories

● ● ●   Saturated fat

● ● ●   Salt

STATISTICS PER SERVING

Energy 441kcals/1842kJ

Protein 35g

Fat 17g
Saturated fat 5g

Carbohydrate 24g
Sugar 1.6g

Fiber 7.2g

Salt 0.4g

2 tbsp olive oil
1 red onion, finely chopped
1lb 2oz (500g) lamb leg steaks, trimmed
  of fat and cut into bite-sized pieces
salt and freshly ground pepper
pinch of chili flakes
pinch of dried oregano
1 tbsp gluten-free all-purpose flour
3 garlic cloves, finely sliced

²/₃ cup white wine
1¼ cups hot gluten-free vegetable
  stock (see page 108)
14oz (400g) can cannellini beans,
  drained and rinsed
14oz (400g) can flageolet beans,
  drained and rinsed
lemon wedges, steamed greens, and
  gluten-free crusty bread, to serve

1 Heat half the oil in a large, heavy frying pan, add the onion, and cook on low heat for 5 minutes, then remove the onion and set aside. Add the remaining oil to the pan. Season the lamb with salt and pepper, the chili flakes, and the oregano, then toss in the flour and add to the pan.

2 Cook on medium-high heat for 10–15 minutes until golden on all sides, then add the onion back to the pan, add the garlic, and cook for 2 more minutes. Increase the heat, add the wine, and boil for a minute, then add the stock and boil for 1 more minute.

3 Reduce to a simmer and stir the beans into the mixture. Cover with a lid, leaving it slightly ajar, and cook gently for 30–40 minutes; make sure it doesn't dry out and add more stock or hot water if needed. Season to taste and serve with lemon wedges, steamed greens, and crusty bread.

Variation

Add some vegetables to the pan if you like, such as 2 large or 3 medium carrots, roughly diced, at the same time as the beans, or 1 fennel bulb, trimmed and sliced, and then fried with the onions.

GREEK ROAST LEG OF LAMB

The sweet and sharp flavors of the tomatoey crust cut through the rich lamb perfectly.

leg of lamb, approx. 4½lb (2kg)
olive oil, for rubbing
salt and freshly ground pepper
fava beans and baby roast potatoes, or
  hot pitas and salad, to serve

FOR THE CRUST
4 slices of gluten-free white bread
  (see page 38)

1¾oz (50g) sun-dried tomatoes
2 tsp capers
grated zest and juice of 2 lemons
pinch of chili flakes
handful of flat-leaf parsley
3 garlic cloves, peeled

SERVES   8
PREP   20 mins
           PLUS RESTING
COOK   2¼ hours

GUIDELINES PER SERVING

●●○ Calories

●●○ Saturated fat

●●● Salt

STATISTICS PER SERVING

Energy 377kcals/1578kJ

Protein 40g

Fat 20g
Saturated fat 7g

Carbohydrate 9.5g
Sugar 0.7g

Fiber 0.3g

Salt 0.8g

1 Preheat the oven to 400°F (200°C). Set the lamb in a large roasting pan, slash it a few times, rub with oil, and season well with salt and pepper.

2 Pulse all the ingredients for the crust in a food processor until well minced. Season to taste; add more lemon or sun-dried tomatoes if you want a stronger taste. Now smother the lamb with the crust mixture, pressing it onto the meat so it sticks and pushing it into the slashes.

3 Cook the lamb in the oven for 15 minutes until it starts to turn golden, then reduce the oven temperature to 325°F (160°C) and continue to cook for another 1½–2 hours. Cover loosely with foil if it starts to dry out. Remove from the oven and leave to rest for 20 minutes before carving the meat. Serve with the juices from the pan and some fava beans and baby roast potatoes, or with hot pitas and a lightly dressed salad.

Variation
You could pour some warmed rosé wine into the roasting pan halfway through cooking—it adds a wonderful flavor to the pan juices.

THAI-STYLE STIR-FRIED GROUND BEEF

This is a quick and delicious meal that the whole family will love. For children, consider leaving out the chile.

SERVES 4–6
PREP 5 mins
COOK 10 mins

GUIDELINES PER SERVING

● ● ○ Calories

● ● ● Saturated fat

● ● ● Salt

STATISTICS PER SERVING

Energy 300kcals/1244kJ

Protein 20g

Fat 22g
Saturated fat 8g

Carbohydrate 4g
Sugar 4g

Fiber 1.5g

Salt 2.3g

salt
3½oz (100g) broccoli florets,
  cut very small
2 tbsp sunflower or vegetable oil
bunch of scallions, finely
  chopped
2 garlic cloves, crushed
1in (3cm) fresh ginger,
  finely chopped
1 tbsp finely chopped cilantro stalks,
  plus a handful of cilantro leaves,
  roughly chopped

1 red chile, seeded and finely
  chopped (optional)
14oz (400g) ground beef
1 tbsp gluten-free nam pla
  (fish sauce)
2 tbsp tamari (gluten-free soy sauce)
1 tbsp lime juice
1 tsp granulated sugar
rice, to serve

1 Bring a large pan of salted water to a boil and blanch the broccoli for 1 minute, then drain and refresh it under cold water. Set aside.

2 Heat the sunflower oil in a wok or a large, deep-sided frying pan. Add the scallions, garlic, ginger, cilantro stalks, and chile (if using), and cook for a couple of minutes until colored slightly.

3 Add the ground beef and continue to cook over high heat until the meat is well browned.

4 Return the broccoli and add the nam pla, tamari, lime juice, and sugar. Mix well, cooking for a minute or two until the broccoli is piping hot. Stir in the cilantro leaves and serve with rice.

BEEF BURGERS

Homemade burgers can't be beaten, and you know exactly what's gone into the mixture.

SERVES 6
PREP 20 mins
PLUS CHILLING
COOK 20 mins
FREEZE 1 month

GUIDELINES PER SERVING

● ● ○ Calories

● ● ○ Saturated fat

● ○ ○ Salt

STATISTICS PER BURGER

Energy 212kcals/879kJ

Protein 18g

Fat 15g
Saturated fat 6g

Carbohydrate 1.5g
Sugar 1.1g

Fiber 0.5g

Salt 0.2g

GREAT FOR KIDS

1lb 2oz (500g) ground beef
1 large red onion, finely diced
1 garlic clove, finely chopped
1 tsp paprika
handful of flat-leaf parsley, finely chopped
1 tbsp finely chopped fresh cilantro leaves
1 large egg
salt and freshly ground pepper
small handful of gluten-free bread crumbs (optional)
gluten-free all-purpose flour, for dusting
vegetable oil, for frying
gluten-free hamburger buns or rolls (see pages 218–20), lettuce, tomato, and gluten-free relish, to serve

1 Add the first 8 ingredients to a large bowl and season well. Use your hands to pound the mixture to a thick paste: this way it will stay together when you cook it. To check that the mixture has a good flavor, before you shape it into burgers break off a small piece and fry until cooked through. Taste it and then alter the seasoning accordingly. If the burgers are too dense, add the bread crumbs to lighten the texture.

2 With floured hands, divide the mixture into 6 balls, then roll each one and flatten into a burger shape. Place on a baking sheet and chill in the fridge for 20 minutes to firm up. If freezing, open-freeze on the sheet at this point until solid, transfer to plastic bags, and label.

3 Heat a large frying pan on high heat and add a little oil. Cook the burgers for 2–3 minutes on each side. Remove and let them rest for 2 minutes before serving on gluten-free buns or rolls with lettuce leaves, sliced tomato, and a dollop of gluten-free relish of your choice.

STEAK WITH MUSTARD SAUCE

Steak and mustard is a match made in heaven. Swap the milk for heavy cream if you prefer a richer sauce, and try whole-grain mustard for more texture and less heat.

SERVES   4
PREP   15 mins
COOK   10 mins

4 x 10oz (300g) beef fillet steaks
1 tbsp olive oil
salt and freshly ground pepper
new potatoes and steamed broccoli,
  to serve

FOR THE SAUCE
2 tbsp butter
2 tbsp gluten-free all-purpose flour
1¼ cups milk
2 tsp Dijon mustard, or more
  if you like it hot
salt and freshly ground pepper

GUIDELINES PER SERVING

● ● ○   Calories

● ● ●   Saturated fat

● ○ ○   Salt

STATISTICS PER SERVING

Energy 570kcals/2378kJ

Protein 67g

Fat 29g
Saturated fat 14g

Carbohydrate 9g
Sugar 3.5g

Fiber 0g

Salt 0.8g

1 First make the sauce. In a small saucepan, melt the butter, remove from the heat, add the flour, and combine well. Pour in a little milk and stir again. Return to the heat and, still stirring to combine well, gradually add the remaining milk to make a fairly thin white sauce. Add the mustard and season to taste. Place over low heat and simmer, stirring constantly, for 5 minutes to cook out the flour.

2 Heat a grill pan on high heat, brush the steaks with the oil, and season well. Add 2 steaks at a time to the hot pan and cook undisturbed for 2–3 minutes, then turn and cook the other side for the same amount of time.

3 Cook all the steaks as above and leave to rest for 5 minutes. Ladle over the hot mustard sauce and serve with new potatoes and steamed broccoli.

NUTRIENT BOOST
Red meat provides iron, vital for the manufacture of red blood cells.

BEEF AND BEER CASSEROLE

A really hearty dish with slow-cooked beef simmered in a light beer. Perfect comfort food.

SERVES 6
PREP 40 mins
COOK 2 hours

GUIDELINES PER SERVING

● ● ○ Calories
● ● ● Saturated fat
● ○ ○ Salt

STATISTICS PER SERVING

Energy 691kcals/2885kJ

Protein 49g

Fat 30g
Saturated fat 12g

Carbohydrate 44g
Sugar 7.5g

Fiber 0.7g

Salt 1.4g

1 tbsp rice flour
salt and freshly ground pepper
2¼lb (1kg) braising steak, chuck, or skirt,
   cut into large bite-sized pieces
3 tbsp olive oil
10oz (300g) carrots, cut into chunks
1 celery root, peeled and chopped into
   bite-sized pieces
3 leeks, trimmed, washed, and cut
   into chunks
1¼ cups gluten-free beer
2½ cups hot gluten-free vegetable stock
   or hot water
1¾oz (50g) quinoa

FOR THE HERB DUMPLINGS
½ onion, finely chopped
½ tbsp olive oil
small handful of flat-leaf parsley,
   finely chopped
a few rosemary leaves, finely chopped
2½oz (75g) gluten-free bread crumbs
1 tsp gluten-free, ready-grated
   horseradish (from a jar)
1 tsp Dijon mustard
1 large egg

1 Preheat the oven to 325°F (160°C). Season the flour and toss the beef to coat. Heat 2 tablespoons of the oil in a flameproof casserole and brown the beef in batches over medium heat for 5 minutes per batch, until the meat is sealed. Remove and set aside.

2 Add the remaining oil to the casserole and cook the vegetables for 5–6 minutes, until golden. Pour in a little of the beer, raise the heat, and stir to scrape up any bits from the bottom of the casserole. Add the remaining beer and simmer on a medium heat for 5 minutes. Pour in the stock, bring to a boil, reduce to a simmer, and add the meat back to the casserole along with the quinoa. Season, cover, and cook in the oven for 1½ hours before adding the dumplings; add more hot water if it looks dry.

3 For the dumplings, cook the onion in the oil over medium heat until soft. Add the remaining ingredients, season, and stir until it comes together. Form 12 dumpling balls and set aside. When ready, remove the casserole and add the balls, pushing them down into the sauce. Re-cover and cook for 30 minutes, removing the lid for the last 5 minutes.

BEEF POT WITH DUMPLINGS

Gluten-free, lard-free dumplings accompany this rich beef casserole for a hearty supper or Sunday lunch.

SERVES 4
PREP 20 mins
COOK 3 hours
FREEZE 1 month
NOT DUMPLINGS

GUIDELINES PER SERVING

● ● ○ Calories
● ● ● Saturated fat
● ● ○ Salt

STATISTICS PER SERVING

Energy 704kcals/2940kJ

Protein 35g

Fat 38g
Saturated fat 15g

Carbohydrate 44g
Sugar 9g

Fiber 7g

Salt 0.8g

3 tbsp gluten-free all-purpose flour
1 tbsp paprika
salt and freshly ground black pepper
1lb 2oz (500g) stewing beef, diced into
   bite-sized pieces
5 tbsp olive oil
3 carrots, sliced
2 celery stalks, sliced
12 whole shallots
9oz (250g) crimini mushrooms
3 garlic cloves, finely chopped
$\frac{3}{4}$–1$\frac{1}{4}$ cups red wine

1$\frac{1}{4}$ cups gluten-free beef stock
1 bouquet garni
green beans or gluten-free crusty bread,
   to serve

FOR THE DUMPLINGS

1 cup gluten-free all-purpose flour
   or cornflour
5 tbsp butter, softened
1 tbsp chopped thyme leaves or
   1 tsp paprika

1 Preheat the oven to 325°F (160°C). In a large bowl, add the flour and paprika, season to taste, and combine well. Add the beef and mix, ensuring that all the meat is covered. Heat half the oil in a large flameproof casserole on medium heat and add the beef. Cook for 6–8 minutes until browned, remove, and set aside.

2 Heat the remaining oil in the pan, add the carrots, and cook for 5 minutes. Add the celery and shallots and cook for 5 more minutes until it begins to turn golden. Add the mushrooms and garlic and cook for 2 more minutes. Add the wine, stock, and bouquet garni, combine, and bring to a boil. Reduce to a simmer, add the beef, and cover. Bake in the oven for 2–2$\frac{1}{2}$ hours, occasionally adding a little more hot water if it starts to dry out.

3 For the dumplings, mix the flour, butter, seasoning, and chopped thyme or paprika until the mix is flaky, then add a little cold water to form a dough. Divide and roll into balls, then drop the dumplings into the pot for the last 30 minutes of cooking, gently poking them just below the surface. Uncover the casserole for the last 10 minutes to allow the dumplings to turn golden. Remove the bouquet garni and serve with green beans or crusty bread.

BEEF AND HORSERADISH WELLINGTON

Perfectly cooked beef encased in crisp gluten-free pastry, with a surprise kick from the horseradish, this dish would make an impressive centerpiece for a dinner party.

2 tbsp olive oil
1¾lb (800g) beef fillet or loin
salt and freshly ground black pepper
14oz (400g) gluten-free rough puff pastry
  (see pages 46–7)
gluten-free all-purpose flour, for dusting

1–2 tbsp hot gluten-free
  horseradish sauce
1 large egg, lightly beaten, to glaze
watercress and roasted new potatoes,
  to serve

GUIDELINES PER SERVING

● ● ●   Calories

● ● ●   Saturated fat

● ● ●   Salt

STATISTICS PER SERVING

Energy 484kcals/2019kJ

Protein 32g

Fat 29g
Saturated fat 14g

Carbohydrate 22g
Sugar 1g

Fiber 1.5g

Salt 0.6g

1 Preheat the oven to 400°F (200°C). In a large frying pan, heat the oil over medium heat. Season the beef, add to the pan, and cook for 8 minutes or until evenly browned all over. Remove from the pan and set aside.

2 Carefully roll out the pastry on a lightly floured surface to a rectangle with a thickness of ⅛–¼in (3–5mm), then spread over the horseradish sauce, leaving a 1in (2.5cm) border. Sit the meat on top toward one end, then very carefully roll the pastry over the meat, ensuring that it is all covered. Press and seal the seam with a little water. Transfer to a baking sheet, making sure the seam is on the underside and the ends are tucked in and sealed.

3 Brush the pastry with the beaten egg and bake in the oven for 40–50 minutes or until evenly golden. Cover loosely with foil if the pastry starts to color too quickly. Remove from the oven and leave to rest for at least 10 minutes, then slice to serve with watercress and roasted new potatoes.

Cook's Tip
You can prepare this ahead and keep it in the refrigerator until ready to bake.

Variation
Use a pâté instead of the horseradish sauce, if you like.

VEGETABLE MAIN DISHES

MUSHROOM BURGERS

Served with miso-roasted chips and tahini dip, these burgers have lots of gutsy flavors. Make mini ones for the kids.

SERVES 4
PREP 20 mins
PLUS CHILLING
COOK 50 mins

GUIDELINES PER SERVING

● ● ○ Calories

● ○ ○ Saturated fat

● ● ● Salt

STATISTICS PER SERVING

Energy 509kcals/2143kJ

Protein 13.6g

Fat 21.4g
Saturated fat 3.3g

Carbohydrate 65.3g
Sugar 14g

Fiber 10.8g

Salt 2.8g

GREAT FOR KIDS

3 tbsp olive oil
1 onion, finely chopped
1lb 2oz (500g) cremini mushrooms,
  pulsed in a food processor
  or blender
4 anchovies, finely chopped
splash of tamari (gluten-free
  soy sauce)
1 cup gluten-free bread crumbs
1 large egg, lightly beaten
salt and freshly ground pepper

FOR THE MISO CHIPS
4 sweet potatoes, peeled and cut
  into thin chips
1 tbsp olive oil
1 tbsp sweet miso or tamari
  (gluten-free soy sauce)

FOR THE TAHINI DIP
2 garlic cloves, grated
pinch of sea salt
3 tbsp tahini
juice of 1 lemon

1 Preheat the oven to 400°F (200°C). Heat 1 tablespoon oil in a large frying pan, add the onion, and cook on low heat for 3–4 minutes. Add the mushrooms and cook for 6 minutes or until they start to release their juices. Stir in the anchovies and tamari and cook for 1 minute. Transfer to a large bowl. Add the bread crumbs and trickle in the egg until the mixture binds well. Add more bread crumbs if it's too wet and season well. Make 4 large balls from the mixture and form into burgers. Set them on a baking sheet lined with waxed paper and chill in the fridge for 30 minutes.

2 For the chips, toss the sweet potatoes with the oil and miso or tamari, and spread out in a roasting pan. Roast in the oven for 20 minutes until the chips begin to turn golden and the thinner ones are crisp. For the tahini dip, grind the garlic and sea salt in a pestle and mortar. Add the tahini and mix. Add about 2 tablespoons of water to loosen it. Stir in the lemon juice.

3 To cook the burgers, heat half the remaining oil in a large frying pan on medium heat, add the burgers two at a time, and cook for 3–5 minutes on each side, until golden brown. Repeat until all burgers are cooked. Serve with the sweet potato chips and tahini dip.

BEAN PATTIES

Mashed beans are a great vegetarian alternative to burgers. If making for children, omit the chile and replace half the onion with grated carrot for additional sweetness.

SERVES	4
PREP	20 mins PLUS CHILLING
COOK	50 mins

1 onion, quartered
2 tbsp chopped flat-leaf parsley
14oz (400g) can butter or navy beans, drained and rinsed
14oz (400g) can kidney beans, drained and rinsed
1 tsp cayenne pepper
2 tbsp gluten-free all-purpose flour
1 large egg, lightly beaten
salt and freshly ground pepper
3 tbsp olive oil
green salad, to serve

FOR THE AVOCADO SALSA

2 ripe avocados, pitted and diced
1 large garlic clove, grated
1 red or jalapeño chile, seeded and finely chopped
2 tbsp olive oil
1 tbsp chopped fresh cilantro leaves, chopped
juice of 1 lime
1 tsp sugar

GUIDELINES PER SERVING

● ● ○ Calories
● ● ○ Saturated fat
● ● ○ Salt

STATISTICS PER SERVING

Energy 424kcals/1761kJ

Protein 11.5g

Fat 31g
Saturated fat 5.6g

Carbohydrate 25g
Sugar 4g

Fiber 11.5g

Salt 1.4g

1 Place the onion in a food processor and pulse until roughly chopped. Add the parsley and pulse again a couple of times. Then add the beans and pulse again. Transfer to a bowl and stir in the cayenne pepper, flour, and egg. Season to taste and mix well. Shape the mixture into 8 patties and chill in the fridge until firm.

2 For the salsa, add all the ingredients to a bowl and combine well. Leave for 15 minutes, then stir and season to taste, as needed.

3 Heat a little oil in a large frying pan on medium-high heat. Add the patties a few at a time and cook for 5 minutes on each side until crisp and golden brown. Repeat until all are cooked, adding more oil as needed. Serve with a green salad and the salsa on the side.

Variation
Other beans, such as cannellini, flageolet, or red kidney beans will work just as well.

NUTRIENT BOOST
Avocados contain vitamins E and B6 for a healthy heart and nervous system.

GREAT FOR KIDS

GNOCCHI WITH BLUE CHEESE

A few ingredients make up this delicious dish—delicate gnocchi tossed in sage butter and topped with Gorgonzola.

SERVES 4
PREP 30 mins
COOK 1 hour
FREEZE 3 months
UNCOOKED GNOCCHI

GUIDELINES PER SERVING

● ● ○ Calories
● ● ● Saturated fat
● ○ ○ Salt

STATISTICS PER SERVING

Energy 532kcals/2222kJ

Protein 14.5g

Fat 22g
Saturated fat 14g

Carbohydrate 65g
Sugar 1.5g

Fiber 5g

Salt 1.1g

2¼lb (1kg) starchy potatoes, such as
 Yukon Gold, Russet, or Red Potatoes,
 skin on
salt and freshly ground pepper
1 cup rice flour, plus extra to dust
pinch of nutmeg (optional)

sea salt
4 tbsp butter
4 sage leaves, torn
4½oz (125g) Gorgonzola cheese, cubed
arugula and tomato salad, to serve

1 Cook the whole potatoes in a pan of boiling salted water until tender, about 30–40 minutes. Drain and leave until cool enough to handle. Peel and press the potatoes through a potato ricer onto a lightly floured surface; if you don't have a ricer, use a medium sieve but take care not to overwork the potato. Add half the rice flour, nutmeg (if using), and the sea salt. Lightly knead until the mixture starts to come together, adding more flour as needed. Don't over-knead or the gnocchi will be tough when cooked. Divide the dough into four. Roll each piece into a sausage shape about ½in (1cm) thick, then slice into ¾in (2cm) pieces, about 80–90 in total.

2 Preheat the oven to 375°F (190°C). Bring a large pan of water to a rolling boil. Add 10 gnocchi at a time, as they need lots of room; they will float to the top once cooked, about 2 minutes. Remove with a slotted spoon, transfer to a warmed ovenproof serving dish, and season with sea salt.

3 Heat the butter in a small frying pan, add the sage leaves, and cook on medium heat for 2–3 minutes until the butter melts. Pour over the gnocchi and turn to coat. Sprinkle over the cubed cheese, then bake for 5–6 minutes or until the cheese has melted. Serve with an arugula and tomato salad.

Cook's Tip
To freeze, lay the uncooked gnocchi on a parchment-lined baking sheet and freeze until solid, then transfer to an airtight container. Cook from frozen, as above, for 3–5 minutes or until the gnocchi float to the surface.

MUSHROOM AND SPINACH CURRY

SERVES 4
PREP   15 mins
COOK   30 mins

*Try this as a side dish with Chicken tikka skewers
(see page 174), or as a main course for a vegetarian.*

GUIDELINES PER SERVING

● ● ○   Calories

● ● ○   Saturated fat

● ○ ○   Salt

STATISTICS PER SERVING

Energy 87kcals/363kJ

Protein 2.5g

Fat 4.5g
Saturated fat 0.8g

Carbohydrate 6g
Sugar 5g

Fiber 4g

Salt 0.3g

1 tbsp vegetable oil
2 onions, sliced
4 garlic cloves, finely chopped
1½in (4cm) piece of fresh ginger root,
   finely chopped
4 cardamom pods
1 red chile, seeded and finely chopped
   (optional)
1 cinnamon stick
1 tsp ground coriander
1 tsp ground cumin
1 tsp turmeric

½ tsp ground nutmeg
9oz (250g) crimini or portabello
   mushrooms, roughly chopped
9oz (250g) button mushrooms
1¼ cups vegetable stock (see
   page 108)
salt and freshly ground black pepper
7oz (200g) spinach
¼ cup plain yogurt
toasted cashew nuts and gluten-free
   naan bread or chapatis, to serve

1 Heat the oil in a large saucepan over medium heat and cook the
onions for 5 minutes. Add the garlic and ginger and cook for 2 minutes,
stirring occasionally.

2 Add the spices to the pan and stir well. Add the mushrooms and stir to
coat in the spices.

3 Pour in the stock, season, and bring to a boil, then cover and reduce the
heat to a simmer. Cook for 15 minutes.

4 Stir in the spinach and cook for another 2 minutes. Remove the cinnamon
stick and cardamom pods (if possible), then stir in the yogurt, sprinkle in
the cashew nuts, and serve with gluten-free naan bread or chapatis.

CHARGRILLED POLENTA WITH SUMAC-ROASTED TOMATOES

Polenta is elevated to new heights in this dish packed with added flavor and served with juicy vine tomatoes.

SERVES 4
PREP 10 mins
COOK 40 mins

GUIDELINES PER SERVING

● ● ○ Calories

● ● ○ Saturated fat

● ○ ○ Salt

STATISTICS PER SERVING

Energy 304kcals/1267kJ

Protein 8g

Fat 18g
Saturated fat 6.5g

Carbohydrate 26g
Sugar 4.5g

Fiber 3g

Salt 0.9g

about 40 baby vine tomatoes
1 tbsp olive oil
2 tsp sumac
2 tbsp capers, rinsed
arugula leaves and salad dressing,
   to serve

FOR THE POLENTA
1 cup instant polenta or fine cornmeal
2 tbsp butter
large handful of freshly grated
   Parmesan cheese

pinch of chili flakes
salt and freshly ground pepper
olive oil, to coat

SPECIAL EQUIPMENT
8in (20cm) square pan, at least 1in
   (2.5cm) deep, or similar serving dish,
   lined with parchment paper
grill pan

1 Preheat the oven to 400°F (200°C). Cook the instant polenta mix as per package instructions, adding it to the water in a steady stream and stirring as it simmers. Cook for 10 minutes, then beat in the butter, Parmesan, and chili flakes, and season well with salt and pepper. Spoon into the prepared pan or serving dish, and set aside to cool.

2 Add the tomatoes to a roasting pan and pour over the oil to cover, then sprinkle with the sumac and season to taste. Roast in the oven for 15–20 minutes or until just beginning to char, then add the capers for the last 5 minutes of cooking. Remove and set aside.

3 Remove the polenta from the pan and cut into 8 triangles or stamp out circles, then coat the pieces lightly with the oil. Heat a grill pan until hot and add the polenta pieces a few at a time. Cook for 2–3 minutes on each side until char lines appear. Serve topped with the tomatoes and capers and a lightly dressed arugula salad.

SICHUAN CRISPY BEAN CURD

Hot and spicy and incredibly simple to make, this recipe relies on good-quality bean curd—buy it from an Asian market where you'll often find it's homemade.

SERVES   4
PREP   15 mins
COOK   20 mins

10oz (300g) firm bean curd or tofu, cut
  into ½in (1cm) squares
3 tbsp sunflower or vegetable oil,
  or more if needed
½ tsp ground Sichuan pepper
3 tomatoes, cut in half lengthwise, then
  each half into 4 wedges
2in (5cm) piece of fresh ginger, peeled
  and finely sliced

pinch of brown sugar
2 tbsp tamari (gluten-free soy sauce)
1 tbsp rice vinegar
bunch of scallions, cut into
  2in (5cm) lengths
cooked basmati rice, to serve

SPECIAL EQUIPMENT
large, deep nonstick frying pan or wok

GUIDELINES PER SERVING

● ● ●   Calories

● ● ●   Saturated fat

● ● ●   Salt

STATISTICS PER SERVING

Energy 174kcals/725kJ

Protein 9g

Fat 13g
Saturated fat 2g

Carbohydrate 6g
Sugar 5g

Fiber 1.5g

Salt 1.4g

1 Toss the bean curd with a drizzle of the oil and the Sichuan pepper. Heat the remaining oil in a wok on medium-high heat, add the bean curd, and fry for 2 minutes until golden, then turn and cook the other side for the same amount of time.

2 Add the tomatoes and ginger and stir-fry for 2 minutes, trying not to break up the bean curd.

3 Add the sugar and stir-fry until caramelized, add the tamari and vinegar, and cook for a further 2–3 minutes. Stir in the scallions and serve hot with rice.

Cook's Tip
Make sure you drain and press the curd before using: it needs to be really dry before frying to ensure it crisps nicely.

STUFFED BUTTERNUT SQUASH

SERVES 4
PREP 15 mins
COOK 1¼ hours

A vibrantly colored autumnal dish that would work just as well with pumpkin. You could use Cheddar, Parmesan, or goat cheese instead of the Gruyère.

GUIDELINES PER SERVING

● ● ○ Calories

● ● ● Saturated fat

● ○ ○ Salt

STATISTICS PER SERVING

Energy 555kcals/2320kJ

Protein 23g

Fat 38g
Saturated fat 14g

Carbohydrate 31g
Sugar 18g

Fiber 11g

Salt 1g

2 medium, or 4 small, butternut squash, halved lengthwise and seeded
1 tbsp olive oil, plus extra for oiling
8oz (225g) Gruyère cheese, grated

FOR THE FRUIT AND NUT MIX
3½oz (100g) hazelnuts, toasted and roughly chopped

2½oz (75g) dried cranberries, roughly chopped
small handful of flat-leaf parsley, finely chopped
pinch of dried chili flakes
salt and freshly ground pepper
arugula salad, to serve

1 Preheat the oven to 375°F (190°C). Brush two baking sheets with oil. With a sharp knife, score a crisscross pattern on the flesh of each butternut squash half and brush with the oil. Sit the squash on the oiled tray, flesh side down, and roast for about 1 hour until the flesh begins to soften. Now scoop out most of the flesh, leaving a thin layer still attached to the skins, and reserve the hollowed squash halves.

2 Place the flesh in a bowl and mash with a fork. Add all the fruit and nut mix ingredients to the mashed squash and mix well. Divide the mixture between the squash skins.

3 Sprinkle over the cheese and return the squashes to the oven. Bake for a further 10–15 minutes until the cheese is bubbling. Serve the squash with a lightly dressed arugula salad.

GREAT FOR KIDS

NUTRIENT BOOST
Butternut squash is exceptionally rich in vitamin B6.

CHINESE PUMPKIN FRITTERS

These crisp, bite-sized fritters, fried in a gluten-free beer batter, make a light supper accompanied by rice.

SERVES 4
PREP 15 mins
PLUS CHILLING
COOK 40 mins

GUIDELINES PER SERVING

● ○ ○ Calories
● ○ ○ Saturated fat
● ○ ○ Salt

STATISTICS PER SERVING

Energy 180kcals/755kJ

Protein 5g

Fat 7.5g
Saturated fat 2.5g

Carbohydrate 22.5g
Sugar 2.5g

Fiber 5g

Salt trace

1lb 2oz (500g) pumpkin or butternut
  squash, peeled and grated
2in (5cm) piece of fresh ginger,
  peeled and grated
½ tsp turmeric
1 red or jalapeño chile, seeded
  and finely chopped
1 tbsp rice flour, plus extra for dusting
salt and freshly ground black pepper
oil, for deep frying
tamari (gluten-free soy sauce) and
  rice, to serve

FOR THE BATTER
½ cup gluten-free beer
¼ cup rice flour
½ cup gram (chickpea) flour
¼ cup carbonated water

SPECIAL EQUIPMENT
wok or large, deep, nonstick frying pan

1 Put the pumpkin in a colander or steamer basket and sit it over a pan of simmering water, covered, for 10–15 minutes until the pumpkin is tender. Remove, leave to cool slightly, then squeeze out any excess water. Add to a bowl and mix in the ginger, turmeric, chile, and rice flour and season to taste.

2 Dust your hands with the extra rice flour, then take a tablespoonful of the pumpkin mixture and shape it into a ball. Repeat to make 19 more round balls. Chill them in the fridge on a lightly floured baking sheet while you make the batter. Add all the batter ingredients to a bowl and season. Stir together until combined, but still lumpy. If the batter is too thin, add more of the flours in equal amounts.

3 Pour the oil to a depth of 2in (5cm) into the pan or wok and heat on medium-high heat until hot. Don't leave the pan or wok unattended, take off the heat when not using, and keep a fire blanket nearby in case of fire. Dip the pumpkin balls into the batter one at a time, making sure they are well coated. Fry them in the hot oil, about 5 at a time, cooking each side for 2–3 minutes until golden and crisp. Remove and sit on paper towels to drain. Serve with a small bowl of tamari.

MUSHROOM STEW WITH FETA AND HERB TOPPING

A hearty vegetarian stew made with meaty mushrooms for a rich depth of flavor. Try baking individual portions if you have some mini ovenproof casserole dishes.

2 tbsp olive oil
1 red onion, finely chopped
2 garlic cloves, finely chopped
2 tsp dried oregano
1 tsp paprika
grated zest of ½ lemon
salt and freshly ground pepper
2 green bell peppers, halved, seeded, and
  sliced
7oz (200g) cremini mushrooms, halved
  and quartered
7oz (200g) baby button mushrooms

1 small glass of white wine
1¾ cups hot gluten-free vegetable
  or mushroom stock

FOR THE TOPPING
5½oz (150g) feta cheese, crumbled
2 large eggs
handful of flat-leaf parsley,
  finely chopped

SERVES 4
PREP 15 mins
COOK 50 mins
FREEZE 3 months
WITHOUT TOPPING

GUIDELINES PER SERVING

Calories
Saturated fat
Salt

STATISTICS PER SERVING

Energy 259kcals/1076kJ

Protein 13g

Fat 18g
Saturated fat 7g

Carbohydrate 8g
Sugar 7g

Fiber 3.5g

Salt 1.5g

1 Heat the oil in a flameproof casserole, add the onion, and cook for 2–3 minutes on low heat. Stir in the garlic, oregano, paprika, lemon zest, and some seasoning and cook for a further 1–2 minutes.

2 Add the peppers and cook on low heat for 5 minutes or until beginning to soften, then add the mushrooms and cook for 5 minutes. Increase the heat, add the wine, and boil for 1 minute. Add the stock and bring to a boil. Partly cover and cook on medium-low heat for 20 minutes; it should begin to thicken slightly. If it is too thin, uncover, turn up the heat a little, and cook for 3–4 minutes more. Preheat the oven to 350°F (180°C).

3 To make the topping, mix together the feta, eggs, half the parsley, and a little seasoning; you may not need much salt as feta is already salty. Pour this over the mushroom mixture and bake in the oven for 15–20 minutes until the egg has set and the top is golden brown. Remove and sprinkle with the remaining parsley to serve.

BREAD
AND PIZZA

BROWN BREAD

A spongy and moist gluten-free loaf that rises well and has a good color and flavor. This dough can also be used to make a tasty, seeded loaf (see Cook's Tip).

MAKES	12 slices
PREP	20 mins
	PLUS RISING
COOK	35–40 mins
FREEZE	3 months

GUIDELINES PER SERVING

● ● ○ Calories

● ○ ○ Saturated fat

● ○ ○ Salt

STATISTICS PER SLICE

Energy 222kcals/941kJ

Protein 8g

Fat 5g
Saturated fat 2g

Carbohydrate 36g
Sugar 3.5g

Fiber 7g

Salt 0.3g

GREAT FOR KIDS

oil, for greasing
3 cups gluten-free brown bread flour
  blend (see page 38), plus
  extra for dusting
2 tsp fast-action dried yeast
½ tsp salt
2 tbsp molasses

1 egg
2 tbsp vegetable oil
1 tsp vinegar
beaten egg, for brushing

SPECIAL EQUIPMENT
1lb (450g) loaf pan

1 Lightly oil the pan. Sift the flour into a large bowl; add the yeast and salt. Measure 1¼ cups lukewarm water into a liquid measuring cup and add the molasses, egg, vegetable oil, and vinegar. Whisk together with a fork.

2 Make a well in the center of the dry ingredients, add the wet ingredients, and mix well to form a dough. Turn onto a lightly floured surface and knead for about 5 minutes, until smooth.

3 Shape the dough into a rectangle the same size as the pan and place in the prepared pan. Cover loosely with oiled plastic wrap and leave in a warm place to rise for 1 hour or until doubled in size.

4 Preheat the oven to 400°F (200°C). Brush the top of the loaf with the beaten egg and bake in the oven for 35–40 minutes or until it is risen and golden brown. Remove from the oven and allow to cool for 5 minutes in the pan, then turn out and cool on a wire rack.

Variation
SEEDED LOAF Simply sprinkle a mix of seeds (poppy, pumpkin, and sunflower are all good) into the oiled pan before adding the dough. Once risen, finish with a final flourish of more seeds after brushing with egg.

SEEDED BROWN ROLLS

Golden-colored and studded with crunchy seeds, these flavorsome rolls are a sure-fire success.

MAKES 12

PREP 15 mins
PLUS RISING

COOK 15–20 mins

FREEZE 3 months

GUIDELINES PER SERVING

● ● ● Calories

● ● ○ Saturated fat

● ○ ○ Salt

STATISTICS PER ROLL

Energy 200kcals/844kJ

Protein 7.5g

Fat 7g
Saturated fat 1g

Carbohydrate 26g
Sugar 2g

Fiber 4g

Salt 0.2g

2 tbsp vegetable oil, plus extra
 for greasing
6 tbsp mixed seeds (see Cook's Tip)
2½ cups gluten-free brown bread flour
 blend (see page 38), plus extra
 for dusting

1 cup buckwheat flour
2 tsp fast-acting dried yeast
1 tsp xanthan gum
½ tsp salt
2 tbsp molasses
2 large eggs

1 Lightly oil 2 baking sheets and sprinkle over 1 tablespoon of the seeds. Sift the flours into a large bowl, add the yeast, xanthan, and salt. Measure 1¼ cups lukewarm water into a liquid measuring cup, then add the molasses, 1 egg, and the vegetable oil. Whisk together with a fork.

2 Make a well in the center of the dry ingredients, add 4 tablespoons of the seeds, then gradually add the wet mixture until a soft, workable dough is formed. Turn onto a lightly floured surface and knead for about 5 minutes until smooth. Divide the dough into 12 balls. Place on the prepared baking sheets, cover loosely with oiled plastic wrap, and leave in a warm place for about 1 hour, until doubled in size.

3 Preheat the oven to 400°F (200°C). Beat the remaining egg. Brush the rolls all over with the egg and sprinkle on the remaining seeds. Bake for 15–20 minutes, or until the rolls are risen and golden brown. Remove from the oven and cool for 5 minutes on the baking sheets, then transfer to a wire rack to cool completely.

Cook's Tip
Vary the seeds according to preference: pumpkin, caraway, and sesame work particularly well with the flavor of the bread. Alternatively, bags of premixed seeds are often cheaper than buying separately.

SOFT WHITE ROLLS

These rolls are great for sandwiches, and also make excellent hamburger buns.

MAKES   8
PREP   20 mins
         PLUS RISING
COOK   15–20 mins
FREEZE   3 months

3 cups gluten-free white bread flour blend (see page 38), plus extra for dusting
2 tsp fast-action dried yeast
1 tsp xanthan gum
½ tsp salt
1¼ cups milk, plus extra for glazing
2 tbsp granulated sugar
1 large egg
2 tbsp vegetable oil, plus extra for greasing

GUIDELINES PER SERVING

● ● ○ Calories
● ● ○ Saturated fat
● ○ ○ Salt

STATISTICS PER ROLL

Energy 271kcals/1147kJ

Protein 8g

Fat 6g
Saturated fat 1.5g

Carbohydrate 47g
Sugar 6g

Fiber 2.5g

Salt 0.4g

1 Lightly flour 2 baking sheets. Sift the flour, yeast, xanthan, and salt into a large bowl. Heat the milk in a small pan until lukewarm, then add the sugar, egg, and oil and whisk together with a fork.

2 Make a well in the center of the dry ingredients, pour in the wet ingredients, and mix until you have a soft workable dough. Turn the dough out onto a lightly floured surface and knead for about 5 minutes, until smooth.

3 Divide the dough into 8 balls. Place well apart on the prepared baking sheets and flatten each slightly. Cover loosely with oiled plastic wrap and leave in a warm place for about 1 hour, until doubled in size.

4 Preheat the oven to 400°F (200°C). Brush the rolls all over with milk and dust with a little flour. Cover the rolls with a roasting pan turned upside down (see Cook's Tip) and bake for 15–20 minutes, or until the rolls have risen. Remove from the oven and cool for 5 minutes on the baking sheets, then transfer to a wire rack to cool completely.

Cook's Tip
Baking the rolls under a roasting pan makes them crisp on the outside and soft on the inside.

BRIOCHE ROLLS

Brioche needs a long rising time. If you prefer, start it the night before and leave it out somewhere cool—you can then have warm brioche for breakfast!

MAKES   12
PREP   15 mins
     PLUS RISING
COOK   20–25 mins
FREEZE   3 months

GUIDELINES PER SERVING

● ● ○   Calories

● ● ●   Saturated fat

● ● ○   Salt

STATISTICS PER ROLL

Energy   308kcals/1296kJ

Protein   7g

Fat   18g
Saturated fat   10g

Carbohydrate   31g
Sugar   4g

Fiber   1.5g

Salt   0.5g

1¼ cups milk
14 tbsp unsalted butter, softened
2 tbsp granulated sugar
4 large eggs
2¾ cups gluten-free white bread flour
   blend (see page 38)
2 tsp fast-acting dried yeast

2 tsp xanthan gum
1 tsp salt
oil, for greasing

SPECIAL EQUIPMENT
12 brioche molds or a 12-hole deep
   muffin pan

1 Warm the milk in a small pan, stir in the butter and sugar until the butter melts and the sugar is dissolved, then take off the heat. Lightly beat 3 eggs in a small bowl.

2 Sift the flour, yeast, xanthan, and salt into a large bowl, make a well in the center, and add the milk mixture and beaten egg. Mix well to a sticky dough, similar to cake mixture. Cover with oiled plastic wrap, then leave to rise in a warm place for at least 3 hours (or a cool place overnight) until it doubles in size.

3 Preheat the oven to 400°F (200°C). Grease the brioche molds or the muffin pan and beat the remaining egg. Divide the dough into 12 lumps about the size of small oranges. Pass each lump back and forth between the palms of your hands to make rough balls and drop them into the holes; wet your hands if the dough is particularly sticky. Brush with the beaten egg.

4 Bake for 20–25 minutes or until golden and risen. Cool in the pan for 5 minutes before serving warm.

FOCACCIA

This versatile Italian loaf, richly flavored with olive oil, should be crisp on top with a light, airy crumb.

2¾ cups gluten-free white bread flour blend (see page 38), plus extra to dust
2 tsp xanthan gum
2 tsp fast-acting dried yeast
2 tsp granulated sugar
1 tsp salt

6 tbsp olive oil, plus extra for greasing
few sprigs of rosemary
coarse sea salt, to sprinkle

SPECIAL EQUIPMENT
9 x 13in (23 x 33cm) rectangular pan

SERVES	6
PREP	15 mins
	PLUS RISING
COOK	30–35 mins
FREEZE	3 months

GUIDELINES PER SERVING

● ● ● Calories

● ● Saturated fat

● ● Salt

STATISTICS PER SERVING

Energy 361kcals/1522kJ

Protein 7g

Fat 12g
Saturated fat 2g

Carbohydrate 56g
Sugar 3g

Fiber 3g

Salt 0.9g

1 Sift the flour, xanthan, yeast, sugar, and salt into a large bowl. Add 1¼ cups lukewarm water and 3 tablespoons oil to the flour, and mix to a slightly sticky, soft dough using your hands. Place on a floured surface and knead for 10 minutes until smooth and elastic. Return to the bowl, cover with oiled plastic wrap, and leave in a warm place for about 1 hour until doubled in size.

2 Lightly grease the pan. Place the dough out onto a floured surface, knead lightly, and roll out to roughly the same size as the pan. Lift the dough into the pan and push it into the corners. Cover with oiled plastic wrap and leave to rise in a warm place for 30 minutes or until doubled again in size.

3 Preheat the oven to 400°F (200°C). Firmly press the surface of the dough with your fingertips to give a dimpled effect. Scatter the rosemary, drizzle over the remaining olive oil, and sprinkle over the sea salt. Bake for 30–35 minutes or until the top is pale golden.

Variations

RED ONION AND FETA Finely slice a small red onion, scatter over the top of the dough instead of the rosemary, along with 4oz (115g) crumbled feta cheese.

OLIVE AND ANCHOVY Roughly chop 5oz (140g) pitted green and black olives and scatter over the dough with 2oz (60g) chopped anchovy fillets. Drizzle with the oil and scatter over a few fresh or dried oregano leaves instead of the rosemary.

PIZZA MARGHERITA

Add different toppings to this basic recipe: wilted spinach and ricotta; sliced mushrooms and Parma ham; pepperoni and chiles, sprinkled with arugula after baking.

SERVES 4
PREP 20 mins
PLUS RISING
COOK 20–25 mins

GUIDELINES PER SERVING

● ● ○ Calories
● ● ○ Saturated fat
● ● ○ Salt

STATISTICS PER SERVING

Energy 759kcals/3190kJ

Protein 28g

Fat 32g
Saturated fat 13g

Carbohydrate 89g
Sugar 9g

Fiber 6g

Salt 1.9g

GREAT FOR KIDS

oil, for greasing
1lb (450g) gluten-free white
  bread flour blend (see page 38),
  plus extra to dust
1 tsp xanthan gum
2 tsp yeast
2 tsp granulated sugar
1 tsp salt
1 large egg
2 tbsp olive oil, plus extra to drizzle
10oz (300g) mozzarella cheese, drained
  and torn into pieces
a few black olives
basil leaves

FOR THE TOMATO SAUCE
2 tbsp olive oil
1 small onion, finely chopped
2 garlic cloves, crushed
14oz (400g) can chopped tomatoes
1 tbsp tomato paste
1 tsp dried oregano
pinch of sugar
salt and freshly ground pepper

1 Lightly oil two baking sheets. Sift the flour, xanthan, yeast, sugar, and salt into a large bowl. Combine 1¼ cups warm water, the egg, and 2 tablespoons oil in a measuring cup and whisk with a fork. Make a well in the center of the dry ingredients, add the wet ingredients, and mix to form a dough. Turn the dough out onto a floured surface and knead for 5 minutes until smooth. Return the dough to a lightly oiled bowl and cover with oiled plastic wrap. Leave in a warm place to rise until doubled in size, for 1 hour.

2 For the tomato sauce, heat the oil in a medium pan, add the onion, and sauté for 5 minutes. Stir in the garlic and cook for 1 minute. Add the remaining ingredients and simmer, uncovered, for 10 minutes. Set aside.

3 Preheat the oven to 450°F (230°C). Knock back the dough, divide into two balls and roll each out to a large circle. Place on the baking sheets. Divide the sauce, mozzarella, and olives between the pizza bases. Season with pepper and drizzle over a little oil. Bake for 10 minutes or until golden and the cheese is bubbling. Sprinkle the basil over each pizza and serve.

CALZONE

This folded pizza is especially delicious with a moist filling of pesto sauce and a combination of cheeses.

MAKES 6
PREP 30 mins
PLUS RISING
COOK 20–25 mins

GUIDELINES PER SERVING

● ● ○ Calories
● ● ● Saturated fat
● ○ ○ Salt

STATISTICS PER CALZONE

Energy 473kcals/1989kJ

Protein 19g

Fat 18g
Saturated fat 7g

Carbohydrate 57.5g
Sugar 3.5g

Fiber 3.5g

Salt 1g

GREAT FOR KIDS

2¾ cups gluten-free white bread flour blend, extra to dust (see page 38)
1 tsp xanthan gum
2 tsp fast-acting dried yeast
2 tsp granulated sugar
salt and freshly ground pepper
1 large egg, plus 1 large egg, beaten, to glaze

2 tbsp olive oil, plus extra for greasing
6 tsp gluten-free pesto (store-bought or see page 137)
1 red onion, finely sliced
4½oz (125g) mozzarella ball, diced
2oz (60g) Dolcelatte or Gorgonzola cheese, crumbled
6 slices of prosciutto ham

1 Sift together the flour, xanthan, yeast, sugar, and 1 teaspoon salt in a large bowl. Mix 1¼ cups lukewarm water with the whole egg and oil, pour into the flour mixture, and use your hands to mix to a slightly sticky, soft dough. Put onto a floured surface and knead for 5 minutes until smooth and elastic. Return to the bowl, cover with oiled plastic wrap, and leave in a warm place for about 1 hour until doubled in size.

2 Preheat the oven to 425°F (220°C). Divide the mixture into 6 and, on a floured surface, roll each into a 8in (20cm) round. Divide between 2 large, lightly oiled baking sheets. Spread 1 teaspoon pesto on one half of each round. Scatter over some onion, the cheeses, ham, and season with black pepper. Glaze the outside edge of the circle with the beaten egg and fold. Pinch and twist the edges to seal and make a steam hole on top. Brush with more egg and lightly dust with flour. Repeat for all 6 rounds. Bake for 20–25 minutes or until golden and puffy. Serve hot with salad.

Variations
BRIE AND BACON Scatter over 5oz (40g) sliced brie with sliced, cooked smoked bacon slices and a few sliced green olives.
SPICY PEPPER AND SALAMI Scatter over 4½oz (125g) sliced mozzarella, a sliced red pepper, 2½oz (75g) salami, and a sprinkle of dried chili flakes.

SOCCA

*These crispy, nutty pancakes made with chickpea flour
are served as street food in the south of France.*

MAKES   6
PREP   10 mins
       PLUS RESTING
COOK   20 mins

1 cup gram (chickpea) flour
2 tsp ground cumin
½ tsp salt

3 tbsp olive oil, plus extra to serve
sea salt flakes, to serve

GUIDELINES PER SERVING

 Calories

 Saturated fat

Salt

STATISTICS PER SOCCA

Energy 139kcals/581kJ

Protein 5g

Fat 9g
Saturated fat 1g

Carbohydrate 11g
Sugar 0.5g

Fiber 3.5g

Salt 0.4g

1 Mix together the flour, cumin, and salt in a large bowl, make a well
in the center, add 1¼ cups water, then use a hand whisk to beat until
smooth. Pour into a large liquid measuring cup and leave to stand for
at least 10 minutes for the batter to thicken.

2 Preheat the broiler and line a baking sheet with parchment paper.
Heat a little of the oil in a large nonstick frying pan and, when hot, pour
in enough of the batter to cover the bottom of the pan, tilting the pan
to cover it quickly. Cook over medium heat until the base is golden.

3 Transfer the socca to the baking sheet and put under the hot broiler.
Cook for a further 2–3 minutes until the top is lightly charred. Transfer to
a board. Repeat with remaining oil and batter to make 5 more pancakes.

4 To serve, sprinkle the pancakes with sea salt flakes and a drizzle of olive
oil, then roughly chop into bite-sized pieces. Heap onto a platter and
serve as an appetizer with drinks.

Cook's Tip

These are finished off under the broiler to speed up the
process, but if you prefer, simply turn over the pancakes and
cook the other side in the pan until golden brown. They should
become crisp and almost charred at the edges.

GARLIC BREAD

For variety, try adding a few chopped tarragon leaves, a pinch of chili flakes, or some grated Cheddar cheese.

MAKES 12 slices
PREP 35 mins
PLUS RISING
COOK 1 hour 5 mins
FREEZE 3 months
UNBUTTERED LOAF

GUIDELINES PER SERVING

● ● ● Calories

● ● ● Saturated fat

● ● ○ Salt

STATISTICS PER SLICE

Energy 274kcals/1155kJ

Protein 5g

Fat 16g
Saturated fat 8.5g

Carbohydrate 24g
Sugar 2g

Fiber 1.5g

Salt 0.5g

2¾ cups gluten-free white bread flour blend (see page 38), plus extra to dust
2 tsp fast-acting dried yeast
1 tbsp granulated sugar
1 tsp xanthan gum
salt and freshly ground pepper
1 large egg, plus 1 large egg, beaten, to glaze

2 tbsp vegetable oil
2–3 garlic cloves, crushed or finely chopped
12 tbsp unsalted butter, softened, plus extra for greasing
2 tbsp finely chopped flat-leaf parsley
1 tbsp dried oregano

1 Lightly grease a baking sheet. Sift together the flour, yeast, sugar, xanthan, and salt in a large bowl. In a measuring cup, whisk together 1¼ cups lukewarm water, the whole egg, and oil. Make a well in the center of the dry ingredients, add the wet ingredients, and mix until it comes together in a ball. Transfer to a floured surface and knead for 5–6 minutes until smooth and springy to the touch. Shape into a fat sausage 6in (15cm) long, place on the baking sheet, and make several slashes across the top. Cover with oiled plastic wrap and leave in a warm place for 1 hour or until doubled in size.

2 Preheat the oven to 425°F (220°C). Add a little salt to the beaten egg and brush over the loaf. Bake for 35–40 minutes or until risen, golden brown, and crusty. The loaf should make a hollow sound when tapped from below. Remove from the oven and cool completely on a wire rack.

3 Reduce the heat to 400°F (200°C). For the garlic butter, mix the garlic, butter, parsley, oregano, a little salt, and plenty of pepper. Beat well. Make diagonal slices in the loaf, about 1¼in (3cm) apart. Don't slice all the way through. Place on a piece of foil large enough to wrap the loaf and spread the garlic butter on both sides of each slice. Lightly press together. Wrap in the foil and seal, making the seam on the top.

4 Place on a baking sheet and bake for 10 minutes. Loosely unwrap the foil and bake for 6–8 minutes more or until the bread is crusty. Serve right away.

CHEESE AND ONION BREAD

A great loaf to serve with soup. The onions are caramelized before adding to the dough for a sweeter flavor.

MAKES   8 slices
PREP   30 mins
        PLUS RISING
COOK   30 mins
FREEZE 3 months

1 tbsp butter

3 tbsp olive oil, plus extra for greasing

3 onions, sliced

4 tsp granulated sugar

salt and freshly ground pepper

2¾ cups gluten-free white bread flour blend (see page 38), plus extra to dust

2 tsp xanthan gum

2 tsp fast-acting dried yeast

2 tsp ground mustard

4oz (115g) aged Cheddar cheese, coarsely grated

1 large egg, plus 1 large egg, beaten, to glaze

GUIDELINES PER SERVING

●●● Calories

●●● Saturated fat

●●○ Salt

STATISTICS PER SLICE

Energy 350kcals/1463kJ

Protein 11g

Fat 13g
Saturated fat 5g

Carbohydrate 46g
Sugar 5g

Fiber 3g

Salt 0.9g

1 Melt the butter and 1 tablespoon oil in a large frying pan, add the onions, and fry over medium heat for 6 minutes until just golden. Reduce the heat, add 2 teaspoons sugar and a pinch of salt, then cook the onions for a further 5–10 minutes or until soft and caramelized. Allow to cool.

2 Sift together the flour, xanthan, yeast, mustard, the remaining sugar, and 1 teaspoon salt in a large bowl, add a good grinding of pepper, and stir in three-quarters of the onions and cheese. Mix 1 cup lukewarm water with the whole egg and remaining oil, then pour into the flour mixture. Use your hands to mix to a slightly sticky, soft dough, transfer to a floured surface, and knead for 5 minutes until smooth and elastic. Shape the dough into a 6½in (16cm) round, place on a lightly oiled baking sheet, and cover loosely with oiled plastic wrap. Leave in a warm place for 1 hour or until doubled in size.

3 Preheat the oven to 425°F (220°C). Add a good pinch of salt to the beaten egg and brush over the loaf. Sprinkle over the remaining onions and cheese and bake for 30 minutes until golden and crusty. Cool and then slice.

Variation
Omit the caramelized onion and use 5 sliced scallions instead. They add a lovely green color.

CARAWAY SEED BREAD

This crunchy, crusty loaf, peppered with caraway seeds, is particularly good served with cured meats and cheese.

MAKES	12 slices
PREP	20 mins
	PLUS PROVING
COOK	40–50 mins
FREEZE	1 month

GUIDELINES PER SERVING

● ● ○ Calories

● ● ○ Saturated fat

● ● ○ Salt

STATISTICS PER SLICE

Energy 190kcals/802kJ

Protein 6g

Fat 4.5g
Saturated fat 1g

Carbohydrate 31.5g
Sugar 5g

Fiber 1.6g

Salt 0.7g

oil, for greasing
2¾ cups gluten-free white
   bread flour blend (see page 38)
2 tsp fast-acting dried yeast
2 tsp salt
2 tbsp brown sugar
2 tsp caraway seeds
1¼ cups milk

2 large eggs
2 tbsp vegetable oil
1 tsp balsamic vinegar
2 tsp superfine granulated sugar

SPECIAL EQUIPMENT
9 x 5in (23 x 13cm) loaf pan

1 Lightly oil the loaf pan. Sift the flour, yeast, and 1 teaspoon salt into a large bowl. Stir in the sugar and 1 teaspoon of the caraway seeds. Heat the milk until lukewarm (see Cook's Tip). Add one of the eggs, the oil, and vinegar to the milk, and whisk with a fork. Make a well in the center of the dry ingredients, add the wet ingredients, and mix well to form a dough. Knead on a floured surface for 5 minutes, until smooth.

2 Shape the dough into a fat roll and transfer to the loaf pan. Use a sharp knife to make diagonal slashes across the dough. Cover loosely with oiled plastic wrap and leave in a warm place to rise for 1 hour or until doubled in size.

3 Preheat the oven to 425°F (220°C). To glaze, beat together the remaining egg, salt, and sugar, generously brush it over the loaf, and sprinkle the remaining caraway seeds. Bake for 35–40 minutes or until the loaf is risen and golden brown. Remove from the pan and bake for a further 5–10 minutes to crisp the crust. Remove from the oven and cool on a wire rack.

Cook's Tip
The ideal temperature for yeast to work is 95°F (35°C). Temperatures above 140°F (60°C) will kill the yeast, so it's important the milk is heated until warm but not hot to the touch.

SUN-DRIED TOMATO BREAD

Colorful and packed with intense Mediterranean flavors, this loaf is perfect for summer.

MAKES 8 slices
PREP 20 mins
PLUS RISING
COOK 30 mins
FREEZE 3 months

GUIDELINES PER SERVING

● ● ● Calories
● ● ○ Saturated fat
● ● ○ Salt

STATISTICS PER SLICE

Energy 305kcals/1284kJ

Protein 9g

Fat 10g
Saturated fat 1.9g

Carbohydrate 42g
Sugar 2g

Fiber 2.5g

Salt 0.6g

3oz (85g) sun-dried tomatoes
  in oil, drained
2¾ cups gluten-free white bread flour
  blend (see page 38), plus extra
  to dust
2 tsp xanthan gum
2 tsp fast-acting dried yeast
1 tsp granulated sugar

salt and freshly ground pepper
1 tsp dried oregano
1oz (30g) freshly grated
  Parmesan cheese
2 tbsp tomato paste
3 tbsp olive oil, from the tomatoes
1 large egg, plus 1 large egg, beaten,
  to glaze

1 Roughly chop the sun-dried tomatoes. Sift together the flour, xanthan, yeast, sugar, and 1 teaspoon salt in a large bowl, add a good grinding of black pepper, then stir in the oregano, tomatoes, and two-thirds of the cheese.

2 Mix 1 cup lukewarm water with the tomato paste and oil, pour into the flour mix with the whole egg, and use your hands to mix to a slightly sticky, soft dough. Transfer the dough to a floured surface and knead for 5 minutes until smooth and elastic. Shape the dough into a 9in (23cm) long fat loaf shape. Use a sharp knife to make diagonal slashes across the dough. Place on a floured baking sheet and cover loosely with oiled plastic wrap. Leave in a warm place for 1 hour or until doubled in size.

3 Preheat the oven to 425°F (220°C). Add a good pinch of salt to the beaten egg and brush all over the loaf. Sprinkle with the remaining Parmesan and bake for 30 minutes or until golden and crusty. Cool slightly before slicing.

Variation
ROAST PEPPER BREAD Use an equal drained weight of roasted peppers in oil instead of the sun-dried tomatoes.

SPICED LAMB FLATBREAD

A street food recipe—in Turkey, these are served garnished with a sprinkling of flat-leaf parsley and a squeeze of lemon.

MAKES   6
PREP   20 mins
   PLUS RISING
COOK   20–25 mins

2¾ cups gluten-free white bread flour blend (see page 38), plus extra to dust
3 tsp fast-acting dried yeast
2 tsp xanthan gum
1 tsp salt
1 tsp granulated sugar
3 tbsp olive oil
2 tsp ground cumin

½–1 tsp chili powder
1 red bell pepper, seeded and roughly chopped
1 red onion, roughly chopped
1 garlic clove
handful of flat-leaf parsley, plus extra to garnish
6oz (175g) ground lamb
lemon and salad, to serve

GUIDELINES PER SERVING

- Calories
- Saturated fat
- Salt

STATISTICS PER FLATBREAD

Energy   371kcals/1565kJ

Protein   13g

Fat   9.5g
Saturated fat   2.4g

Carbohydrate   58g
Sugar   4g

Fiber   4g

Salt   0.8g

1 Sift the flour, yeast, xanthan, salt, and sugar into a large bowl. Pour 1¼ cups lukewarm water and 2 tablespoons oil into the flour, mix to a slightly sticky, soft dough, and knead on a floured surface for 5 minutes until smooth and elastic. Divide into 6 balls, place on oiled baking sheets, and cover with damp kitchen towels. Set aside in a warm place.

2 Preheat the oven to 400°F (200°C). For the topping, purée together the spices, pepper, onion, garlic, and parsley in a food processor until finely chopped. Strain and discard the juice. Transfer to a bowl, add 1 tablespoon oil and the ground lamb, and season.

3 Roll out the dough balls into thin, flat ovals and place on oiled baking sheets. Spread a thin layer of the lamb mixture over each oval, leaving a thin border clear around the edges. Bake for 20–25 minutes or until the bread is crisp, and the topping is cooked. Top with parsley and a squeeze of lemon, fold in half lengthwise, and serve warm with a salad for a light supper.

Variations

CHICKEN Instead of the lamb, grind an equal weight of chicken with the vegetables.

VEGETARIAN Omit the lamb and add 1 chopped eggplant to the food processor. Strain out the excess liquid and stir through 1 tablespoon gluten-free tahini.

PITA BREAD

These are pale and soft when baked, and take on a slight golden hue when reheated. Cooling them wrapped in a damp kitchen towel gives them their soft texture.

MAKES 8
PREP 15 mins
PLUS RISING
COOK 10–15 mins
FREEZE 3 months

GUIDELINES PER SERVING

● ● ○ Calories
● ○ ○ Saturated fat
● ○ ○ Salt

STATISTICS PER PITA

Energy 217kcals/917kJ

Protein 5g

Fat 3.5g
Saturated fat 0.5g

Carbohydrate 41g
Sugar 1g

Fiber 2.5g

Salt 0.5g

GREAT FOR KIDS

2¾ cups gluten-free white bread flour blend (see page 38), plus extra for dusting
3 tsp fast-acting dried yeast
2 tsp xanthan gum
1 tsp salt
1 tsp granulated sugar
2 tbsp olive oil, plus extra for greasing
hummus and dips (see page 188), to serve (optional)

1 Sift together the flour, yeast, xanthan, salt, and sugar in a large bowl. Mix 1½ cups lukewarm water with the oil, pour into the flour mix, and use your hands to mix to a slightly sticky, soft dough.

2 Transfer the dough to a lightly floured surface and knead for 5 minutes until smooth and elastic. Divide the dough into 8 balls. Place the balls on 2 large oiled baking sheets and cover loosely with oiled plastic wrap. Leave in a warm place for 10 minutes.

3 On a lightly floured surface, roll out each ball into a flat oval, place on oiled baking sheets, cover with a damp kitchen towel, and leave in a warm place for 20 minutes or until puffy.

4 Preheat the oven to 425°F (220°C). Bake for 10–15 minutes or until pale golden and puffed up. Remove from the oven, wrap the pitas in a damp kitchen towel and leave on a wire rack until cold. To serve, put under a hot broiler or in a toaster until warm. Serve with hummus and dips or split the pitas and add a filling of your choice.

Cook's Tips

Make these with gluten-free brown bread flour blend (see page 38), if preferred, adding a little more water if required. You can freeze the cold pitas in a plastic bag, then thaw before toasting to warm through.

TORTILLA

These Mexican flatbreads are simple to make and cook on the stove top. Serve them with a choice of delicious fillings.

MAKES   6
PREP   20 mins
COOK   20–30 mins

1 cup gluten-free all-purpose flour, plus extra for dusting
½ cup fine cornmeal or polenta
2 tsp xanthan gum
1 tsp salt

1 tsp gluten-free baking powder
1 tbsp vegetable shortening, lard, or butter, cubed
ready-made salsa, guacamole, or sour cream, to taste

GUIDELINES PER SERVING

● ● ○ Calories
● ● ○ Saturated fat
● ● ○ Salt

STATISTICS PER TORTILLA

Energy 141kcals/592kJ

Protein 3g

Fat 3g
Saturated fat 1g

Carbohydrate 24g
Sugar 0.5g

Fiber 1g

Salt 0.9g

1 Sift together the flours, xanthan, salt, and baking powder in a large bowl, and rub in the fat. Stir in ²⁄₃ cup lukewarm water and mix to a soft dough. Knead on a floured surface for 2–3 minutes until smooth and elastic. Leave for 20 minutes in a bowl covered loosely with oiled plastic wrap. Divide into 6 balls. Roll out each ball between 2 pieces of parchment paper to a thin, flat round, approximately 8in (20cm) in diameter. Dust with flour.

2 Heat a large, heavy frying pan, add a tortilla, and cook for 5–6 minutes, turning once, until speckled with brown spots. Keep warm in a dry kitchen towel. Cook the remainder in the same way. Prepare a filling of your choice (see below). Divide the mixture between the tortillas, adding a spoonful of salsa, guacamole, or sour cream to taste. Roll up and serve.

Choose Your Filling

Spicy chicken filling Heat 2 tablespoons vegetable oil in a large, heavy frying pan. Add 4 thinly sliced chicken breasts and sauté for 10 minutes. Add 1 red pepper, cut into strips, 1 sliced red onion, and 1 crushed garlic clove. Sauté for 6–8 minutes. Add 1 teaspoon each of cumin, ground coriander, paprika, and ½ teaspoon dried chili flakes. Cook for 30 seconds and remove. Stir through juice of 1 lime and chopped cilantro.

Mixed pepper filling Substitute the chicken with 3 mixed color peppers, cut into strips, and 4oz (115g) frozen corn kernels, defrosted. Add the corn with the garlic after the peppers and onions have cooked, and sauté for 1 minute, before adding the spices.

GREAT FOR KIDS

MASALA DOSA

These spicy vegan pancakes, made from ground lentils and rice, are traditionally served for breakfast in southern India.

SERVES 6

PREP 20 mins
PLUS SOAKING

COOK 40–50 mins

FREEZE 1 month

GUIDELINES PER SERVING

● ● ●   Calories

● ● ●   Saturated fat

● ● ●   Salt

STATISTICS PER SERVING

Energy 250kcals/1049kJ

Protein 6.5g

Fat 6g
Saturated fat 0.7g

Carbohydrate 40g
Sugar 2.3g

Fiber 3g

Salt 0.3g

6oz (175g) basmati rice
2oz (60g) urad dal
1 tsp fenugreek seeds
salt
vegetable oil, for frying

FOR THE POTATO FILLING
2 tbsp vegetable oil
1 onion, finely chopped
1 jalapeño chile, seeded and chopped
1 garlic clove, finely chopped
1in (2.5cm) fresh ginger, grated
2 tsp black mustard seeds

¼ tsp turmeric
6 dried curry leaves
1lb (450g) potatoes, cubed
zest and juice of ½ lemon
2 tbsp finely chopped cilantro

FOR THE DIPPING SAUCE
1oz (30g) cilantro
1 small tomato
½ jalapeño chile, seeded
juice of 1 lemon
½ tsp granulated sugar

1 Place the rice, dal, and fenugreek seeds in a large bowl, cover with cold water, and soak for 6–8 hours or overnight. Drain and coarsely grind in a food processor with a pinch of salt. Add 1¼ cups cold water and process to a smooth batter the consistency of thin cream.

2 For the spicy potato filling, heat the oil in a medium-sized pan and fry the onion for 4 minutes, or until soft. Add the chile, garlic, ginger, mustard, turmeric, and curry leaves and cook for 30 seconds, or until the mustard seeds start to pop. Add the potatoes, lemon zest and juice, a generous pinch of salt, and 1 cup water. Bring to a boil, cover, and simmer for 15–20 minutes until tender. Remove the lid and simmer until soft and breaking up. Stir in the cilantro and keep warm. For the sauce, place all the ingredients with a pinch of salt in a food processor and puree to a rough paste.

3 Heat 1 teaspoon oil in a small frying pan. Cover the pan with a ladleful of batter and cook over medium heat for 2–3 minutes. Flip and cook for another 1–2 minutes. Keep warm. Repeat to make 5 pancakes. Divide the potato filling between pancakes, fold over, and serve with the sauce.

NAAN BREAD

Using fizzy lemonade in a bread recipe sounds strange, but it really does work. The naan puff up to give a wonderfully soft-textured bread—and they don't taste of lemonade at all!

1¾ cups gluten-free all-purpose flour, plus extra to dust
2 tsp xanthan gum
2 tsp gluten-free baking powder
1 tsp salt

1–2 tsp black onion (nigella) seeds (optional)
⅔ cup clear sparkling lemonade
2 tbsp butter, melted

1 Sift together the flour, xanthan, baking powder, and salt in a large bowl. Stir in the black onion seeds (if using), pour the lemonade into the mixture, and mix with your hands to a slightly sticky, soft dough.

2 Transfer the dough to a floured surface and knead for 5 minutes until smooth and elastic. Transfer to a bowl, cover with a damp kitchen towel, and leave for 10 minutes. Divide the mixture into 4 pieces. Roll out each ball into a flat teardrop-shaped oval.

3 Heat a heavy frying pan, brush one side of each naan with the melted butter, and cook butter-side down in the frying pan for 3–4 minutes, or until the base is golden. Brush the top with butter, then turn over and cook for a further 3–4 minutes or until puffed up and golden. Transfer to a kitchen towel while you cook the remainder in the same way. Serve warm.

Variations

GARLIC AND CILANTRO Once cooked on both sides, scatter a little chopped garlic and a small handful of chopped cilantro leaves over the top, flip over, and cook for 30 seconds or until the garlic is golden.

PESHWARI Mix 2 tablespoons unsweetened, dried coconut with 1 teaspoon sugar. Once cooked on both sides, brush the top with more butter, scatter over the coconut, flip over, and cook for 30–45 seconds or until the coconut is toasted.

CORNBREAD WITH OLIVES

Cornbread is served alongside spicy stews and fried chicken—it's great for mopping up juices. If making for kids, omit the olives.

11½oz (326g) can corn, juice reserved
1½ cups fine cornmeal or polenta
1 cup gluten-free all-purpose flour
¼ cup granulated sugar
1 tbsp gluten-free baking powder
1 tsp xanthan gum
½ tsp salt
½ cup milk

2 large eggs, beaten
4 tbsp butter, melted, plus
  extra for greasing
4oz (115g) pimento-stuffed green olives,
  halved

SPECIAL EQUIPMENT
8in (20cm) round cake pan

SERVES   12
PREP   10 mins
COOK   30–35 mins
FREEZE   3 months

GUIDELINES PER SERVING

● ● ●   Calories

● ● ●   Saturated fat

● ● ○   Salt

STATISTICS PER SERVING

Energy 288kcals/1201kJ

Protein 5g

Fat 16g
Saturated fat 4.5g

Carbohydrate 30g
Sugar 7g

Fiber 1.5g

Salt 0.8g

1 Preheat the oven to 400°F (200°C). Grease the pan and line the base with parchment paper. Drain the corn, saving the juice in a measuring cup. Add half the corn to the cup, then purée with a immersion blender until creamed or transfer to a food processor. Sift together the cornmeal, flour, sugar, baking powder, xanthan, and salt in a large bowl.

2 Beat the milk and eggs together, add to the dry ingredients along with the butter, creamed corn, and the remaining whole kernels, and beat together until just mixed.

3 Spoon the mixture into the cake pan, level the surface, and scatter over the olives. Bake for 30–35 minutes or until risen and golden. Leave to cool in the pan for 5 minutes. Run a knife around the edge of the loaf and turn out from the pan. Cool slightly on a wire rack, then serve warm in wedges.

Cook's Tips
If you like a bit of heat, add a couple of chopped chiles to the mixture. If freezing, leave to cool completely, then pack into a plastic bag and freeze for up to 3 months. Reheat for 10 minutes in a hot oven after defrosting.

GREAT FOR KIDS

BRAZILIAN CHEESE ROLLS

Crisp on the outside and chewy within, these pão de queijo *are a popular street food in their native land.*

MAKES 16
PREP 10 mins
COOK 30 mins

GUIDELINES PER SERVING

● ● ● Calories
● ● ○ Saturated fat
● ● ○ Salt

STATISTICS PER SERVING

Energy 121kcals/510kJ

Protein 4g

Fat 6g
Saturated fat 2g

Carbohydrate 12g
Sugar 0.6g

Fiber trace

Salt 0.4g

½ cup whole milk
3–4 tbsp sunflower or vegetable oil
1 tsp salt
1¾ cups tapioca (manioc or cassava) flour, plus extra for dusting

2 eggs, beaten, plus extra for glazing
4½oz (125g) Parmesan cheese, grated

SPECIAL EQUIPMENT
food processor

1 Put the milk, oil, ½ cup of water, and the salt in a small saucepan and bring to a boil. Put the flour into a large bowl and quickly mix in the hot liquid. The mixture will be very sticky. Set aside to cool.

2 Preheat the oven to 375°F (190°C). Once the tapioca mixture has cooled, put it into a food processor with a blade attachment. Add the eggs and process until the lumps disappear and it is a smooth paste. Add the cheese and process until the mixture is sticky and elastic.

3 Turn the mixture out onto a well-floured work surface and knead for 2–3 minutes until smooth and pliable. Divide into 16 equal pieces. Roll each into golf ball–sized balls and place, spaced well apart, on a baking sheet lined with wax paper.

4 Brush the balls with a little beaten egg, and bake in the middle of the oven for 30 minutes until well risen and golden brown. Remove from the oven and cool for a few minutes before eating. These are best eaten the same day they are made, preferably while still warm.

How to freeze

These rolls can be open-frozen on the baking sheet at the end of step 3, transferred to freezer bags, and frozen for up to 6 months. Simply defrost for 30 minutes and bake as in step 4.

PUMPKIN BREAD WREATH

Gently spiced, this lovely moist bread makes an impressive centerpiece for a party, especially around Halloween.

SERVES   12
PREP   25 mins
          PLUS RISING
COOK   1 hour 5 mins–
          1¼ hours

GUIDELINES PER SERVING

● ● ●   Calories

● ● ●   Saturated fat

● ● ○   Salt

STATISTICS PER SERVING

Energy 304kcals/1283kJ

Protein 8g

Fat 8g
Saturated fat 2.5g

Carbohydrate 50g
Sugar 9g

Fiber 3.5g

Salt 0.9g

GREAT FOR KIDS

vegetable oil, for greasing
1lb 2oz (500g) pumpkin or butternut
  squash, peeled, deseeded, and cut into
  2in (5cm) cubes, or 15oz (400g) canned
  pumpkin purée
2 tbsp olive oil
salt and freshly ground black pepper
4¼ cups gluten-free white bread flour
  blend (see page 38),
  plus extra for dusting
2 tsp xanthan gum

1 tbsp fast-acting dried yeast
2½ tsp salt
1 tsp ground cinnamon
1 tsp ground ginger
½ tsp ground cloves
⅔ cup brown sugar
2 tbsp butter
¾ cup milk
3 large eggs
1 tsp granulated sugar
2 tbsp pumpkin seeds

1 Oil a large baking sheet. Place the butternut cubes in a roasting pan and drizzle over the olive oil, 3 tablespoons water, and seasoning. Cover with foil and roast for 30–35 minutes, or until tender. Transfer to a food processor and pulse until smooth. Spread in the roasting pan and leave until cold.

2 Sift the flour, xanthan, yeast, 1½ teaspoons of the salt, and the spices into a large bowl and stir in the brown sugar. Melt the butter in a pan, add the milk and heat to lukewarm, then add 1 egg and beat with a fork. Pour the mixture over the dry ingredients, add the squash, and mix to form a dough. Knead the dough on a lightly floured surface for 5 minutes, until smooth. Roll it into 12 even-sized balls. Place 9 of these in a circle on a large baking sheet and 3 in the center to make a wreath. Cover with oiled plastic wrap and leave in a warm place for 1 hour, until doubled in size.

3 Preheat the oven to 400°F (200°C). Beat the remaining egg, granulated sugar, and 1 teaspoon salt, and brush over the rolls. Scatter over the pumpkin seeds and bake for 35–40 minutes until golden brown. Cool for 30 minutes. Serve the bread warm on a large board, so guests can break off the rolls.

SAVORY TARTS AND PIES

FENNEL AND GRUYÈRE TART

The light aniseed flavor of fennel and sweet, tangy Gruyère make a winning combination in this recipe.

SERVES 6
PREP 20 mins
PLUS CHILLING
COOK 40 mins

GUIDELINES PER SERVING

● ● ○ Calories
● ● ● Saturated fat
● ● ○ Salt

STATISTICS PER SLICE

Energy 698kcals/2886kJ

Protein 14g

Fat 58g
Saturated fat 31g

Carbohydrate 31g
Sugar 2.5g

Fiber 1g

Salt 1.2g

14oz (400g) gluten-free shortcrust pastry
(see pages 44–5)
gluten-free all-purpose flour, to dust

FOR THE FILLING
3 tbsp olive oil
1 onion, sliced
1 large fennel bulb, trimmed, quartered,
and sliced
salt and freshly ground pepper

½ tsp freshly grated nutmeg
3 large eggs
1 cup heavy cream
3½oz (100g) Gruyère cheese, grated
salad leaves, to serve

SPECIAL EQUIPMENT
9in (23cm) round, 1¼in (3cm)
deep, fluted tart pan

1 Preheat the oven to 400°F (200°C). For the filling, heat the oil in a frying pan, add the onion, and fry on medium heat for 2–3 minutes. Add the fennel and sauté for 6–8 minutes, stirring occasionally, until golden. Season with salt, pepper, and nutmeg and set aside. Beat the eggs and cream together in a large measuring cup.

2 Roll out the pastry on a lightly floured surface to a thickness of ¼in (5mm). Lift it over the pan and press into the base and sides. (Gluten-free pastry is delicate, so if you get a few cracks, "glue" them with a little water.) Trim the edges. Pierce the base with a fork, fill with parchment paper and baking beans, and bake for 15 minutes. Remove the beans and paper, then return to the oven for another 5 minutes to crisp up.

3 Scatter the onions and fennel over the base and sprinkle the cheese. Pour the egg and cream mixture into the pastry case. Return the tart to the oven. Reduce the temperature to 350°F (180°C) and bake for 20–25 minutes or until the filling is set and golden brown. Serve warm or cold with salad leaves.

RED PEPPER AND CHILE TART

These hot flavors are tempered with cool sheep cheese. Swap the cheese for your favorite—blue, Brie, or feta.

SERVES   6
PREP   25–30 mins
COOK   1¼–1½ hours
FREEZE   1 month

GUIDELINES PER SERVING

●●○ Calories

●●● Saturated fat

●●○ Salt

STATISTICS PER SLICE

Energy 597kcals/2481kJ

Protein 13g

Fat 45g
Saturated fat 20g

Carbohydrate 35g
Sugar 6.5g

Fiber 4g

Salt 1.1g

14oz (400g) gluten-free shortcrust pastry
  (see pages 44–5)
gluten-free all-purpose flour, to dust

FOR THE FILLING
3 red bell peppers
2 red or jalapeño chiles
2 tbsp olive oil
1 red onion, finely chopped
salt and freshly ground pepper

leaves from a few sprigs of thyme
5½oz (150g) soft sheep cheese, crumbled
⅔ cup heavy cream
2 large eggs
2 garlic cloves, grated

SPECIAL EQUIPMENT
8in (20cm) round, loose-bottomed
  tart pan

1 Preheat the oven to 400°F (200°C). For the filling, place the peppers and chiles on a baking sheet and coat with half the oil. Cook in the oven for 30–40 minutes until the skins begin to char. Transfer the peppers to a plastic bag to cool. Chop and seed the chiles. When the peppers are cool, remove the skins and seeds, roughly chop, and add to the chiles.

2 Carefully roll out the pastry on a lightly floured surface to a thickness of ¼in (5mm). Lift it over the pan and press into the base and sides. Line with parchment paper and baking beans and bake for 15 minutes. Remove the beans and paper and return to the oven for another 5 minutes to crisp up. Reduce the oven temperature to 350°F (180°C).

3 Heat the remaining oil in a frying pan, add the onion, and cook for 6–8 minutes on medium-low heat until softened. Season to taste, then stir in half the thyme. Leave to cool a little, then transfer to the pastry case. Add the peppers and chile, spreading them out evenly, and tuck in the cheese so it covers all the tart. Mix together the cream and egg and season. Add the remaining thyme and the garlic and stir well. Pour the mixture over the tart evenly, set the pan on a baking sheet, and bake for 20–25 minutes or until the top is set and golden. Remove and leave to cool before releasing from the pan.

GOAT CHEESE TARTLETS

Sweet prunes pair well with goat cheese and the tartlets can be served with sun-dried tomato bread (see page 230).

MAKES 6
PREP 30 mins
PLUS CHILLING
COOK 25–35 mins

GUIDELINES PER SERVING

● ● ● Calories
● ● ● Saturated fat
● ○ ○ Salt

STATISTICS PER TARTLET

Energy 435kcals/1818kJ

Protein 12g

Fat 26g
Saturated fat 16g

Carbohydrate 36g
Sugar 10g

Fiber 4g

Salt 1g

7 tbsp butter, cubed, plus extra
  for greasing
2 cups gluten-free all-purpose flour,
  plus extra for dusting
pinch of salt
1 tsp xanthan gum
1 tbsp olive oil
1 large red onion, sliced
a few sprigs of thyme, leaves only

8oz (225g) semi-hard, mild goat cheese,
  finely cubed
4½oz (125g) pitted soft
  prunes, chopped
freshly ground pepper

SPECIAL EQUIPMENT
6 x 3½in (9cm) round, 1in (2.5cm) deep
  tart pans

1 Preheat the oven to 400°F (200°C). Grease the pans with butter. Mix the flour, salt, and xanthan gum in a bowl. Rub the butter in with your fingertips until it resembles crumbs. Gradually add 1–2 tablespoons cold water until the mixture forms a dough. Lightly knead the dough on a floured surface, wrap in plastic wrap, and chill for 10 minutes.

2 Cut the pastry into 6 even pieces. Roll out each piece between two pieces of plastic wrap and cut 6 x 5in (12cm) rounds. Lift the pastry into the tart pans, pushing it into the base and sides. If it tears, patch it up. Trim the top, pierce the bases with a fork, and line with parchment and baking beans. Bake for 10–15 minutes or until the edges turn pale golden. Remove the beans and paper, and set the crusts aside.

3 For the filling, heat the oil in a small pan, add the onion and thyme leaves, and cook on medium heat for 5 minutes until the onion begins to soften and turn transparent. Reduce the heat and cook for a further 5 minutes, to sweeten them a little, then spoon them into the pastry crusts.

4 Mix the goat cheese and prunes and season with pepper. Divide between the crusts and bake for 15–20 minutes or until the mixture is bubbling and the pastry is golden brown. Remove and serve warm.

SOUTHWEST CORN AND JALAPEÑO TART

A jumble of sweet and hot ingredients make this colorful tart, which can be served hot or at room temperature.

SERVES 6
PREP 20 mins
COOK 45 mins–1 hour
FREEZE 1 month

GUIDELINES PER SERVING

● ● ○   Calories

● ● ●   Saturated fat

● ● ○   Salt

STATISTICS PER SLICE

Energy 590kcals/2454kJ

Protein 10g

Fat 41g
Saturated fat 17g

Carbohydrate 45g
Sugar 8g

Fiber 3.5g

Salt 1.2g

GREAT FOR KIDS

14oz (400g) gluten-free shortcrust pastry (see pages 44–5)
gluten-free all-purpose flour, for dusting
2 tbsp olive oil
bunch of scallions, finely chopped
pinch of cayenne pepper or paprika (optional)
1 large red bell pepper, halved, seeded, and finely chopped
14oz (400g) can corn, drained
salt and freshly ground pepper

⅔ cup heavy cream
1 large egg, beaten
1–2 tbsp canned chopped green chiles
2oz (60g) Monterey Jack or Cheddar cheese, sliced or grated

SPECIAL EQUIPMENT
8in (20cm) round, loose-bottomed, straight-sided tart pan

1 Preheat the oven to 400°F (200°C). Roll out the pastry on a lightly floured surface to a thickness of ¼in (5mm). Line the pan with the pastry, letting it overlap, then trim the surplus and line with parchment paper and baking beans. Bake for 15 minutes. Remove the beans and paper, and return to the oven for 5 minutes to crisp up. Reduce the oven temperature to 350°F (180°C).

2 Meanwhile, heat the oil in a large pan, add the scallions, and cook on low heat for 2 minutes. Stir in the cayenne or paprika (if using) and add the bell pepper. Cook for 5 more minutes, add the corn, and season to taste.

3 Remove from the heat and leave to cool. Stir in the cream and egg to coat. Spoon the mixture into the pastry crust and top with the green chiles and cheese. Bake for 20–30 minutes or until set and golden. Remove and leave to cool for 10 minutes. Slice and serve with a tomato and avocado salad.

Variations
Children will love a corn pie minus the green chiles and cayenne. You can also add cooked chicken to the mix and top with pastry for a pie rather than a tart.

WILD MUSHROOM AND TALEGGIO TART

An earthy, robust tart that is good for entertaining, served with roasted new potatoes and a lightly dressed watercress and orange salad.

SERVES   6
PREP   20 mins
COOK   50 mins
FREEZE   1 month

GUIDELINES PER SERVING

● ● ○ Calories

● ● ● Saturated fat

● ● ○ Salt

STATISTICS PER SLICE

Energy 567kcals/2358kJ

Protein 15g

Fat 43g
Saturated fat 16g

Carbohydrate 30g
Sugar 1g

Fiber 3g

Salt 1.2g

14oz (400g) gluten-free shortcrust pastry
  (see pages 44–5)
gluten-free all-purpose flour, for dusting

FOR THE FILLING
2 tbsp olive oil
5½oz (150g) mixed wild or exotic
  mushrooms, larger ones sliced
5½oz (150g) button mushrooms,
  roughly chopped
scant 1oz (25g) dried porcini mushrooms,
  soaked in boiling water for 30 minutes
  and drained
3 garlic cloves, finely chopped

1¾oz (50g) hazelnuts, toasted
  and roughly chopped
salt and freshly ground pepper
handful of flat-leaf parsley,
  finely chopped
3 tbsp heavy cream
1 large egg, lightly beaten
7oz (200g) Taleggio cheese, sliced
pinch of paprika

SPECIAL EQUIPMENT
14 x 5in (35 x 12cm) rectangular,
  loose-bottomed tart pan,
  1in (2.5cm) deep

1 Preheat the oven to 400°F (200°C). Roll out the pastry on a lightly floured surface to a thickness of ¼in (5mm). Line the pan with the pastry, patching up any holes. Trim to neaten. Fill with parchment paper and baking beans and bake in the oven for 15 minutes or until the edges start turning golden. Remove the beans and paper and return to the oven for 5 minutes to crisp up.

2 Meanwhile, for the filling, heat the oil in a large frying pan, add all the mushrooms, and cook on medium-high heat for 10 minutes. Stir in the garlic and nuts and season to taste.

3 Transfer the mixture to a large bowl and toss with the parsley, cream, and egg. Spoon the mixture into the tart crust and top with the cheese. Sprinkle with paprika and bake for 15–20 minutes until golden and set. Remove and leave for at least 10 minutes before releasing from the pan.

ZUCCHINI, MINT, AND FETA FRITTATA

SERVES 4
PREP 10 mins
COOK 15 mins
PLUS RESTING

GUIDELINES PER SERVING

● ● ○   Calories

● ● ●   Saturated fat

● ● ○   Salt

STATISTICS PER SERVING

Energy 326kcals/1353kJ

Protein 19g

Fat 28g
Saturated fat 11g

Carbohydrate 1.5g
Sugar 1.5g

Fiber 0.8g

Salt 1.4g

This light, summery frittata is perfect for a summer picnic, cut into wedges and served cold.

2 tbsp olive oil
9oz (250g) zucchini, cut into
   1cm ($\frac{1}{2}$in) cubes
1 garlic clove, crushed
6 large eggs
1 tbsp heavy cream
scant 1oz (25g) finely grated
   Parmesan cheese
2 tbsp chopped mint leaves

salt and freshly ground black pepper
3$\frac{1}{2}$oz (100g) feta cheese, cut into
   $\frac{1}{2}$in (1cm) cubes
1 tbsp butter

SPECIAL EQUIPMENT
10in (25cm) heavy-bottomed, ovenproof
   frying pan

1 Heat the oil in a 10in (25cm) heavy-bottomed, ovenproof frying pan and fry the zucchini over medium heat for 3–5 minutes until it starts to brown. Add the garlic and cook for 1 minute. Transfer to a plate and wipe the pan with paper towels. Preheat the broiler to its highest setting.

2 Whisk together the eggs, cream, Parmesan cheese, and mint, then season well. Add the garlicky zucchini and the feta cheese and mix well.

3 Melt the butter in the frying pan over medium heat and pour the egg mixture into the pan. Cook for 5 minutes, without moving it at all, until the edges start to set.

4 Transfer the pan to the broiler and cook for another 5 minutes, until the frittata is set and the top golden brown. Rest for 5 minutes before cutting into wedges to serve.

SALMON AND SPINACH QUICHE

The classic combination of salmon and spinach means this delicious tart has high nutritional values, too.

SERVES 6
PREP 20 mins
PLUS CHILLING
COOK 1 hour 10 mins
FREEZE 2 months
PASTRY CASE ONLY

GUIDELINES PER SERVING

● ● ● Calories

● ● ● Saturated fat

● ● ● Salt

STATISTICS PER SERVING

Energy 375kcals/1576kJ

Protein 9g

Fat 31g
Saturated fat 15g

Carbohydrate 14.5g
Sugar 4g

Fiber 0.9g

Salt 1.6g

FOR THE PASTRY
14oz (400g) gluten-free shortcrust
  pastry (see pages 44–5)
gluten-free plain flour, for dusting

FOR THE FILLING
7oz (200g) baby spinach
2 tbsp olive oil
1 garlic clove, crushed
salt and freshly ground black pepper

$3\frac{1}{2}$oz (100g) cooked salmon,
  broken into pieces
9fl oz (250ml) single cream
2 eggs, plus 1 egg yolk
1 tsp grated lemon zest

EQUIPMENT
9in (22cm) deep-sided, loose-bottomed
  fluted tart pan, baking beans

1 Preheat the oven to 400°F (200°C). Roll out the pastry on a well-floured surface to a thickness of about $\frac{1}{4}$in (5mm). Line the tart pan, then neaten and trim the edges. Prick the base with a fork, line with parchment paper, and fill with baking beans. Place on a baking tray and bake in the oven for 15 minutes. Remove the beans and paper and bake for a further 5 minutes to crisp. Trim off any ragged edges while it is still warm, and set aside. Reduce the oven temperature to 350°F (180°C).

2 Meanwhile, cook the baby spinach in a large saucepan with the olive oil and garlic for 2–3 minutes until soft. Season well. Place the spinach in a sieve and press out any excess water. Set aside to cool.

3 Spread the cooled spinach evenly over the bottom of the tart. Arrange the salmon pieces on top of the spinach. Whisk together the cream, eggs, yolk, lemon zest, and seasoning. Place the tart case on a baking tray and pour the cream mixture over the filling.

4 Bake for 45 minutes until just set. Cool for 30 minutes before eating warm or cold. The quiche is best eaten the day it is made, but can be chilled overnight.

SHALLOT TARTE TATIN

Shallots are caramelized and topped with pastry in this savory version of tarte Tatin, which is surprisingly easy to make and always looks impressive.

SERVES   4
PREP   20 mins
COOK   1 hour

1 tbsp olive oil, plus extra if needed
about 20 shallots, peeled
salt and freshly ground pepper
drizzle of thick balsamic vinegar
leaves from a few sprigs of thyme
14oz (400g) gluten-free shortcrust pastry
  (see pages 44–5)

gluten-free plain all-purpose, to dust
1 large egg, lightly beaten, to glaze
mixed leaf salad, to serve

SPECIAL EQUIPMENT
small, deep, nonstick ovenproof
  frying pan

GUIDELINES PER SERVING

⚫⚫⚪ Calories

⚫⚫⚫ Saturated fat

⚫⚫⚪ Salt

STATISTICS PER SLICE

Energy   527kcals/2203kJ

Protein   9.5g

Fat   33g
Saturated fat   10g

Carbohydrate   48g
Sugar   6g

Fiber   5g

Salt   1.1g

1 Preheat the oven to 400°F (200°C). Heat the oil in the ovenproof frying pan and arrange the shallots to fill the pan. Season with salt and pepper and cook on medium heat for 5 minutes or until light golden. Reduce the heat and cook for 20–30 minutes until they begin to caramelize, adding more oil if needed and turning the shallots halfway through cooking. Drizzle with the vinegar and cook for a further 2–3 minutes, then sprinkle over the thyme.

2 Roll out the pastry on a lightly floured surface to a thickness of $\frac{1}{8}$–$\frac{1}{4}$in (3–5mm). Cut out a circle the same size as the top of the pan and discard any surplus pastry. Set the circle over the shallots and tuck the edges in neatly.

3 Brush all over with the beaten egg. Bake in the oven for 20–30 minutes until the pastry is cooked and golden all over, then remove from the oven; be careful, the handle will be extremely hot. Leave to stand for 2–3 minutes, then invert onto a plate. Slice and serve with a mixed leaf salad.

Variation
You can also make this with gluten-free rough puff pastry (see pages 46–7).

SPICY PEPPER EMPANADAS

A variety of savory or sweet fillings—pumpkin and cheese to mixed berries—work well in this South American snack.

SERVES	5
PREP	30 mins
COOK	30 mins
FREEZE	1 month
	UNCOOKED

GUIDELINES PER SERVING

● ● ○ Calories

● ● ● Saturated fat

● ● ○ Salt

STATISTICS PER SERVING

Energy 424kcals/1774kJ

Protein 8g

Fat 24g
Saturated fat 12g

Carbohydrate 42g
Sugar 4g

Fiber 3g

Salt 1.2g

GREAT FOR KIDS

1 tbsp olive oil
1 large onion, sliced
salt and freshly ground pepper
1 red bell pepper, seeded, chopped
2 garlic cloves, finely chopped
3 red or green jalapeño chiles
2 tbsp dry sherry
14oz (400g) can chickpeas, drained

2 tbsp fresh cilantro, chopped
2 tbsp finely chopped flat-leaf parsley
7 tbsp butter
juice of 1 lemon
2 cups gluten-free all-purpose flour,
 plus extra for dusting
1 tsp paprika
sunflower or vegetable oil, for frying

1 For the filling, heat the oil in a medium pan, add the onion, and season. Cook on low heat for 2–3 minutes until soft. Chop the chiles. Add the red pepper, garlic, and chiles, and cook for 10 minutes—until the pepper softens.

2 Add the sherry to the pan, raise the heat, and cook for 2 minutes. Add in the chickpeas, cilantro, and parsley, and stir. Season to taste. Pulse the mixture in a food processor to break it up, but not overwork it.

3 To make the pastry, melt the butter in a pan, add the lemon juice and ½ cup water. Combine the flour, 1 teaspoon salt, and paprika in a mixing bowl. Add the melted butter liquid and mix to a thick paste. Knead gently for 2 minutes. Leave to rest for 2–3 minutes at room temperature.

4 To form the empanadas, roll the pastry out on a floured board to about ⅛in (3mm) thick, adding more flour if needed. Cut out 10 rounds, 4in (10cm) in diameter. Spoon a generous amount of filling onto one half of each round, wet around the edges with water, fold over, and seal with a pinch.

5 Pour sunflower oil into a small, deep-sided frying pan, to a depth of ½in (1cm), and heat to medium. Add 3 empanadas at a time and cook for 2–3 minutes on each side until golden. Transfer to a plate lined with paper towels. Serve hot or warm.

LAMB MASALA PASTIES

MAKES 8
PREP 30 mins
COOK 1 hour 20 mins
FREEZE 1 month

GUIDELINES PER SERVING

● ● ○ Calories
● ● ● Saturated fat
● ● ○ Salt

STATISTICS PER PASTY

Energy 396kcals/1655kJ

Protein 14g

Fat 25g
Saturated fat 10g

Carbohydrate 29g
Sugar 3.5g

Fiber 1g

Salt 0.7g

These pasties can be made with either puff or shortcrust pastry. You can also add peas or fava beans to the filling.

2 tbsp cashew nuts
2in (5cm) piece of fresh ginger, peeled and roughly chopped
1 tsp coriander seeds, crushed
½ tsp cumin seeds
1 tsp turmeric
1 tbsp garam masala
1–2 jalapeño chiles, seeded and finely chopped
salt and freshly ground pepper
1 tbsp olive oil, plus extra if needed
1 onion, chopped

10oz (300g) lamb shoulder, cut into bite-sized pieces
4 tomatoes, peeled and roughly chopped
1 tbsp tomato paste
handful of fresh cilantro leaves, finely chopped (optional)
1lb 5oz (600g) gluten-free rough puff pastry (see pages 46–7, scaling up quantities by one half)
gluten-free all-purpose flour, for dusting
1 large egg, lightly beaten, to glaze
1 tbsp black onion (nigella) seeds, to top (optional)

1 Preheat the oven to 400°F (200°C). Place the first 7 ingredients, up to and including the chiles, in a food processor and purée to a paste. Season well and set aside. Heat the oil in a large, deep frying pan, add the onion, and cook on low heat for 3–4 minutes, then push to one side of the pan. Season the lamb and add to the pan, increasing the heat a little; add a drop of oil if needed. Cook for 6–8 minutes or until the lamb is sealed.

2 Add the spice paste, tomatoes, and paste, and stir. Pour in ⅔–¾ cup hot water to just cover and simmer for 30 minutes or until the meat is tender. Add more water if needed; the sauce should have a thick consistency. Taste, season, and stir in the cilantro (if using). Set aside.

3 Roll out the pastry on a lightly floured surface to a thickness of ¼in (5mm). Cut eight 6in (15cm) circles and wet the edges. Divide the lamb between the circles of pastry, spooning it onto one side. Fold the pastry over to make a half-moon and set them on a lightly oiled baking sheet. Brush with the beaten egg and sprinkle with onion seeds (if using). Bake for 30–40 minutes or until golden. Remove and leave to cool a little before serving.

CHEESE AND ASPARAGUS TURNOVERS

These flaky, crumbly parcels are perfect for a light lunch or picnic on a sunny summer's day.

salt and freshly ground pepper
3½oz (100g) asparagus spears, cut into ½in (1cm) lengths
1¾oz (50g) aged Cheddar cheese, grated
3 tbsp snipped fresh chives

14oz (400g) gluten-free rough puff pastry (see pages 46–7)
gluten-free all-purpose flour, for dusting
1 large egg, beaten, to glaze
ground paprika, to dust
salad leaves, to serve

1 Bring a small pan of salted water to the boil and blanch the asparagus tips for 2 minutes. Drain and refresh in cold water. Drain again and cool. Mix the asparagus with the cheese, chives, and plenty of pepper. Set aside.

2 Carefully roll out the pastry on a lightly floured surface to form a 12in (30cm) square, ¼in (5mm) in thickness. Trim the edges, then cut out 9 equal squares. Brush the edges of each square with water. Divide the asparagus filling between the squares, heaping it over one diagonal half of each. Fold the pastry over the filling and pinch the edges together to seal. Use a knife to flute and crimp the edges together.

3 Place the triangles well apart on a large baking sheet. Make a steam hole on top of each, then glaze with beaten egg and dust with paprika. Bake for 20–25 minutes or until golden and risen. Serve warm or cold with salad leaves.

Variation
Vary the cheese and herbs if you like—goat cheese and mint would taste great with the asparagus.

MAKES	9
PREP	40 mins
	PLUS CHILLING
COOK	20–25 mins

GUIDELINES PER TURNOVER

● ● ○ Calories
● ● ● Saturated fat
● ○ ○ Salt

STATISTICS PER TURNOVER

Energy 200kcals/840kJ

Protein 5g

Fat 13g
Saturated fat 6.5g

Carbohydrate 15.5g
Sugar 0.8g

Fiber 0.3g

Salt 0.5g

NUTRIENT BOOST
Asparagus is a source of folic acid, vital for women planning a pregnancy.

SPANAKOPITA

Rolling out gluten-free pastry thin enough for filo is difficult for the home cook. This version works just as well with thin shortcrust and saves you the Herculean challenge!

SERVES 6
PREP 20 mins
COOK 1 hour

GUIDELINES PER SERVING

● ● ○ Calories
● ● ● Saturated fat
● ● ● Salt

STATISTICS PER SLICE

Energy 524kcals/2182kJ

Protein 20g

Fat 35g
Saturated fat 13g

Carbohydrate 33g
Sugar 4g

Fiber 6.5g

Salt 2.9g

GREAT FOR KIDS

1 tbsp olive oil
½ onion, very finely chopped
2¼lb (1kg) spinach
salt and freshly ground pepper
9oz (250g) feta cheese, crumbled
pinch of freshly grated nutmeg
handful of dill, finely chopped
3 large eggs
14oz (400g) gluten-free shortcrust pastry
  (see pages 44–5)

gluten-free all-purpose flour, for dusting
1 large egg, beaten, to glaze
tomato salad, to serve

SPECIAL EQUIPMENT
8in (20cm) square, 1¾in (4cm) deep
  baking dish or pan

1 Preheat the oven to 400°F (200°C). Heat the oil in a large frying pan, add the onion, and cook for 2–3 minutes. Season to taste. In a separate large pan, cook the spinach in 4 batches of 9oz (250g) each on low heat for 4–5 minutes until it wilts. Remove and set aside.

2 In a bowl, stir together the feta, nutmeg, and dill, and season to taste with more pepper. Add the eggs and combine. Squeeze any excess water from the spinach, then add this and the onion to the feta mixture and mix.

3 Halve the pastry and roll out each piece as thinly as possible on a lightly floured surface, or between sheets of plastic wrap, if easier. Cut a square the size of the base of the dish or pan, trim any extra pastry, and neaten the edges. Spoon a little of the mixture into the bottom of the dish and add a layer of pastry, patching up any holes. Spoon the rest of the mixture on top and finish with a layer of pastry. Brush with the beaten egg to cover and bake in the oven for 30–40 minutes until golden. Cool for 15 minutes before slicing into 6 rectangles and serving with a tomato salad.

Variations
Add some toasted pine nuts to the spinach mix or a pinch of cayenne pepper for a little heat. For a lighter dish, substitute half the feta with ricotta.

SMOKED SALMON AND CREAM CHEESE PICNIC PIES

Baked in a muffin pan, these delightful little pies are perfect for a summer picnic or buffet lunch.

MAKES 12
PREP 30 mins
COOK 40 mins

1lb 5oz (600g) gluten-free shortcrust pastry (see pages 44–5, scaling up quantities by one half)
gluten-free all-purpose flour, for dusting
10oz (300g) cream cheese
3–4 tbsp crème fraîche
10oz (300g) smoked salmon slices, chopped, or use trimmings
handful of dill, finely chopped

1–2 tbsp canned chopped green chiles
salt and freshly ground pepper
1 egg, beaten

SPECIAL EQUIPMENT
12-hole 1¾in (3cm) deep nonstick muffin pan
4in (10cm) and 3in (7.5cm) round cutters

GUIDELINES PER SERVING

● ● ● Calories
● ● ● Saturated fat
● ● ● Salt

STATISTICS PER PIE

Energy 392kcals/1632kJ

Protein 11g

Fat 29g
Saturated fat 13g

Carbohydrate 22g
Sugar 0.5g

Fiber 1.5g

Salt 1.9g

1 Preheat the oven to 375°F (190°C). Roll out two-thirds of the pastry on a lightly floured surface to a thickness of ¼in (5mm). Using the larger cutter, cut out 12 circles and use them to line the lightly oiled muffin pan, patching up any holes. You will have to keep gathering and re-rolling. Put in the fridge while you mix the filling.

2 In a bowl, mix together the cream cheese, crème fraîche, smoked salmon, dill, green chiles (if using), and season well with salt and pepper.

3 Roll out the remaining pastry as before and cut out the tops using the smaller cutter. Remove the muffin pan from the fridge and divide the mixture between the pastry crusts. Wet the rims of the pastry crusts with water, cover with the tops, and pinch the edges to secure. Make a steam hole in each one and brush with the beaten egg. Bake in the oven for 30–40 minutes until golden, then remove and leave to cool completely before turning each one out of the pan.

CHICKEN AND PARSLEY POT PIES

These pies are great to make after a roast chicken dinner or to use up leftover ham. They can be prepared ahead and stored in the refrigerator overnight before glazing and baking.

SERVES 4
PREP 20 mins
PLUS CHILLING
COOK 25–30 mins
FREEZE 1 month

GUIDELINES PER SERVING

● ● ○ Calories
● ● ● Saturated fat
● ● ○ Salt

STATISTICS PER SERVING

Energy 703kcals/2942kJ

Protein 43g

Fat 39g
Saturated fat 19g

Carbohydrate 46g
Sugar 9g

Fiber 4g

Salt 2.3g

GREAT FOR KIDS

5½oz (150g) frozen fava beans, or 14oz can corn, drained
4 tbsp butter
1 onion, finely chopped
salt and freshly ground black pepper
½ cup gluten-free all-purpose flour, plus extra for dusting
1¾ cups milk
1 tsp Dijon mustard
10oz (300g) cooked chicken, cut into chunky bite-sized pieces
5½oz (150g) gluten-free cooked ham, cubed

3 tbsp finely chopped curly or flat-leaf parsley
1 tbsp finely chopped marjoram leaves (optional)
10oz (300g) gluten-free rough puff pastry (see pages 46–7) or shortcrust pastry (see pages 44–5)
1 large egg, beaten
boiled potatoes and carrots, to serve

SPECIAL EQUIPMENT
4 x 10oz (300ml) or 1 x 1 quart baking dishes

1 Preheat the oven to 400°F (200°C). Place the fava beans in a bowl and pour over boiling water. Leave for 5–8 minutes, drain, and set aside.

2 Melt the butter in a large pan over low heat, add the onion, season, and cook for 5–7 minutes until soft and transparent. Remove from the heat and stir in the flour. Pour in a little milk, stir, put back on low heat, and gradually add the milk, stirring as you go. You may need to switch to a hand whisk for a lump-free sauce. Bring to a boil, then reduce to a simmer. Cook for 2–3 minutes, remove from the heat, and stir in the mustard, chicken, ham, herbs, and fava beans. Season and set aside to cool.

3 Roll out the pastry onto a lightly floured surface. Cut out 4 small lids or 1 large lid 1½in (4cm) larger than the dishes. Set aside. Spoon the filling into the dishes and wet the edges. Drape the lids and press to secure. Make a hole in the top of each pie. Brush with half the beaten egg and chill for 20 minutes, then brush with the remaining egg and bake for 25–30 minutes until golden; cooking a large pie may take a little longer. Remove and serve.

SQUASH AND CIDER COBBLER

SERVES 6
PREP 20 mins
COOK 1 hour

Autumnal vegetables are simmered in cider and topped with herby dough—great for a Halloween supper.

GUIDELINES PER SERVING

● ● ○ Calories

● ● ● Saturated fat

● ○ ○ Salt

STATISTICS PER SERVING

Energy 389kcals/1632kJ

Protein 8g

Fat 19g
Saturated fat 9g

Carbohydrate 45g
Sugar 12.5g

Fiber 7.5g

Salt 1.3g

1 butternut squash, halved, seeded,
  peeled, and cut into bite-sized cubes
2 tbsp olive oil
pinch of freshly grated nutmeg
few sage leaves, roughly chopped
salt and freshly ground pepper
1 onion, finely chopped
2 garlic cloves, finely chopped
2 leeks, sliced
14oz (400g) can chopped tomatoes

1¼ cups cider
1⅓ cups gluten-free all-purpose flour
3 tsp gluten-free baking powder
7 tbsp cold butter, cubed
few sprigs of rosemary, finely chopped
⅓ cup buttermilk
7oz (200g) Savoy cabbage, cored
  and roughly chopped
baked potatoes, to serve (optional)

1 Preheat the oven to 400°F (200°C). Put the squash in a roasting pan, add half the oil, and toss to coat thoroughly. Add the nutmeg and sage, season well, and toss again. Roast for 15 minutes, then remove and set aside.

2 Heat the remaining oil in a flameproof casserole or ovenproof pot, add the onion, and cook for 2–3 minutes. Season to taste, stir in the garlic and leeks, and cook on low heat for 2 more minutes. Add the tomatoes and cider, then add 1¾ cups hot water, or enough to cover the vegetables. Bring to a boil, reduce to a simmer, and stir through the squash. Simmer gently for 5–10 minutes.

3 For the cobbler topping, add the flour, baking powder, and a pinch of salt to a bowl and mix. Rub in the butter until it forms crumbs and stir in the rosemary. Add the buttermilk, a little at a time, until it forms a soft dough. Alternatively, make it in a food processor, adding the buttermilk a little at a time and pulsing until the dough forms.

4 Stir the cabbage into the simmering vegetables, then tear large lumps of the dough, flatten slightly, and sit on top of the vegetables. Bake for 25–30 minutes or until golden and bubbling. Cover loosely with foil if it starts to brown too much. Serve alone or with baked potatoes.

CORNMEAL CRUST CHILE PIE

A hot and spicy ground beef mixture topped with golden cornmeal pastry.

SERVES   4
PREP   20 mins
COOK   1 hour

¾ cup gluten-free all-purpose flour, plus extra to dust
¾ cup fine cornmeal or polenta
pinch of salt
2 tsp xanthan gum
7 tbsp cold butter, cubed
1 large egg yolk
1 tbsp olive oil
1lb 2oz (500g) ground beef
1 onion, finely chopped
salt and freshly ground pepper

1 jalapeño chile, seeded and finely chopped
1 red bell pepper, finely chopped
14oz (400g) can corn, drained
pinch of cayenne pepper (optional)
⅓ cup gluten-free beer
⅓ cup hot gluten-free vegetable stock
3 tomatoes, seeded and chopped

SPECIAL EQUIPMENT
10in (26cm) round, deep pie dish

GUIDELINES PER SERVING

● ● ●   Calories
● ● ●   Saturated fat
●   Salt

STATISTICS PER SERVING

Energy 801kcals/3342kJ

Protein 34g

Fat 44g
Saturated fat 22g

Carbohydrate 62g
Sugar 12g

Fiber 5g

Salt 1.4g

1 For the pastry, mix the flour, cornmeal, salt, and xanthan, then rub in the butter until it forms crumbs. Add the yolk and 1 tablespoon water and mix until it forms a dough. Wrap in plastic wrap and set aside.

2 For the filling, heat the oil in a large frying pan, add the ground beef, and cook on medium heat for 5–6 minutes, stirring until the meat is no longer pink. Remove from the pan, leaving the fat behind, and set aside. Add the onion to the pan, season, and cook on low heat for 2–3 minutes. Stir in the chile and cook for 1 more minute, then add the pepper and cook for 5 minutes until it softens. Return the ground beef to the pan, add the corn and cayenne (if using), and stir. Increase the heat, add the beer, and boil for 2–3 minutes, then add the stock and simmer, uncovered, over medium heat for 10–15 minutes; the mixture shouldn't be too runny. Stir in the tomatoes, season to taste, spoon into the pie dish, and set aside.

3 Preheat the oven to 400°F (200°C). Roll out the pastry on a lightly floured surface, wet the ridge of the pie dish, and drape the pastry over the top. Press the edges to seal and trim. Make a steam hole and bake for 30 minutes, or until pale golden. Serve on its own or with steamed carrots.

PORK PIE

A great British classic with a unique pastry. It's best to handle the pastry while it's hot and pliable.

SERVES 6
PREP 20 mins
PLUS CHILLING
COOK 1 hour 10-15 mins
FREEZE 1 month

GUIDELINES PER SERVING

● ● ○ Calories

● ● ● Saturated fat

● ● ○ Salt

STATISTICS PER SLICE

Energy 518kcals/2171kJ

Protein 28g

Fat 26g
Saturated fat 10g

Carbohydrate 42g
Sugar 1.3g

Fiber 2.7g

Salt 1.7g

1lb 2oz (500g) pork shoulder, cubed
3½oz (100g) unsmoked back
  bacon, diced
1 tsp dried sage
½ tsp ground mace
¼ tsp ground allspice
salt and freshly ground pepper
oil, for greasing

1lb 2oz (500g) gluten-free hot
  water crust pastry (see page 47)
1 large egg
pickles and salad, to serve

SPECIAL EQUIPMENT
  8in (20cm) springform cake pan

1 For the filling, place the pork, bacon, sage, mace, allspice, and seasoning in a food processor. Pulse until the meat is finely chopped. Chill.

2 Preheat the oven to 400°F (200°C) and put a baking sheet in to heat up. Lightly grease the base and sides of the pan. Roll out two-thirds of the pastry between 2 sheets of parchment paper to a 12in (30cm) wide circle. Press it into the base and sides of the pan—there should be ¾in (2cm) of pastry standing up taller than the pan. Trim any excess pastry.

3 Spoon in the filling, compacting it down. Roll out the remaining pastry between the parchment paper and cut to make a 8in (20cm) lid. Place on top of the filling. Beat the egg with a pinch of salt and glaze the pie. Bend the ¾in (2cm) of pastry down and over the lid. Roll and turn over to form a seal, crimp with a knife, and make a steam hole in the center. Glaze with the egg, place on the hot baking sheet, and bake for 40 minutes.

4 Remove the pie and cool slightly. Loosen the sides with a butter knife and remove the sides of the pan. Reduce the temperature to 375°F (190°C). Place the pie back on the sheet and glaze the sides with the beaten egg. Bake for 30–35 minutes. Remove, cool, and chill. Cut into wedges and serve with pickles and a crisp salad.

GALA LOAF PIE

SERVES 8
PREP 40 mins
COOK 2 hours

A great pie to make ahead for a picnic. Serve with a dollop of English mustard or some homemade chutney.

GUIDELINES PER SERVING

● ● ● Calories

● ● ● Saturated fat

● ○ ○ Salt

STATISTICS PER SERVING

Energy 642kcals/2684kJ

Protein 28g

Fat 39g
Saturated fat 12g

Carbohydrate 44g
Sugar 2.5g

Fiber 2.6g

Salt 0.3g

1lb 10oz (750g) gluten-free hot
   water crust pastry, freshly made (see
   page 47, doubling quantities)
gluten-free all-purpose flour, for dusting
9oz (250g) gluten-free pork sausages,
   casings removed
6oz (175g) pork tenderloin, diced
12oz (350g) gluten-free cooked
   ham, diced
1 onion, finely chopped
bunch of flat-leaf parsley,
   finely chopped

1 tsp paprika
1/4 tsp ground allspice
1/4 tsp cayenne pepper
salt and freshly ground pepper
2 large eggs, lightly beaten
4 large hard-boiled eggs, peeled
1 tsp powdered gelatin

SPECIAL EQUIPMENT
long, shallow 9 x 5in (23 x 13cm)
   nonstick loaf pan

1 Preheat the oven to 400°F (200°C). Set aside one-third of the warm
pastry for the lid. Roll out the remaining pastry on a lightly floured surface.
Use it to line the pan with an overhang, patching up any holes. Line with
parchment paper and baking beans and bake for 15 minutes. Remove the
beans and paper and return to the oven for 5 minutes to crisp up.

2 In a large bowl, use your fingers to mix the sausage, pork, ham, onion,
parsley, and spices together until well combined, then season. Add half the
beaten egg and mix again. Spoon half the mixture into the pan and pack it
down evenly. Place the hard-boiled eggs lengthwise down the middle.
Spoon over the remaining mixture and press so it's tightly packed.

3 Roll out the remaining pastry to make the lid. Brush the sides of the pastry
crust with beaten egg, set the lid on top, pinch to secure, and trim. Brush
the lid with the remaining egg. Make a fairly large steam hole in the center.
Bake for 30 minutes, then reduce the temperature to 350°F (180°C) and
cook for 1 1/2 hours. Cover with foil if it starts to brown. Remove and leave to
cool slightly. Now, mix the gelatin with 1 1/4 cups water and pour the mixture
through the hole. Leave to cool for another 20 minutes, loosen edges with a
butter knife, and cool completely before removing from pan.

GAME PIE

A rich, comforting pie to keep out the cold on a crisp winter's day. Serve with spiced, slow-cooked red cabbage.

SERVES 6
PREP 30 mins
COOK 1 hour 40 mins

GUIDELINES PER SERVING

● ● ○ Calories
● ● ● Saturated fat
● ● ◐ Salt

STATISTICS PER SLICE

Energy 618kcals/2585kJ

Protein 43g

Fat 33g
Saturated fat 12g

Carbohydrate 31g
Sugar 2g

Fiber 3g

Salt 1.9g

1–2 tbsp olive oil
4½oz (125g) bacon, chopped
2lb (900g) mixed game, such as
  pheasant, rabbit, and venison,
  cut into chunky bite-sized pieces
salt and freshly ground pepper
1 onion, finely chopped
3 celery stalks, finely chopped
¾ cup red wine
few sprigs of rosemary
1 bay leaf
1⅔ cups hot gluten-free vegetable stock

2 tbsp butter
9oz (250g) cremini mushrooms,
  roughly chopped
14oz (400g) gluten-free shortcrust pastry
  (see pages 44–5)
gluten-free all-purpose flour, to dust
1 large egg, lightly beaten, to glaze
mashed potato, red cabbage, and
  gluten-free gravy, to serve

SPECIAL EQUIPMENT
large pie dish

1 Preheat the oven to 375°F (190°C). Heat the oil in a large frying pan, add the bacon, and fry on medium-high heat for 5–6 minutes until golden, then remove and set aside. Season the game meat, add to the pan in batches, and cook until browned all over, adding more oil if needed. Remove the meat and set aside. Now add the onion and celery to the pan and cook on medium heat for 5–6 minutes until beginning to soften. Then increase the heat, add the wine, and boil for 2–3 minutes. Add the rosemary and bay leaf and pour over the stock. Return the meat to the pan and simmer gently for 40 minutes or until tender. Season and remove the bay leaf and rosemary.

2 Heat the butter in a frying pan, add the mushrooms, and cook on medium-high heat for 5–6 minutes until golden, then stir them into the meat mixture. Spoon the pie filling into the pie dish.

3 Roll out the pastry on a lightly floured surface to a thickness of ¼in (5mm). Wet the rim of the pie dish with water, top with the pastry, trim away any excess, and pinch to secure. Make a couple of steam holes in the top, brush with the egg, and bake in the oven for 40 minutes or until golden. Serve with mashed potato, red cabbage, and gluten-free gravy.

SWEET TARTS AND PIES

LEMON TART

SERVES	8
PREP	30 mins
COOK	1 hour 10 mins

Take care to ensure there are no holes in the pastry crust or all that delicious lemon cream filling may leak out.

GUIDELINES PER SERVING

● ● ● Calories

● ● ● Saturated fat

● ● ○ Salt

STATISTICS PER SLICE

Energy 535kcals/2232kJ

Protein 8g

Fat 35g
Saturated fat 16g

Carbohydrate 47g
Sugar 26g

Fiber 1.5g

Salt 0.7g

14oz (400g) gluten-free shortcrust pastry
  (see pages 44–5)
gluten-free all-purpose flour, to dust
confectioner's sugar, to dust

FOR THE FILLING
5 large eggs
¾ cup granulated sugar

1⅛ cups heavy cream
½ cup lemon juice and grated zest
  of 4 lemons

SPECIAL EQUIPMENT
8in (20cm) round loose-bottomed
  tart pan

1 Preheat the oven to 400°F (200°C). Roll out the pastry on a lightly floured surface to a thickness of ¼in (5mm). Line the pan with the pastry, patching up any holes. Trim any surplus and neaten. Line with parchment paper and baking beans and bake for 15 minutes. Remove the beans and paper, and return to the oven for 5 minutes to crisp up. Set aside to cool.

2 While the tart is baking, prepare the filling. Add the eggs to a bowl and whisk gently. Add the sugar and mix well, then pour in the cream and the lemon juice and stir. Strain the mixture through a nylon sieve so it is smooth, then stir through the lemon zest. Reduce the oven temperature to 300°F (150°C).

3 Set the pan on a baking sheet, then pour the lemon mixture into the pastry crust to fill. You can put it in the oven, pull out the shelf a bit, and pour it in to save any spills. Bake in the oven for 50 minutes or until the filling is just starting to set; it will continue to set once out of the oven. Remove and leave to cool. To serve, dust with confectioner's sugar.

Variation

ORANGE TART Substitute the lemon for the zest of 2 oranges and ½ cup fresh orange juice, then dust dark cocoa powder over the cooked tart to serve.

STRAWBERRY TARTS

This recipe for easy crème pâtissière tarts can be adapted by topping with whatever fruit is in season.

MAKES 6
PREP 35 mins
PLUS CHILLING
COOK 20–25 mins

GUIDELINES PER SERVING

● ● ● Calories
● ● ● Saturated fat
● ● ○ Salt

STATISTICS PER TART

Energy 542kcals/2255kJ

Protein 7g

Fat 34g
Saturated fat 19g

Carbohydrate 52g
Sugar 22g

Fiber 1g

Salt 1g

1⅓ cups gluten-free all-purpose flour,
   plus extra to dust
1 tsp xanthan gum
2 tbsp confectioner's sugar
pinch of salt
7 tbsp butter, cubed
zest and juice of 1 large lemon
1 large egg, beaten, plus 3 egg yolks
¼ cup granulated sugar

3 tbsp cornstarch
1¼ cups milk
⅔ cup heavy cream
½ tsp pure vanilla extract
14oz (400g) ripe strawberries, hulled and
   sliced or halved

SPECIAL EQUIPMENT
6 x 5in (12cm) loose-bottomed fluted
   tart pans

1 Pulse the first 5 ingredients and the lemon zest in a food processor until the mixture resembles bread crumbs. Add the whole beaten egg and 3 tablespoons lemon juice and pulse until a ball of dough forms. Lightly knead it on a floured surface, wrap in plastic wrap, and chill for 10 minutes.

2 Preheat the oven to 400°F (200°C). Cut the pastry into 4 pieces and roll each out to a thickness of ¼in (5mm), then line 4 pans with the pastry. Re-roll the trimmings and line the other 2 pans in the same way. Prick the base of each with a fork. Line each tart with waxed paper and fill with baking beans, and bake for 15 minutes. Remove the paper and baking beans and bake for 5–10 minutes more or until pale golden. Set aside to cool.

3 For the crème pâtissière, beat the egg yolks, granulated sugar, and cornstarch with a splash of milk to form a smooth paste. Heat the remaining milk to just below boiling in a small pan, pour into the cornstarch mix, stirring, then return to the rinsed-out pan. Bring to a boil, stirring continuously, and cook for 1 minute. Spoon into a bowl, place damp waxed paper directly on the surface to prevent skin from forming and cool completely. Once cool, whip the heavy cream until soft peaks form. Fold into the crème pâtissière with the vanilla extract. To serve, spoon the crème pâtissière into each tart crust. Arrange the strawberries on top and serve.

APRICOT FRANGIPANE TART

An impressive dessert of crisp buttery pastry filled with a sweet almond paste and topped with apricots.

SERVES 10
PREP 20 mins
COOK 25–35 mins

GUIDELINES PER SERVING

● ● ● Calories
● ● ● Saturated fat
● ● ○ Salt

STATISTICS PER SLICE

Energy 499kcals/2079kJ

Protein 7.5g

Fat 37.4g
Saturated fat 14g

Carbohydrate 33g
Sugar 25g

Fiber 1g

Salt 0.6g

9oz (250g) gluten-free shortcrust pastry
  (see pages 44–5)
gluten-free all-purpose flour, for dusting

FOR THE FILLING
14 tbsp butter
¾ cup granulated sugar
1 tsp pure vanilla extract

5 large egg yolks
7oz (200g) ground almonds
4–5 ripe apricots, halved and pitted
crème fraîche, to serve

SPECIAL EQUIPMENT
10in (25cm) tart pan

1 Preheat the oven to 400°F (200°C). Roll the pastry out on a lightly floured surface to a 14in (35cm) circle, about ⅛in (3mm) thick. Place it into the base of the pan, with the edges overlapping, patching up any rips in the pastry. Ease it into the corners and sides of the pan, and trim the edges. Prick the base with a fork and line with parchment paper and baking beans. Bake for about 15 minutes, until the edges begin to turn pale golden. Remove from the oven, take out the beans and paper, and return to the oven for another 5 minutes. Set aside. Reduce the oven temperature to 350°F (180°C).

2 To make the filling, beat the butter in a large bowl with an electric mixer for 2 minutes. Add the sugar and beat until pale and creamy. Add the vanilla extract and mix. Now add the egg yolks, one at a time, and beat gently until they are all incorporated. Gently stir in the ground almonds.

3 Pour the filling into the pastry crust and arrange the apricots, cut side down, in the mixture, pressing them in slightly so they fit snugly. Bake for 25–35 minutes, or until the mixture is cooked and golden. Leave to cool and serve at room temperature with crème fraîche.

Variations
Try other seasonal fruits like peaches, blackberries, or pitted cherries. For a sweeter tart, spread the pastry base with strawberry or raspberry jam before filling.

BANOFFEE PIE

This version of the modern classic is incredibly rich and sweet, just as it should be, and is great for a party.

SERVES 8
PREP 20 mins
PLUS CHILLING
COOK 5 mins

GUIDELINES PER SERVING

● ● ● Calories
● ● ● Saturated fat
● ● ○ Salt

STATISTICS PER SLICE

Energy 665kcals/2785kJ

Protein 7g

Fat 44g
Saturated fat 27g

Carbohydrate 60g
Sugar 44g

Fiber 0.6g

Salt 0.7g

9oz (250g) gluten-free plain cookies or
  shortbread cookies (see page 333)
7 tbsp unsalted butter, melted
  and cooled

FOR THE CARAMEL
4 tbsp unsalted butter
¼ cup soft light brown sugar
14oz (400g) can condensed milk

FOR THE TOPPING
2 large, ripe bananas
1 cup heavy cream
a little dark chocolate, for grating

SPECIAL EQUIPMENT
9in (22cm) round springform cake pan
  or loose-bottomed tart pan

1 Line a 9in (22cm) round springform cake pan or loose-bottomed tart pan with parchment paper. Put the cookies in a plastic bag and crush with a rolling pin. Mix the cookies with the butter, pour into the pan, and press down. Cover and refrigerate.

2 To make the caramel, melt the butter and sugar in a small, heavy-bottomed saucepan over medium heat. Add the condensed milk and bring to a boil. Reduce the heat and simmer for 2–3 minutes, stirring. It will thicken and take on a light caramel color. Pour over the base and leave to set.

3 Once set, remove from the pan and transfer to a serving plate. Slice the bananas into ¼in (5mm) disks on the diagonal, and use them to cover the caramel.

4 Whip the cream and smooth it over the pie. Decorate with grated chocolate and chocolate curls, made by paring chocolate with a vegetable peeler.

 Cook's Tip
This pie will keep in an airtight container in the refrigerator for 2 days, and can be frozen for up to 8 weeks.

CHERRY LATTICE PIE

Sweet plump cherries encased in crisp gluten-free pastry with an impressive looking lattice crust.

SERVES 6
PREP 30 mins
COOK 1 hour

GUIDELINES PER SERVING

● ● ● Calories
● ● ○ Saturated fat
● ● ○ Salt

STATISTICS PER SLICE

Energy 470kcals/1967kJ

Protein 6g

Fat 20g
Saturated fat 6g

Carbohydrate 65g
Sugar 35g

Fiber 3.5g

Salt 0.7g

2lb (900g) cherries, stoned
juice of ½ lemon
1 vanilla bean, split lengthwise
⅓ cup granulated sugar, plus extra
  to sprinkle
1 tbsp cornstarch
14oz (400g) gluten-free shortcrust pastry
  (see pages 44–5)

gluten-free plain all-purpose, for dusting
1 large egg, beaten, to glaze
cream or gluten-free ice cream
  (see page 299), to serve

SPECIAL EQUIPMENT
8in (20cm) round pie pan

1 Preheat the oven to 375°F (190°C). Toss the cherries with the lemon juice and add them to a pan along with the vanilla bean. Sprinkle in the sugar and simmer gently on low heat, stirring occasionally, until it dissolves.

2 Continue to simmer on low heat until the cherries begin to soften. Mix the cornstarch with a little water until it forms a paste, stir it into the cherry mixture, and cook for 5–8 minutes or until the mixture begins to thicken. Remove and set aside to cool completely.

3 Roll out two-thirds of the pastry on a lightly floured surface to a thickness of ¼in (5mm). Use it to line the pan, draping the pastry over the edge. Remove the vanilla bean from the cherries and spoon them into the crust.

4 Roll out the remaining pastry and cut 8 long strips to lay over the pie; each strip should be about ½in (1cm) wide and ¼in (5mm) thick. Wet the edges of the pastry with water, drape 4 strips one way, and 4 the other way for a crisscross lattice effect. Press around the edges to secure and trim off any excess. Brush the pastry with the beaten egg and sprinkle the lattice top with the sugar.

5 Bake for 40–45 minutes, covering loosely with foil if the pastry starts to burn. Remove and leave to cool in the pan for 15 minutes. Transfer to a wire rack to cool completely. Slice and serve warm with cream or ice cream.

PUMPKIN TART

If serving this American classic at a Halloween party, you could make smaller individual tarts and drizzle them with dark chocolate.

SERVES   8
PREP   20 mins
COOK   1½ hours

14oz (400g) gluten-free shortcrust pastry
  (see pages 44–5)
gluten-free all-purpose flour, for dusting
pinch of ground cinnamon
cream, to serve (optional)

drizzle of sunflower or vegetable oil
¾ cup evaporated milk
¾ cup granulated sugar
2 large eggs
2 tsp pumpkin pie spice

FOR THE FILLING

1 small pumpkin or 1 medium butternut
  squash, peeled, halved, seeded, and
  roughly chopped

SPECIAL EQUIPMENT

8in (20cm) round, loose-bottomed
  tart pan

GUIDELINES PER SERVING

● ● ●   Calories

● ● ○   Saturated fat

● ● ○   Salt

STATISTICS PER SLICE

Energy 404kcals/1695kJ

Protein 7g

Fat 20g
Saturated fat 6.5g

Carbohydrate 49g
Sugar 28g

Fiber 2g

Salt 0.7g

1 Preheat the oven to 400°F (200°C). Add the pumpkin or squash to a large roasting pan and toss with the oil, using your hands to coat. Roast for 25 minutes or until soft, then remove and transfer to a food processor and purée until smooth. Transfer to a bowl and leave to cool. Drain the purée in a sieve if it looks a little watery.

2 Roll out the pastry on a lightly floured surface to a thickness of ¼in (5mm), then line the tart pan with it, patching up any holes. Trim away the surplus and neaten. Line with parchment paper and baking beans, and bake in the oven for 15 minutes. Remove the beans and paper, then return to the oven for another 5 minutes to crisp up.

3 In another bowl, mix together the milk, sugar, eggs, and pumpkin pie spice, then pour into the pumpkin or squash purée and stir well to combine. Pour the mixture into the pastry crust and smooth the top, then sprinkle over the cinnamon and bake in the oven for 40–50 minutes until set. If it starts to color too much, cover loosely with foil. Leave to cool and continue to set in the pan before releasing, then serve at room temperature with a trickle of cream, if you like.

GREAT FOR KIDS

CHOCOLATE MOCHA TART

SERVES	8
PREP	20 mins
COOK	40 mins

A chocolate tart for grown ups! This version uses coffee-flavored chocolate, but you could vary it with different flavors or chocolate with nuts to add texture.

GUIDELINES PER SERVING

●●● Calories

●●● Saturated fat

●●○ Salt

STATISTICS PER SLICE

Energy 516kcals/2152kJ

Protein 7g

Fat 34g
Saturated fat 16g

Carbohydrate 46g
Sugar 24g

Fiber 2g

Salt 0.8g

14oz (400g) gluten-free shortcrust pastry
  (see pages 44–5)
gluten-free all-purpose flour, for dusting
confectioner's sugar or dark cocoa
  powder, for dusting
crème fraîche, to serve

FOR THE FILLING
3½oz (100g) dark chocolate (at least
  70% cocoa solids), broken into
  even pieces

3½oz (100g) coffee-flavored dark
  chocolate (at least 70% cocoa solids),
  broken into even pieces
7 tbsp butter
3 large eggs
⅓ cup granulated sugar

SPECIAL EQUIPMENT
5 x 14in (12 x 35cm) rectangular
  loose-bottomed tart pan

1 Preheat the oven to 400°F (200°C). Roll out the pastry on a lightly floured surface to a thickness of ¼in (5mm). Line the pan with the pastry, patching up any holes, and trim away any surplus. Line with parchment paper and baking beans, and bake for 15 minutes. Remove the beans and paper and return to the oven for 5 minutes to crisp up. Remove the tart crust from the oven and reduce the temperature to 340°F (170°C).

2 For the filling, add the chocolate and butter to a heatproof bowl, sit it over a pan of barely simmering water, and stir occasionally until melted. Remove and leave to cool. In another bowl, whisk together the eggs and sugar using an electric whisk for 5 minutes or until thick and creamy.

3 Fold the cooled chocolate mixture into the egg mixture until combined, then pour it into the pastry crust. Bake in the oven for 15–20 minutes until set and the top just forms a crust; it should still be slightly wobbly. Remove from the oven and leave to cool completely before releasing from the pan; it will continue to set. Dust with confectioner's sugar or dark cocoa powder, slice, and serve with crème fraîche.

TREACLE TART

Made with sweet shortcrust pastry, this most English of tarts is a great family favorite.

1½ cups gluten-free all-purpose flour,
  plus extra for dusting
2 tbsp confectioner's sugar
1 tsp xanthan gum
7 tbsp butter, cubed
pinch of salt
2 large eggs, beaten
cream, to serve

FOR THE FILLING
1¾ cups corn syrup
7oz (200g) gluten-free white bread,
  crusts removed
2 large eggs, beaten
zest and juice of ½ lemon
½ tsp ground ginger

SPECIAL EQUIPMENT
9in (23cm) round, loose-bottomed
  tart pan

SERVES 8
PREP 30 mins
  PLUS CHILLING
COOK 55 mins–1 hour

GUIDELINES PER SERVING

● ● ●   Calories
● ● ●   Saturated fat
● ● ●   Salt

STATISTICS PER SLICE

Energy 455kcals/1912kJ

Protein 7g

Fat 14.5g
Saturated fat 7.5g

Carbohydrate 73g
Sugar 42g

Fiber 0.5g

Salt 1.4g

1 Preheat the oven to 400°F (200°C). Pulse the flour, confectioner's sugar, xanthan, butter, and salt in a food processor until the mix looks like crumbs. Add 1 egg and 1 tablespoon cold water and continue to pulse until the mixture forms a ball of dough. Lightly knead it on a floured surface, wrap in plastic wrap, and chill for 10 minutes.

2 Gently roll out the pastry on a lightly floured surface, place it over the pan, and push it into the base and sides. Trim the edges. Prick the base with a fork, fill with parchment paper and baking beans, place on a baking sheet, and bake for 15 minutes. Remove the paper and beans, brush with the remaining egg, and bake for a further 5 minutes.

3 Reduce the oven temperature to 350°F (180°C). For the filling, warm the syrup in a small pan. Place the bread in a food processor and pulse to make fine bread crumbs. In a large bowl, beat the eggs, lemon zest and juice, and ginger. Add the bread crumbs and syrup and beat again. Pour the mixture into the pastry crust and bake for 35–40 minutes or until the filling is golden and set. Serve warm or cold with cream.

BLACKBERRY AND APPLE PIE

A classic dessert using late summer fruits. Omit the spices and serve with vanilla ice cream to make this perfect for kids.

SERVES 6
PREP 15 mins
PLUS CHILLING
COOK 40–50 mins
FREEZE 3 months

GUIDELINES PER SERVING

● ● ● Calories

● ● ○ Saturated fat

● ○ ○ Salt

STATISTICS PER SLICE

Energy 323kcals/1362kJ

Protein 4.5g

Fat 13g
Saturated fat 4g

Carbohydrate 47g
Sugar 30g

Fiber 5g

Salt 0.5g

GREAT FOR KIDS

1lb (450g) gluten-free shortcrust pastry
   (see pages 44–5)
gluten-free all-purpose flour, for dusting
1 egg, lightly beaten
1 tbsp granulated sugar

FOR THE FILLING
3 cooking apples, peeled, cored,
   and sliced
1 star anise

1 vanilla bean, split lengthwise
pinch of freshly grated nutmeg
1/2 cup brown sugar
9oz (250g) blackberries
zest of 1/2 lemon or 1/2 orange

SPECIAL EQUIPMENT
7in (18cm) round pie dish

1 Set aside one-third of the pastry for the lid. On a lightly floured surface, roll out the remaining pastry into a circle large enough to line the pie dish and overlap the sides. Chill in the refrigerator while you prepare the filling.

2 Place the apple slices in a pan with 6 tablespoons cold water, add the star anise, vanilla bean, nutmeg, and half the sugar, and heat over very low heat for 10–15 minutes, until the apples begin to soften. Remove from the heat and set aside for 20 minutes to allow the flavors to infuse.

3 Sprinkle the pastry base with the remaining sugar. Remove the vanilla pod, star anise, and any excess liquid from the apples. Arrange the apple slices over the pastry, then add the blackberries and lemon or orange zest.

4 Wet the edges of the pastry with a little water. Roll out the pastry for the lid and drape, pressing the edges to seal. Trim the edges and slash the top a couple of times. Brush with half the egg and chill for 20 minutes.

5 Preheat the oven to 400°F (200°C). Brush the pie with the remaining egg and sprinkle with granulated sugar. Bake for 40–50 minutes, until golden. If it starts to brown too much, cover the top with a little foil, since you need the underside of the pastry to cook.

MINCE PIES

Mincemeat often contains gluten from the suet, but this easy homemade recipe does without. At other times of year, substitute the mincemeat with jam to make jam tarts.

MAKES	18
PREP	30 mins
	PLUS SOAKING
COOK	20–30 mins

GUIDELINES PER SERVING

● ● ○ Calories

● ○ ○ Saturated fat

● ○ ○ Salt

STATISTICS PER PIE

Energy 250kcals/1053kJ

Protein 2.5g

Fat 7g
Saturated fat 2g

Carbohydrate 44g
Sugar 36g

Fiber 2g

Salt 0.3g

GREAT FOR KIDS

14oz (400g) gluten-free shortcrust pastry (see pages 44–5)
gluten-free all-purpose flour, for dusting
1 large egg, beaten, to glaze
confectioner's sugar, for sprinkling
clotted cream, to serve

FOR THE MINCEMEAT
1lb 2oz (500g) dried fruits, such as golden raisins, currants, and raisins
pinch of freshly grated nutmeg
2 tsp pumpkin pie spice

1¾oz (50g) soft prunes, finely chopped
1lb (450g) apples, grated
grated zest and juice of 1 lemon
grated zest and juice of 1 orange
½ cup granulated sugar
½ cup brown sugar
2 tbsp dessert wine

SPECIAL EQUIPMENT
2 x 12-hole muffin top pans, about ¾in (2cm) deep, 2½in (6cm) round metal cutter, star cutter

1 For the mincemeat, add all the ingredients to a bowl and stir, then cover and leave to soak overnight. Preheat the oven to 375°F (190°C). Roll out the pastry on a lightly floured surface to a thickness of ⅛in (3mm). Cut out 18 rounds, re-rolling if needed, and neatly tuck them into the pans.

2 Fill each case with about 1½ teaspoons mincemeat; don't overfill or it will spill out during cooking. Re-roll the remaining pastry, cut out 18 star shapes, and sit them on top of each pie. Brush with the egg and bake for 20–30 minutes until golden brown. Remove and leave to cool for 10 minutes, then release the pies from the pans. Serve warm or cold with a sprinkling of confectioner's sugar and a dollop of clotted cream.

Cook's Tips
For full pie lids, cut out the pastry using a 1½–2in (4–5cm) round cutter. Wet the edges to seal, then make a steam hole in each lid. There will be plenty of mincemeat left over. Store in a sterilized, sealed jar for up to 6 months..

TARTE TATIN

An impressive dessert for a dinner party, it can be prepared ahead and baked when needed. Choose apples with a good flavor—Pink Lady, Braeburn, and Jazz all work well.

SERVES	8
PREP	20 mins
	PLUS CHILLING
COOK	30–35 mins

1⅓ cups gluten-free all-purpose flour, plus extra for dusting
1 tsp xanthan gum
pinch of salt
3 tbsp granulated sugar
10 tbsp cold unsalted butter, cubed
1 egg

FOR THE FILLING
4 tbsp unsalted butter
½ cup granulated sugar
1lb (450g) sweet apples

SPECIAL EQUIPMENT
9in (23cm) round, springform cake pan

GUIDELINES PER SERVING

● ● ● Calories
● ● ○ Saturated fat
● ● ○ Salt

STATISTICS PER SLICE

Energy 401kcals/1692kJ

Protein 4g

Fat 22g
Saturated fat 4g

Carbohydrate 47g
Sugar 27g

Fiber 3g

Salt 0.3g

1 Sift the flour, xanthan, and salt into a large bowl, then stir in the sugar. Add the butter and mix with your fingertips until fine crumbs form; alternatively, mix in a food processor. Add the egg and mix it in with your hands until it starts to form a dough, then bring it together into a ball with your hands. Wrap with plastic wrap and refrigerate.

2 For the filling, melt the butter in a small, heavy frying pan, add the sugar along with 6 tablespoons water, and stir until the sugar dissolves, then cook until caramelized and golden. Pour into the pan and swirl to coat the bottom. Peel, core, and quarter the apples, then cut each quarter into 3 slices. Pack the apples tightly into the cake pan, leaving no gaps.

3 On a lightly floured surface, or between 2 pieces of parchment paper, roll out the pastry to a round slightly larger than the pan and to a thickness of ¼in (5mm). Place on top of the apples and tuck the pastry under at the edges of the pan. Prick with a fork and chill for 10 minutes.

4 Preheat the oven to 400°F (200°C). Bake the tart on a baking sheet for 30–35 minutes until it is golden. Remove from the oven. Place a large plate on top of the pan, invert it, and leave to stand for about 1 minute before carefully removing the pan.

DESSERTS, CAKES, AND OTHER SWEET TREATS

APPLE FRITTERS AND CUSTARD

SERVES 4
PREP 20 mins
COOK 50 mins–1 hour

Custard is easier to make at home than you might think and is the perfect partner to these fruity fritters.

GUIDELINES PER SERVING

● ● ● Calories

● ● ○ Saturated fat

● ○ ○ Salt

STATISTICS PER SERVING

Energy 441kcals/1851kJ

Protein 8g

Fat 14g
Saturated fat 4g

Carbohydrate 68g
Sugar 38g

Fiber 4g

Salt 0.15g

GREAT FOR KIDS

4 small, sweet apples, each cored
  and sliced into 4–5 rings
vegetable oil, for frying

FOR THE CUSTARD
1 vanilla bean, halved lengthwise
¾ cup milk, or half milk and half
  heavy cream
3 large egg yolks
1 tbsp granulated sugar

FOR THE BATTER
1 cup rice flour
1 tbsp cornstarch
pinch of ground cinnamon, plus extra
¼ cup granulated sugar, plus extra
⅔ cup milk, or more if needed

SPECIAL EQUIPMENT
 deep-fat fryer (optional)

1 For the custard, pour the milk, or half milk and half cream (if using) into a pan, add the vanilla bean, and leave to infuse for 20 minutes. In a large bowl, beat the egg yolks and sugar. Add the infused milk and vanilla bean to a pan and heat gently to near boiling point, but do not boil. Remove, discard the vanilla bean, and pour over the egg mixture, whisking as you go. Return the mixture to the pan and heat gently over low heat, stirring constantly, for 10–20 minutes until the custard begins to thicken and coats the back of a wooden spoon; do not allow it to boil or it will turn lumpy and split. If need be, pass the prepared custard through a fine metal sieve, so it's smooth and lump-free. Set aside.

2 For the fritters, add the dry batter ingredients to a bowl and whisk in the milk until it has the consistency of heavy cream; you may not need it all.

3 Heat the oil in a large pan or deep-fat fryer to 375°F (190°C), if using a thermometer, or until hot enough to crisp a piece of bread, and maintain this temperature. Do not leave the pan or fryer unattended, turn off when not using, and keep a damp kitchen towel nearby in case of fire. Dip the apple slices into the batter, add to the oil a couple at a time, and fry for 2–3 minutes until golden. Remove and transfer to paper towels. Keep the finished fritters warm while you fry the remaining slices. Dust the fritters with the sugar and the cinnamon. Gently reheat the custard and serve with the fruit fritters.

BLACK CHERRY CLAFOUTIS

This simple French dessert is nothing more than fruit and batter, baked until golden, but it tastes divine.

SERVES   4
PREP   20 mins
COOK   30 mins

1lb 2oz (500g) cherries, pitted
grated zest of 1 orange
1 tbsp kirsch or cherry brandy (optional)
²/₃ cup granulated sugar
2 large eggs

²/₃ cup heavy cream
¼ cup rice flour
1 tbsp ground almonds
confectioner's sugar, for dusting

GUIDELINES PER SERVING

● ● ●   Calories

● ● ●   Saturated fat

● ○ ○   Salt

STATISTICS PER SERVING

Energy 514kcals/2152kJ

Protein 7g

Fat 26g
Saturated fat 14g

Carbohydrate 60g
Sugar 52g

Fiber 2g

Salt 0.1g

1 Preheat the oven to 350°F (180°C). Add the cherries, orange zest, kirsch (if using), and half the sugar to a frying pan and cook on very low heat for 5 minutes to dissolve the sugar and soften the cherries just a little. Then transfer it all to a baking dish.

2 For the batter, add the eggs and the remaining sugar to a bowl and whisk until creamy, then mix in the cream, rice flour, and almonds. Pour over the cherries to cover, then bake in the oven for 20–30 minutes until the batter is puffed and golden. Remove from the oven, dust with confectioner's sugar, and serve with cream and a drizzle of kirsch or cherry brandy, if you like.

Variations
You could use frozen berries if cherries are not available, or try fresh apricots or peaches.

PITTING CHERRIES
If you don't own a cherry pitter, take a clean metal paper clip and unfold it so that it looks like an "S." Press the larger end of the paper clip into the stalk end of the cherry until you feel the pit, twist it around, and the pit should pull out easily.

RASPBERRY AND WHITE CHOCOLATE TRIFLE

Tart raspberries contrast well with sweet white chocolate, and a trickle of cassis liqueur transforms this dessert into an indulgent, special-occasion trifle.

SERVES 6
PREP 20 mins

GUIDELINES PER SERVING

● ● ●   Calories
● ● ●   Saturated fat
● ○ ○   Salt

STATISTICS PER SERVING

Energy 644kcals/2676kJ

Protein 8g

Fat 50g
Saturated fat 25g

Carbohydrate 39g
Sugar 33g

Fiber 2g

Salt 0.4g

7oz (200g) white chocolate, broken into
  even-sized pieces, plus extra
  for grating to decorate
6oz (175g) gluten-free sponge
  (see page 40) or amaretti cookies
  (see page 339), crumbled
juice of 1–2 oranges

2 tbsp cassis (optional)
1¼ cups heavy cream, lightly whipped,
  or mascarpone cheese
10oz (300g) raspberries
1¾oz (50g) sliced almonds,
  lightly toasted

1 Put the chocolate in a heatproof bowl over a pan of barely simmering water and stir occasionally until melted. Remove the bowl from the pan and leave to cool slightly.

2 Place the crumbled sponge or cookies in the base of a glass serving dish. Pour over just enough orange juice to wet the sponge, then add half the cassis (if using). Set aside for the sponge or cookies to absorb the juice.

3 Mix the melted chocolate with half the whipped cream or mascarpone and stir well to combine. Mix the remaining cassis with the raspberries. Reserve some raspberries for decoration. Spoon half the cream mixture into the dish and top with half the raspberry mixture. Repeat the layers to use the remaining cream and raspberry mixture.

4 Top with the leftover cream and dot with the reserved raspberries, then sprinkle over the almonds and grated white chocolate. Chill before serving.

Variations
A variety of bases can be used for the trifle—try gluten-free brownies, cookies, or fruit cake for a heavier version—and try stewed fruits for a winter dessert.

SUMMER FRUIT COBBLER

SERVES   8
PREP   20 mins
COOK   35–40 mins

You can vary the fruit in this dessert, but keep a similar ratio of soft berries to firmer fruit, such as peaches or pears, so that the cobbler topping has a firm base to rise on.

GUIDELINES PER SERVING

● ● ○   Calories

● ● ○   Saturated fat

● ● ○   Salt

STATISTICS PER SERVING

Energy 286kcals/1211kJ

Protein 6g

Fat 8g
Saturated fat 4g

Carbohydrate 46g
Sugar 25g

Fiber 3.5g

Salt 0.9g

1½ cups gluten-free all-purpose flour,
   plus extra for dusting
2 tsp gluten-free baking powder
1 tsp xanthan gum
pinch of salt
¼ cup granulated sugar
4 tbsp cold unsalted butter, cubed
¾ cup buttermilk, or half milk
   and half plain yogurt
1 large egg, beaten
2 tsp coarse sugar
half-and-half, to serve

FOR THE FILLING
1lb (450g) ripe peaches or nectarines
¼ cup granulated sugar
2 tbsp cornstarch
7oz (200g) raspberries
7oz (200g) blueberries

SPECIAL EQUIPMENT
2in (5cm) round fluted metal cutter
1 quart oval baking dish

1 Preheat the oven to 400°F (200°C). If using peaches, soak them in boiling water for 1 minute, drain, and peel. Halve the peaches or nectarines, remove the pits, and slice. Mix the granulated sugar and cornstarch in the baking dish. Add the sliced peaches or nectarines and the berries and toss until evenly coated. Tossing the fruit in the cornstarch and sugar mixture makes a lovely sauce. Spread the fruit out in an even layer.

2 For the topping, sift the flour, baking powder, xanthan, and salt into a large bowl and stir in the sugar. Add the butter and rub it in with your fingertips, or pulse in a food processor until it resembles fine bread crumbs. Stir in the buttermilk, or half milk and half plain yogurt, and mix using your hands to make a soft dough. Knead briefly.

3 On a lightly floured surface, roll out the dough to a thickness of ¾in (2cm). Using the cutter, cut out 12 circles, re-rolling the dough as necessary. Lay the circles on top of the fruit, overlapping them slightly. Brush with the egg and sprinkle over the coarse sugar. Bake on a baking sheet, near the top of the oven, for 35–40 minutes or until the cobbler is risen and golden brown on top and the fruit is bubbling. Serve warm with half-and-half.

FRUIT CRUMBLE

A real family favorite. You can swap the fruit to suit the seasons or mix and match the toppings.

SERVES 6
PREP 20 mins
COOK 35 mins
FREEZE 3 months

14oz (400g) rhubarb, trimmed and
  chopped into 2in (5cm) pieces
zest of 1 orange and juice of 2
14oz (400g) strawberries, quartered
9 tbsp cold unsalted butter, cubed

1⅛ cups gluten-free all-purpose flour
⅔ cup coarse sugar
handful of sliced almonds
gluten-free custard or ice cream
  (see pages 286 or 299), to serve

GUIDELINES PER SERVING

● ● ● Calories
● ● ● Saturated fat
● ○ ○ Salt

STATISTICS PER SERVING

Energy 404kcals/1696kJ

Protein 5.5g

Fat 20g
Saturated fat 11g

Carbohydrate 51g
Sugar 28g

Fiber 3.5g

Salt 0.3g

1 Preheat the oven to 350°F (180°C). Put the rhubarb and the orange zest and juice in a shallow pan and simmer gently for 8–10 minutes until the rhubarb softens. If it needs more liquid, add a little water. Transfer to a shallow ovenproof dish and mix in the strawberries.

2 In a bowl, rub the butter into the flour with your fingertips until crumbs form, or pulse in a food processor. Stir in the sugar. Sprinkle the topping over the fruit to cover and scatter with the almonds. Bake in the oven for 25 minutes until golden. Serve with gluten-free custard or ice cream.

Variations

APPLE AND CRANBERRY Peel, core, and slice 2 large apples and simmer for 4–5 minutes with the juice of ½ lemon, 3 tablespoons water, and 3 tablespoons soft brown sugar, until just soft. Transfer to an ovenproof dish and scatter over 7oz (200g) fresh or 3½oz (100g) dried cranberries. Sprinkle 3 tablespoons brown sugar and a pinch of cinnamon. Top with the crumble topping and bake as above.

PEAR AND BLACKBERRY Slice 3 sweet pears and simmer for 3–5 minutes with the juice of ½ lemon, 2 tablespoons water, and ½ vanilla bean, sliced lengthwise, until just soft. Transfer to an ovenproof dish, add 10oz (300g) blackberries and 1–2 tablespoons coarse sugar, and combine. Add a topping and bake as above.

ALMOND TOPPING Replace all-purpose flour with ¾ cup rice flour and 5½oz (150g) ground almonds, and do as above. Try with pear and blackberries.

QUINOA TOPPING Replace the all-purpose flour with ¼ cup rice flour and 1½ cups quinoa flakes. Process with 2½oz (75g) roughly chopped mixed nuts until combined. Add 4 tbsp butter and pulse until it resembles bread crumbs, then add ½ cup coarse sugar and pulse a few more times.

GREAT FOR KIDS

CHINESE-STYLE DUMPLINGS

These simple doughnutlike sweet dumplings are flavored with cinnamon and ginger.

SERVES 4
PREP 20 mins
COOK 28 mins

GUIDELINES PER SERVING

● ● ● Calories
● ● ● Saturated fat
● ● ● Salt

STATISTICS PER SERVING

Energy 680kcals/2835kJ

Protein 10g

Fat 40g
Saturated fat 10g

Carbohydrate 65g
Sugar 12.5g

Fiber 3g

Salt 0.75g

2 cups gluten-free all-purpose flour
½ tsp salt
3 tsp gluten-free baking powder
½ tsp ground cinnamon
4 tbsp cold unsalted butter, cubed
3 balls of preserved stem ginger, or
 ½ cup chopped crystallized ginger,
 finely chopped

½ cup milk
1 large egg
1 quart sunflower, or vegetable oil,
 for frying
granulated sugar, for sprinkling

SPECIAL EQUIPMENT
 deep-fat fryer or large pan

1 Sift the flour, salt, baking powder, and cinnamon into a bowl, then add the butter, rubbing it in with your fingertips until the mixture forms fine crumbs. Stir through the ginger, then beat the milk and egg together and add to the mixture, stirring until you get a smooth dough.

2 Divide and roll the dough into 20 balls, then make a thumb indentation on each one. Heat the oil in a large pan or deep-fat fryer until hot, but not too hot or the dumplings will burn quickly. The pan or fryer should not be more than one-third full. Do not leave the pan or fryer unattended, switch off when not using, and keep a fire blanket nearby in case of fire.

3 Carefully add the dough balls into the pan or fryer, 3 at a time, and deep-fry at a low sizzle for 4 minutes, turning them halfway through cooking so they turn golden brown all over. Remove and drain on paper towels. Repeat until all the dumplings are cooked. Pour the granulated sugar out onto a plate and roll the dumplings in it. Serve piled high in bowls.

Cook's Tip
These dumplings are very delicate. The key is to have the oil at the correct temperature; too hot and they burn, too cold and the inside doesn't cook.

PASSION FRUIT AND LEMON SOUFFLÉS

This is a really easy version of a sweet soufflé that relies on good-quality lemon curd.

2 tbsp unsalted butter, melted

½ cup granulated sugar, plus
  6 tsp for sprinkling

4 passion fruit

4 tbsp gluten-free lemon curd

4 large eggs, separated

confectioner's sugar, for sprinkling

SPECIAL EQUIPMENT
 6 x 5fl oz (150ml) ramekin dishes

MAKES 6
PREP 15 mins
COOK 12–15 mins

GUIDELINES PER SERVING

● ● ○ Calories

● ● ○ Saturated fat

● ○ ○ Salt

STATISTICS PER SOUFFLÉ

Energy 229kcals/964kJ

Protein 5g

Fat 9g
Saturated fat 4g

Carbohydrate 32g
Sugar 30g

Fiber 0.4g

Salt 0.2g

1 Preheat the oven to 400°F (200°C). Grease the ramekin dishes generously with the butter, then dust each with 1 teaspoon granulated sugar. Put them in the fridge while you prepare the soufflé mixture.

2 Scoop the seeds from the passion fruit and strain through a nylon sieve set over a bowl, to collect the juice and remove the seeds. Stir the juice into the lemon curd along with the egg yolks.

3 Whisk the egg whites in a grease-free bowl (see Cook's Tip) using an electric whisk until stiff peaks form. Add the granulated sugar and whisk until the mixture is stiff and shiny. Stir a heaped tablespoonful of the egg whites into the curd mixture to loosen it. Gently fold the remaining egg whites into the mixture; do this slowly so you don't knock out the air.

4 Divide the mixture between the ramekins, tap them on the work surface so that the mixture settles inside, then wipe a clean finger around the inside edge of each dish; this helps the soufflés rise evenly. Bake for 12–15 minutes or until well-risen and golden tinged. Remove from the oven, transfer each ramekin to a plate, and sprinkle with confectioner's sugar before serving.

Cook's Tip
When whisking the egg whites, ensure that the bowl is really clean or you just won't get the volume you need.

CHOCOLATE TAPIOCA PUDDING

An old-fashioned pudding that may take you back to your childhood, but one that's given a more grown-up twist by using dark chocolate.

SERVES 6
PREP 5 mins
COOK 25 mins

GUIDELINES PER SERVING

● ● ● Calories
● ● ● Saturated fat
● ● ○ Salt

STATISTICS PER SERVING

Energy 326kcals/1370kJ

Protein 7g

Fat 13g
Saturated fat 7g

Carbohydrate 45g
Sugar 30g

Fiber 0.6g

Salt 0.6g

3½ cups milk
½ cup tapioca pearls
1–2 tbsp dark cocoa powder
2 large egg yolks
½ cup sugar
pinch of salt

pinch of freshly grated nutmeg
2–3 tbsp heavy cream, to serve (optional)
scant 1oz (25g) dark chocolate,
  grated, to top

1 Add the milk to a pan, then add in the tapioca and cocoa powder, stir, and warm gently on low heat. Mix together the egg yolks, sugar, and a pinch of salt. Pour a little of the warmed milk mixture into the egg and stir to combine, then pour it all back into the pan.

2 Bring to a boil, stirring constantly, then reduce the heat to medium-low. Simmer gently for 20 minutes, stirring frequently, until the tapioca is cooked. Add more milk if it's too thick. Add the nutmeg, stir in the cream (if using), and serve with a topping of grated chocolate.

Cook's Tip
Children will love this, though they may prefer the sweeter flavor of drinking chocolate to the dark cocoa powder, and milk chocolate grated on top.

Variation
Make this without the cocoa powder and chocolate, and stir in jam to serve.

CHOCOLATE LAVA CAKES

Lightly cooked cake on the outside with an oozy, runny center, chocolate lava cakes are far easier to make than their reputation implies—just don't overcook them.

MAKES   6
PREP   20 mins
COOK   10 mins
FREEZE   3 months
          UNCOOKED

10 tbsp butter, plus extra
  for greasing
cocoa powder, for dusting
5oz (140g) dark chocolate (at least
  70% cocoa solids)
4 large eggs and 3 large egg yolks
⅓ cup granulated sugar

3 tbsp gluten-free all-purpose flour
cream or gluten-free ice cream (see
  page 299), to serve

SPECIAL EQUIPMENT
  6 x 6fl oz (175ml) ramekins

GUIDELINES PER SERVING

● ● ●   Calories

● ● ●   Saturated fat

● ● ●   Salt

STATISTICS PER LAVA CAKE

Energy 471kcals/1962kJ

Protein 8g

Fat 34g
Saturated fat 18g

Carbohydrate 33g
Sugar 28g

Fiber 1g

Salt 0.6g

1 Preheat the oven to 400°F (200°C). Generously grease the ramekins, then dust with cocoa powder. Melt the butter and chocolate together in a large heatproof bowl set over a pan of gently simmering water. Once melted, remove from the heat.

2 Using an electric whisk, beat together the eggs, egg yolks, and sugar until pale and thick; the mixture should leave a trail when the whisk is lifted.

3 Pour the egg mixture into the melted chocolate and sift the flour on top. Gently fold everything together using a large rubber spatula. Divide the mixture evenly between the ramekins and chill until required.

4 Bake for 10 minutes. Remove from the oven and leave to rest for 1 minute. Holding the ramekins with a heatproof cloth, run a knife around the edges of each cake, and invert onto a plate. Serve with ice cream or cream.

Cook's Tips
Make these up to 3 days ahead, simply cover the tops with plastic wrap and refrigerate until ready to bake. You can also freeze and bake straight from frozen by adding 4 minutes to the cooking time.

CHOCOLATE CHEESECAKE

A gooey mixture of dark chocolate and mascarpone baked on a crumbly base of almond or ginger cookies.

SERVES 8
PREP 20 mins
PLUS COOLING
COOK 35–40 mins

GUIDELINES PER SERVING

● ● ● Calories
● ● ● Saturated fat
● ● ● Salt

STATISTICS PER SLICE

Energy 598kcals/2501kJ

Protein 7g

Fat 43g
Saturated fat 23.5g

Carbohydrate 41g
Sugar 41g

Fiber 0.6g

Salt 0.4g

6 tbsp butter, plus extra for greasing
6oz (175g) gluten-free amaretti
  or ginger cookies (see pages 338–9),
  crushed
5¹⁄₂oz (150g) dark chocolate
  (70% cocoa solids), broken
  into even-sized pieces
2 large eggs, separated
pinch of salt

14oz (400g) mascarpone cheese
zest and juice of 1 orange
¹⁄₂ cup granulated sugar
2 tbsp cornstarch
heavy cream, to serve

SPECIAL EQUIPMENT
  8in (20cm) round springform cake pan

1 Preheat the oven to 350°F (180°C). Grease the pan and line with parchment paper. Slowly melt the butter in a pan, remove from the heat, and stir in the crushed cookies. Press these into the base and edges of the pan using the back of a wooden spoon. When cool, chill in the refrigerator.

2 Put the chocolate in a heatproof bowl set over a pan of barely simmering water and stir occasionally until melted. Remove the bowl from the pan and leave the chocolate to cool slightly.

3 Place the egg whites and salt in a bowl and beat until stiff. Set aside.

4 Place the mascarpone, melted chocolate, orange zest and juice, granulated sugar, and egg yolks in a large bowl and beat gently with an electric mixer to combine. Fold in the cornstarch and then the egg whites.

5 Pour the mixture over the cookie base and spread it until even and smooth. Bake for 35–40 minutes, or until firm to the touch. Switch off the heat and leave the cheesecake to cool inside the oven; this helps prevent cracking. Once cool, remove from the oven and set aside until completely cold, then release the sides and ease from the pan. Serve with a drizzle of heavy cream.

CHRISTMAS PUDDING

Christmas cakes, puddings, and mincemeat are best made a few weeks in advance to let the flavors mellow and mature.

SERVES 10
PREP 30 mins
PLUS SOAKING
COOK 2 hours

GUIDELINES PER SERVING

● ● ●   Calories

● ● ●   Saturated fat

● ● ○   Salt

STATISTICS PER SERVING

Energy 732kcals/3078kJ

Protein 10g

Fat 2g
Saturated fat 13g

Carbohydrate 100g
Sugar 83g

Fiber 5g

Salt 1g

2oz (60g) each of ready-to-eat
dates, dried apricots, and prunes,
finely chopped
7oz (200g) each of currants, raisins,
and golden raisins
4oz (115g) candied cherries, halved
2oz (60g) mixed citrus peel, chopped
zest and juice of 1 lemon
¾ cup cider
¼ cup each of brandy and rum
3 tbsp black molasses
1 tbsp cocoa powder
2 tsp apple pie spice
1 tsp ground cinnamon

1 sweet apple, cored and grated
16 tbsp unsalted butter, softened,
plus extra for greasing
1¼ cups dark brown sugar
3 large eggs, beaten
½ cup gluten-free all-purpose flour, plus
½ tsp baking powder, ¼ tsp salt
1½ cups gluten-free bread crumbs
2oz (60g) walnut pieces, chopped
½ cup ground almonds

SPECIAL EQUIPMENT
3 x 2 cup souffle dishes or baking dishes

1 Place the first 12 ingredients, up to and including the grated apple, in a large, nonmetallic bowl and mix to combine. Cover with plastic wrap and leave to soak for at least 12 hours or up to 2 days in a cool place.

2 Preheat the oven to 325°F (160°C). Lightly grease the baking dishes and line the base of each one with parchment paper. Cream the butter and sugar in a large bowl until fluffy. Gradually add the eggs, whisking between additions. Fold in the flour, baking powder, and salt. Add the bread crumbs, walnuts, almonds, and the soaked fruit and juices. Mix well, divide the mixture between the dishes, and level the surfaces. Cover each with a square of parchment paper and foil, pleated in the middle to allow the puddings to rise. Tightly pinch around the edges to form a good seal.

3 Stand them in a roasting pan and pour boiling water to halfway up the outside of the baking dishes. Bake for 2 hours, adding more water occasionally. Remove and leave to cool before storing. To reheat, follow the same process, but bake at 350°F (180°C) for 35 minutes.

BROWN BREAD ICE CREAM

In this slightly retro dessert, the toasted bread tastes like toffee. Kids will love this with sliced banana or chocolate.

1⅛ cups whole milk
1⅛ cups heavy cream
1 vanilla bean, split lengthwise
¾ cup gluten-free brown bread crumbs
  (see page 38)
⅓ cup dark brown sugar

5 large egg yolks
¼ cup granulated sugar

SERVES   6
PREP   30 mins
          PLUS INFUSING
          AND FREEZING
COOK   25 mins
FREEZE   3 months

GUIDELINES PER SERVING

●●○ Calories
●●○ Saturated fat
●○○ Salt

STATISTICS PER SERVING

Energy 407kcals/1697kJ

Protein 6g

Fat 29g
Saturated fat 16g

Carbohydrate 31g
Sugar 23g

Fiber 0.4g

Salt 0.3g

1 To make the custard for the ice cream, add the milk, cream, and vanilla to a pan and bring just to a boil. Remove and leave for 30 minutes to cool and for the vanilla to infuse. Then discard the vanilla bean.

2 Preheat the oven to 400°F (200°C). Spread the bread crumbs out on a large roasting pan or baking sheet and toast for 10 minutes until just turning pale golden. Add the dark brown sugar, toss together, and bake for 5 more minutes. Remove and leave to cool, then transfer into a small blender and pulse once or twice to break up the bigger lumps.

3 In a bowl, whisk together the egg yolks and granulated sugar until creamy. Pour in the infused milk and whisk to combine. Pour the custard into the cleaned pan and simmer gently over very low heat for 10–15 minutes, stirring, until it begins to thicken. Stir constantly and do not let it boil or it may split and turn lumpy. Pour the custard through a nylon sieve into a large bowl so it is smooth. Cover the custard with parchment paper so that the paper touches the surface to prevent a skin forming. Cool.

4 Pour the mixture into a freezer-proof container and freeze for 2 hours. Remove, add to the food processor, and pulse until creamy. Add the bread crumb mixture and pulse once more to combine. Put back in the freezer and repeat once the ice cream has frozen, pulsing it again in the food processor. If using an ice cream maker, you can skip this step: simply add the mixture and leave until frozen.

GREAT FOR KIDS

SUMMER PUDDING

SERVES	6
PREP	25 mins
	PLUS CHILLING
COOK	5 mins

This traditional fruit dessert is useful for using up leftover gluten-free bread as it works better than fresh. Children will love it too and it's a great way to get them eating fruit.

GUIDELINES PER SERVING

● ● ○ Calories

● ● ○ Saturated fat

● ● ○ Salt

STATISTICS PER SERVING

Energy 178kcals/756kJ

Protein 6g

Fat 1g
Saturated fat 0.2g

Carbohydrate 31g
Sugar 19g

Fiber 5.5g

Salt 0.5g

GREAT FOR KIDS

NUTRIENT BOOST

Frozen berries are rich in vitamin C and a good option when fresh aren't in season.

2¾lb (1.25kg) frozen mixed berries, or a mixture of fresh summer berries and currants that are in season, reserving a few for decoration

2–3 tbsp granulated sugar, or more if the fruit is tart

8–10 slices of gluten-free white bread
cream, to serve

SPECIAL EQUIPMENT
1 quart bowl

1 Add the fruit to a pan along with the sugar and 3 tablespoons water. Simmer gently on low heat for 3–5 minutes, then set aside until cool; you need to bring out the juices from the fruit to color the bread. Drain the fruit with a slotted spoon and transfer to another bowl. Reserve the juice.

2 Remove the crusts from the bread, reserve 1 slice for the base of the bowl (what will be the top of the pudding), and cut each of the remaining slices into 3 even fingers. Line the pudding bowl with plastic wrap, leaving plenty of overlap. Cut a circle for the base from the reserved slice, dip into the juice, and sit it at the bottom of the bowl. Line the bowl with bread fingers, first dipping them into the juice, and overlapping them slightly, so there are no gaps and they follow the shape of the bowl.

3 Spoon the fruit into the bowl. Dip the remaining bread fingers into the juice and top the pudding, ensuring that it's completely covered. Press them down to secure. Pull the plastic wrap over to cover the top, then set a plate on top and use a can to weigh it down. Chill in the fridge overnight.

4 If you have any leftover juice, you could make a sauce by simmering it in a small pan over medium heat until slightly thickened. Transfer to a bowl and chill with the pudding. To serve, invert the pudding onto a plate and peel away the plastic wrap. Decorate with the reserved berries and serve with the fruit sauce or cream.

STICKY TOFFEE PUDDINGS

These delicious little puddings can also be made into a big one. Just spoon the mixture into a 1-quart pudding mold or soufflé dish and steam for an extra 20 minutes.

SERVES 6
PREP 20–25 mins
COOK 1–1¼ hours
FREEZE 3 months

vegetable oil, for greasing
12 tbsp butter, softened
1 cup dark brown soft sugar
3 large eggs
1 cup gluten-free all-purpose flour
1 tsp baking powder
½ tsp salt
1 tsp xanthan gum
½ cup ground almonds
2oz (60g) fudge, cut into small pieces
3 tbsp milk

FOR THE SAUCE
1⅔ cups milk
3 tbsp cornstarch
¼ cup dark brown soft sugar
1 tsp pure vanilla extract

SPECIAL EQUIPMENT
6 x 6fl oz (175ml) ramekins

GUIDELINES PER SERVING

● ● ● Calories

● ● ● Saturated fat

● ● ○ Salt

STATISTICS PER PUDDING

Energy 654kcals/2737kJ

Protein 11g

Fat 37g
Saturated fat 19g

Carbohydrate 69g
Sugar 50g

Fiber 0.8g

Salt 0.7g

1 Preheat the oven to 350°F (180°C). Oil the ramekins and place a disk of parchment at the base of each. Using an electric mixer, cream together the butter and sugar until fluffy. Add the eggs, one at a time, beating well between additions. Add a spoonful of the flour if it starts to curdle.

2 Sift over the remaining flour, baking powder, salt, and xanthan, and add the almonds, fudge, and milk. Fold together to form a batter and divide between the ramekins. Cover each with squares of parchment and foil, pleated in the middle to allow the pudding to rise. Tie in place with string. Stand the puddings in a roasting pan, pour in enough hot water to come halfway up the outside of the pudding ramekins. Bake for 1–1¼ hours or until the puddings are risen and golden. Let stand and make the sauce.

3 In a large bowl, mix 6 tablespoons milk with the cornstarch, sugar, and vanilla to form a smooth paste. Heat the remaining milk in a nonstick pan until almost boiling, and pour over the cornstarch paste, stirring constantly. Return to the rinsed-out pan and gently bring to a boil, stirring until the mixture thickens. Cook over low heat for 1 minute, continuing to stir constantly. Pour into a warm bowl. To serve, invert the puddings onto serving plates, remove the parchment, and hand out the toffee sauce separately.

CARAMELIZED ORANGE CAKE

Be patient when baking this tangy, orange-topped cake. Don't open the oven for a peep too early or the cake won't rise and it may even sink.

SERVES 10
PREP 20 mins
COOK 30–40 mins

GUIDELINES PER SERVING

● ● ● Calories
● ● ● Saturated fat
● ● ○ Salt

STATISTICS PER SERVING

Energy 643kcals/2646kJ

Protein 7g

Fat 42g
Saturated fat 25g

Carbohydrate 57g
Sugar 44g

Fiber 3g

Salt 0.9g

GREAT FOR KIDS

2 sticks, plus 3 tbsp unsalted butter, plus extra for greasing
3–4 oranges, peeled, pith and seeds removed, and thickly sliced
3–4 tbsp brown sugar
4oz (115g) gluten-free self-raising flour
1 tsp gluten-free baking powder
1 tsp xanthan gum
⅔ cup granulated sugar
3 large eggs
3 tbsp milk
heavy cream, crème fraîche, or gluten-free custard (see page 286), to serve

1 Preheat the oven to 350°F (180°C). Grease an 8 x 8in (20 x 20cm) ovenproof dish with a little butter. Melt 7 tablespoons butter in a large, nonstick frying pan over medium heat. Add the orange slices and brown sugar, and cook for 5–6 minutes until the oranges are golden and caramelized. Don't let the sugar burn. Put the oranges and sauce into the ovenproof dish.

2 Sift the flour, baking powder, and xanthan into a large bowl and set aside. Place the remaining butter and granulated sugar into a bowl and beat with an electric whisk until light and fluffy. Do this for at least 8 minutes so it is really light. Add the eggs, one at a time, with a spoonful of the flour mixture. Beat until well-incorporated, then fold in the remaining flour mix, and stir in the milk.

3 Spoon the mixture over the oranges and bake for 30–40 minutes, or until risen and golden and an inserted skewer comes out clean. Spoon into shallow bowls with the orange slices on top. Serve with heavy cream, crème fraîche, or gluten-free custard.

Cook's Tip
This is a great dessert for children, best when served with gluten-free custard.

VANILLA CHEESECAKE WITH SUMMER-FRUIT COULIS

SERVES	8–10
PREP	20 mins
	PLUS CHILLING
COOK	50 mins

GUIDELINES PER SERVING

● ● ● Calories

● ● ● Saturated fat

● ● ○ Salt

STATISTICS PER SERVING

Energy 738kcals/3070kJ

Protein 7g

Fat 58g
Saturated fat 34g

Carbohydrate 46g
Sugar 34g

Fiber 0.4g

Salt 1g

This is an indulgent dessert but the rich creaminess is cut by the sharp, fruity flavors of the sauce.

FOR THE CHEESECAKE
4 tbsp unsalted butter, plus
  extra for greasing
8oz (225g) gluten-free vanilla
  wafers, finely crushed
1 tbsp demerara sugar
1½lb (675g) cream cheese,
  at room temperature
4 large eggs, separated
¾ cup granulated sugar

1 tsp vanilla extract
2 cups (16oz) sour cream

FOR THE FRUIT COULIS
10oz (300g) frozen summer fruits
¼ cup granulated sugar

SPECIAL EQUIPMENT
9in (23cm) springform cake pan
handheld blender

1 Preheat the oven to 350°F (180°C). Grease the cake pan and line with parchment paper. Gently melt the butter in a pan, remove from the heat, and stir in the wafer crumbs and demerara sugar. Press the crumbs into the base of the pan using the back of a wooden spoon.

2 Beat the cream cheese, egg yolks, ½ cup of the granulated sugar, and the vanilla in a bowl until blended. In a separate bowl, beat the egg whites until stiff. Fold the egg whites into the cream-cheese mixture. Pour the mixture into the pan and smooth the top.

3 Place the pan in the oven and bake for 45 minutes until set. Remove the pan from the oven and let stand for 10 minutes.

4 Meanwhile, increase the oven temperature to 475°F (240°C). Combine the sour cream and remaining ¼ cup of granulated sugar in a bowl and beat well. Pour over the cheesecake and smooth the top. Bake the cheesecake for 5 minutes. Cool, then cover and chill for at least 6 hours.

5 To make the summer fruit coulis, put the frozen fruit, sugar, and 3 tbsp of water into a small saucepan with a lid. Cover, place over medium heat, and bring to a boil, then remove the lid, stir, and simmer the fruit for about 5 minutes or until soft. Blend the fruit with a handheld blender until smooth, then press it through a nylon sieve to remove all the seeds. The coulis can be served warm or cold, and will thicken as it cools.

VANILLA CUPCAKES

Ever popular cupcakes don't come much lighter than these! You can add a few drops of yellow food coloring to the frosting.

MAKES 12
PREP 15 mins
COOK 20 mins

GUIDELINES PER SERVING

● ● ● Calories
● ● ● Saturated fat
● ● ● Salt

STATISTICS PER CUPCAKE

Energy 223kcals/940kJ

Protein 2g

Fat 9g
Saturated fat 5.5g

Carbohydrate 33g
Sugar 26g

Fiber 0.5g

Salt 0.3g

8 tbsp unsalted butter, softened
½ cup granulated sugar
2 large eggs
1 cup gluten-free all-purpose flour,
  plus 1 tsp baking powder and
  ½ tsp salt
3 tbsp milk
1 tsp vanilla extract

gluten-free cake decorations, for sprinkling

FOR THE FROSTING
1²⁄₃ cups confectioner's sugar
½ tsp pure vanilla extract

SPECIAL EQUIPMENT
 12-hole muffin pan lined with paper liners

1 Preheat the oven to 350°F (180°C). Sift the flour, baking powder, and salt into a large bowl. In a separate bowl, mix the butter and sugar with an electric mixer until pale, light, and fluffy. Add the eggs, one at a time, beating well, until fluffy. Add 1–2 tablespoons flour with the last egg to stop the mixture from curdling. Add the flour, milk, and pure vanilla extract and beat for 1 minute.

2 Divide the mixture between the liners and bake for 20 minutes, until the cupcakes look golden and spring back when lightly touched in the center. Leave to cool in the pan for 5 minutes, then transfer to cool on a wire rack.

3 For the frosting, sift the sugar into a bowl, add the vanilla, and gradually add 2–3 tablespoons water, beating well between additions until smooth. Spoon the frosting over each cake, spreading it to the edges. Sprinkle over the decorations and leave to set. Store in an airtight container for up to 4 days.

GREAT FOR KIDS

Variations
LEMON CUPCAKES Omit the pure vanilla extract, beat the finely grated zest of 1 lemon with the butter and sugar. Replace the water with lemon juice in the frosting.
CHOCOLATE CUPCAKES Replace ⅓ cup of the flour with cocoa powder. For the frosting, replace 2 tablespoons of the sugar with cocoa powder and sift together.

CHOCOLATE CAKE

This light-as-a-feather cake, smothered in a wickedly delicious chocolate fudge frosting, makes the perfect treat.

SERVES 12
PREP 25–30 mins
COOK 25–30 mins
FREEZE 3 months

GUIDELINES PER SERVING

● ● ● Calories
● ● ● Saturated fat
● ○ ○ Salt

STATISTICS PER SLICE

Energy 565kcals/2359kJ

Protein 6g

Fat 37g
Saturated fat 21g

Carbohydrate 52g
Sugar 46g

Fiber 2g

Salt 0.8g

GREAT FOR KIDS

butter, for greasing
7oz (200g) dark chocolate, broken into pieces
2 sticks, plus 6 tbsp butter, softened
1¼ cups light brown sugar
3 large eggs, separated
1 cup gluten-free all-purpose flour
1 tsp baking powder
½ tsp salt
½ tsp gluten-free baking soda
¾ cup cocoa powder
½ cup ground almonds
¼ cup milk
½ cup heavy cream
1⅔ cups confectioner's sugar, sifted

SPECIAL EQUIPMENT
2 x 8in (20cm) round cake pans

1 Preheat the oven to 350°F (180°C). Grease the pans and line with parchment paper. Melt 2oz (60g) of the chocolate in a heatproof bowl over a pan of simmering water. Cool slightly.

2 In a large bowl, cream together 2 sticks of the butter and light brown sugar with an electric whisk until light and fluffy. Add the egg yolks and cooled chocolate and whisk again. Sift in the flour, baking powder, salt, soda, and cocoa. Add the almonds and milk and gently fold in until well mixed. Whisk the egg whites in a clean bowl to form stiff peaks. Stir a spoonful into the chocolate mix, then gently fold in the remainder.

3 Divide the mixture between the 2 pans and bake in the center of the oven for 25–30 minutes or until the cakes bounce back when lightly touched in the middle. Place the pans on a wire rack and cover with a damp kitchen towel, which will keep them beautifully moist. Leave until cold.

4 For the frosting, combine the remaining chocolate and the cream in a bowl and place over a pan of gently simmering water. Stir occasionally until the chocolate has melted and the mixture is smooth. Remove and cool. In a separate bowl, whisk remaining butter and confectioner's sugar until fluffy, add the melted chocolate mixture, and whisk until smooth. Turn out the cakes. Spread a third of the frosting over one cake and top with the second. Spread the remaining frosting over the top and sides of the cake.

DEVIL'S FOOD CAKE

This cake gets its name from being so tempting and indulgent—you have been warned!

SERVES 12
PREP 20 mins
COOK 25–30 mins
FREEZE 3 months

GUIDELINES PER SERVING

● ● ● Calories
● ● ● Saturated fat
● ○ ○ Salt

STATISTICS PER SLICE

Energy 463kcals/1949kJ

Protein 6g

Fat 30g
Saturated fat 18g

Carbohydrate 43g
Sugar 30g

Fiber 2g

Salt 0.3g

2oz (60g) cocoa powder
¾ cup dark brown sugar
1⅓ cups gluten-free all-purpose flour
¾ tsp salt
1½ tsp gluten-free baking powder
½ tsp gluten-free baking soda
10 tbsp unsalted butter, plus extra
½ cup granulated sugar
3 large eggs
1 tsp pure vanilla extract

FOR THE FROSTING
12 tbsp unsalted butter, cubed
2 tbsp dark brown sugar
8oz (225g) dark chocolate, chopped
  (70% cocoa solids)
1 tsp pure vanilla extract

SPECIAL EQUIPMENT
 2 x 8in (20cm) round cake pans

1 Preheat the oven to 350°F (180°C). Lightly grease the pans and line with parchment paper. Put the cocoa and brown sugar in a heatproof bowl, add 1 cup boiling water, mix well, and leave to cool.

2 Sift together the flour, baking powder, and soda. Cream the butter and granulated sugar in a large bowl using an electric whisk until pale and fluffy. Add the eggs, whisking well between additions. Add half the flour mixture, vanilla, and half the cocoa mixture, and whisk for 30 seconds. Scrape down the sides of the bowl and repeat with the remaining flour and cocoa mixtures. Divide the cake mix between the pans. Bake for 25–30 minutes or until the cakes bounce back when lightly touched in the center. Remove the cakes from the oven. Cool for 5 minutes in the pans before peeling off the parchment paper and transferring to a wire rack to cool completely.

3 For the frosting, place the butter and sugar in a pan and gently heat until melted and bubbling. Remove from the heat and stir in the chocolate and vanilla until smooth. Allow to cool, stirring once or twice.

4 Whisk the frosting for 30 seconds or until fluffy. Sandwich the cakes with a third of the frosting, then spread the remainder over the top and sides. Swirl with the back of a knife for a decorative effect and serve, or store in an airtight container for up to 3 days.

CHOCOLATE HAZELNUT WHOOPIE PIES

Filled with ready-made hazelnut spread, these are irresistible. Whoopie pies are based on cakes made by the Amish community in the United States.

MAKES	10
PREP	15 mins
COOK	12–15 mins
FREEZE	3 months
	UNFILLED

1 cup gluten-free all-purpose flour
½ tsp xanthan gum
¼ cup cocoa powder
½ tsp gluten-free baking powder
1oz (30g) blanched hazelnuts
4 tbsp unsalted butter, softened,
  plus extra for greasing

⅓ cup light brown sugar
1 large egg
⅓ cup buttermilk
½ cup gluten-free hazelnut spread

GUIDELINES PER SERVING

● ● ○ Calories
● ● ○ Saturated fat
● ○ ○ Salt

STATISTICS PER PIE

Energy 202kcals/843kJ

Protein 3.5g

Fat 12g
Saturated fat 5g

Carbohydrate 20g
Sugar 13g

Fiber 1g

Salt 0.2g

1 Preheat the oven to 350°F (180°C). Lightly grease 2 baking sheets and line with parchment paper. Sift together the flour, xanthan, cocoa, and baking powder. Toast the hazelnuts in the hot oven for 5 minutes and set aside to cool.

2 Cream the butter and sugar together using an electric whisk. Add the egg, whisking well. Add half the sifted ingredients and half the buttermilk, then whisk until fluffy. Repeat with the remaining sifted ingredients and buttermilk. Place heaped teaspoons of the mix, 2in (5cm) apart, on the baking sheets to form 20 mounds. Dip a clean spoon in warm water and use the back to smooth the surface of the cake mounds.

3 Bake for 12–15 minutes or until the tops have risen and spring back when lightly touched in the center. Leave to cool on the baking sheets for 2–3 minutes before transferring to a wire rack to cool completely.

4 Chop the toasted hazelnuts. To finish, spread a little hazelnut spread on the base of half the cakes, sprinkle with some hazelnuts, and then sandwich together with the remaining cakes.

GREAT FOR KIDS

ORANGE AND ROSEMARY POLENTA CAKE

Wonderfully moist, this cake has a rich, grainy texture that easily surpasses those made from wheat flour.

SERVES 8
PREP 30 mins
COOK 50 mins–1 hour
FREEZE 3 months

GUIDELINES PER SERVING

● ● ● Calories
● ● ● Saturated fat
● ● ● Salt

STATISTICS PER SERVING

Energy 475kcals/1990kJ

Protein 9g

Fat 34g
Saturated fat 13.5g

Carbohydrate 34g
Sugar 27g

Fiber 0.5g

Salt 0.3g

juice and finely grated zest of
  1 large orange
³/₄ cup granulated sugar
sprig of rosemary
12 tbsp unsalted butter, softened,
  plus extra for greasing
3 large eggs, lightly beaten
¹/₂ cup coarse or fine polenta

1³/₄ cups ground almonds
1 tsp gluten-free baking powder
crème fraîche, to serve (optional)

SPECIAL EQUIPMENT
  9in (23cm) round springform cake pan
  electric handheld whisk

1 Put the orange juice and scant 1oz (25g) of the sugar in a small pan. Heat over medium heat, stirring from time to time, until the sugar has dissolved. Add the rosemary, remove from the heat, and let infuse.

2 Preheat the oven to 325°F (160°C). Grease the pan and line the bottom with parchment paper. With an electric handheld mixer, cream the butter and remaining sugar until fluffy. Gradually add the eggs, whisking well after each addition. Add the polenta and almonds, and gently fold in with a rubber spatula. Finally, fold in the orange zest and baking powder. The batter will seem quite stiff.

3 Scrape the mixture into the prepared pan and smooth the surface with a palette knife. Bake the cake for 50–60 minutes, until a skewer inserted in the center comes out clean. Leave the cake in the pan, and reheat the syrup over medium heat until hot. Remove and discard the rosemary.

4 While the cake and syrup are both still hot, poke holes in the cake using a thin skewer or toothpick. Pour the syrup a little at a time over the cake, until it is all used up. When cool, remove the cake from the pan and serve at room temperature, with crème fraîche (if using).

How to freeze
This cake will keep in an airtight container for up to 3 days. To freeze, wrap it in parchment paper and seal with foil. Defrost thoroughly before eating, and reheat for 15 minutes at 350°F (180°C) for best results.

RED VELVET CUPCAKES

These chocolate-flavored, vanilla-scented cupcakes look stunning with their deep red color.

MAKES 12
PREP 20 mins
COOK 40–45 mins
FREEZE 2 months

GUIDELINES PER SERVING

● ● ● Calories

● ● ○ Saturated fat

● ○ ○ Salt

STATISTICS PER CUPCAKE

Energy 380kcals/1600kJ

Protein 4.5g

Fat 17g
Saturated fat 2g

Carbohydrate 52g
Sugar 42g

Fiber 1g

Salt 0.2g

1½ cups gluten-free self-rising flour
1 tsp xanthan gum
3 tbsp cocoa powder
1 tsp gluten-free cream of tartar
6 tbsp unsalted butter
⅔ cup granulated sugar
2 large eggs
2 tbsp natural red food coloring
2 tsp pure vanilla extract
1 tsp cider vinegar
¾ cup buttermilk

FOR THE CREAM CHEESE FROSTING
4oz (115g) full-fat cream cheese
4 tbsp unsalted butter, softened
½ tsp pure vanilla extract
2¾ cup confectioner's sugar, sifted

SPECIAL EQUIPMENT
deep 12-hole muffin pan lined
 with paper liners
piping bag equipped with a
 ¾in (2cm) star nozzle

1 Preheat the oven to 325°F (160°C). Combine the flour, xanthan, cocoa, and cream of tartar in a bowl.

2 In another large bowl, beat the butter and sugar with an electric mixer. Add the eggs, one at a time, beating between additions. Add half the flour mixture, coloring, vanilla, vinegar, and half the buttermilk. Whisk well. Add the remaining flour and buttermilk. Whisk again for 30 seconds. Divide the mixture between the paper liners so they are two-thirds full. Bake for 40–45 minutes or until the centers spring back when touched in the middle. Cool for 5 minutes, then transfer to a wire rack.

3 For the frosting, beat the cream cheese, butter, and vanilla in a large bowl using an electric mixer. Gradually add the confectioner's sugar, a little at a time, until it is all incorporated. Beat for 30 seconds until very light and fluffy.

4 Carefully slice and crumble a thin disk from the top of three cupcakes to make crumbs for the topping. Spoon the frosting into a piping bag and pipe it in swirls on top of the cakes. Scatter over the cupcake crumbs to finish.

COCONUT CAKE WITH LIME FROSTING

Crunchy unsweetened, dried coconut adds texture to this cake; a zingy lime buttercream cuts through the richness.

SERVES 12
PREP 20 mins
COOK 25–30 mins
FREEZE 3 months

GUIDELINES PER SERVING

● ● ● Calories
● ● ● Saturated fat
● ● ● Salt

STATISTICS PER SLICE

Energy 474kcals/1997kJ

Protein 4g

Fat 27g
Saturated fat 18g

Carbohydrate 55g
Sugar 44g

Fiber 1.7g

Salt 0.3g

12 tbsp unsalted butter, softened, plus extra for greasing
¾ cup granulated sugar
3 large eggs, beaten
1¼ cups gluten-free all-purpose flour
½ tsp salt
1 tsp gluten-free baking powder
2oz (60g) unsweetened, dried coconut
⅔ cup cream of coconut

FOR THE FROSTING
6 tbsp unsalted butter, softened
1⅔ cups confectioner's sugar
finely grated zest and juice of 2 limes
1 tbsp unsweetened, dried coconut, toasted

SPECIAL EQUIPMENT
2 x 8in (20cm) round cake pans

1 Preheat the oven to 350°F (180°C). Lightly grease the pans and line with parchment paper. Cream the butter and granulated sugar in a large bowl with an electric mixer, until pale and fluffy. Add the eggs, beat well between additions. Sift over the flour, baking powder, and salt, add both kinds of coconut, and whisk briefly. Scrape down the sides of the bowl, then whisk again for 30 seconds.

2 Divide the mixture evenly between the pans and bake for 25–30 minutes or until the cakes bounce back when lightly touched in the center.

3 For the frosting, cream the the butter and confectioner's sugar in a large bowl with an electric mixer until fluffy. Add the lime zest and juice and beat again for 30 seconds until fluffy and light. Cover and chill until firm.

4 Remove the cakes from the oven and cool in the pans for 5 minutes before peeling off the parchment and transferring to a wire rack to cool.

5 Sandwich the cakes together with a third of the frosting, then spread the remainder over the top and sides. Swirl with the back of a knife for decorative effect. Sprinkle over the toasted coconut to finish.

STICKY GINGER CAKE

This moist dark ginger cake, flecked with crystallized ginger, is best made a day in advance for the flavors to deepen.

2 tbsp crystallized ginger syrup, from a jar of ginger in syrup

²⁄₃ cup corn syrup

8 tbsp unsalted butter, plus extra for greasing

½ cup dark brown sugar

1¾ cups gluten-free, all-purpose flour

2 tsp ground ginger

1½ tsp gluten-free baking powder

1 tsp xanthan gum

1 tsp gluten-free baking soda

½ tsp ground cinnamon

pinch of salt

3 balls of stem ginger, from the jar, finely chopped, or ¼ cup chopped, crystallized ginger

3 large eggs

⅓ cup milk

SPECIAL EQUIPMENT

9 x 5in loaf pan

SERVES   12
PREP   15 mins
COOK   50–55 mins
FREEZE   3 months

GUIDELINES PER SERVING

●●○ Calories

●●○ Saturated fat

●●○ Salt

STATISTICS PER SLICE

Energy 264kcals/1109kJ

Protein 4.25g

Fat 10.5g
Saturated fat 6g

Carbohydrate 38g
Sugar 23.5g

Fiber 1g

Salt 0.8g

1 Place the syrups in a pan, add the butter and sugar, and heat, stirring until the mixture is smooth and melted. Set aside to cool slightly.

2 Preheat the oven to 350°F (180°C). Grease and line the pan with parchment paper.

3 Sift the flour, ground ginger, baking powder, xanthan, soda, cinnamon, and salt into a large bowl. Add the cooled syrup mixture to the dry ingredients along with the stem ginger, eggs, and milk. Mix well with a wooden spoon.

4 Pour the mixture into the prepared pan and bake for 50–55 minutes, or until the cake springs back when lightly touched in the center. Leave to cool in the pan for 10 minutes before turning out. Cool on a wire rack. Store in an airtight container for up to 1 week.

Cook's Tip
If preferred, bake 2 loaves in 5¾ x 3in mini loaf pans and freeze the second loaf.

VANILLA AND CHESTNUT CAKE

SERVES 12
PREP 15 mins
COOK 40–45 mins
FREEZE 3 months

GUIDELINES PER SERVING

● ● ○ Calories

● ● ○ Saturated fat

● ○ ○ Salt

STATISTICS PER SLICE

Energy 141kcals/588kJ

Protein 4g

Fat 9g
Saturated fat 5g

Carbohydrate 19g
Sugar 12g

Fiber 1g

Salt 0.3g

You could jazz up this cake with a bit of whipped cream: split the cake in two, spread some cream in the middle, and dust the top with confectioner's sugar.

vegetable oil, for greasing
4 large eggs, separated
1½ cups light brown sugar
¾ cup full-fat crème fraîche
2 tsp pure vanilla extract

1 cup chestnut flour
2 tsp gluten-free baking powder

SPECIAL EQUIPMENT
8in (20cm) round cake pan

1 Preheat the oven to 350°F (180°C). Lightly grease the pan and line the base with parchment paper.

2 Place the egg yolks and sugar in a large bowl and use an electric mixer to beat until light and creamy. Add the crème fraîche and vanilla. Sift in the flour and baking powder and gently fold in.

3 Whisk the egg whites in a clean bowl until they form stiff peaks. Stir 1 heaped tablespoon of the egg whites into the cake mixture, then gently fold through the remainder.

4 Spoon the mixture into the prepared pan and bake for 40–45 minutes or until the cake springs back when lightly touched in the center. Cool in the pan for 5 minutes, then turn out and leave to cool completely on a wire rack. Dust with confectioner's sugar and serve.

Cook's Tip
Chestnut flour is available from good health food stores and Italian delicatessens.

ALMOND CAKE

This moist cake will store for an exceptionally long time and just seems to get better with each day.

vegetable oil, for greasing
12 tbsp unsalted butter, softened
¾ cup granulated sugar
3 large eggs, beaten
2 tsp almond extract
2½ cups ground almonds
¾ cup polenta or fine cornmeal

1½ tsp gluten-free baking powder
⅔ cup Greek yogurt
1oz (30g) sliced almonds

SPECIAL EQUIPMENT
9in (23cm) round springform cake pan

1 Preheat the oven to 325°F (160°C). Grease the pan and line the base with parchment paper.

2 Place the butter and sugar in a large bowl and cream together with an electric mixer until pale and fluffy. Add the eggs, beating well between additions. Stir in the almond extract.

3 Mix the ground almonds, polenta, and baking powder together, add half to the creamed mixture along with half the yogurt, and whisk well. Whisk in the remaining dry ingredients and the yogurt.

4 Spoon into the prepared pan and level the surface. Scatter over the sliced almonds. Bake in the center of the oven for 1–1¼ hours or until a skewer inserted in the center comes out clean. Leave to cool in the pan for 10 minutes before transferring to a wire rack to cool completely. Store in an airtight container for up to 2 weeks.

SERVES 12
PREP 20 mins
COOK 1–1¼ hours

GUIDELINES PER SERVING

● ● ● Calories
● ● ● Saturated fat
● ● ● Salt

STATISTICS PER SLICE

Energy 380kcals/1582kJ

Protein 8.5g

Fat 28g
Saturated fat 9.5g

Carbohydrate 23g
Sugar 16g

Fiber 0.3g

Salt 0.5g

LEMON AND RASPBERRY LAYERED POLENTA CAKE

Polenta gives this moist cake a wonderful lemony color. You can also try strawberries instead of raspberries.

SERVES 12
PREP 20 mins
COOK 25–30 mins
FREEZE 3 months
UNFILLED SPONGES

GUIDELINES PER SERVING

● ● ● Calories

● ● ● Saturated fat

● ● ○ Salt

STATISTICS PER SLICE

Energy 462kcals/1924kJ

Protein 6g

Fat 32g
Saturated fat 16g

Carbohydrate 36g
Sugar 27g

Fiber 1.3g

Salt 0.36g

vegetable oil, for greasing
16 tbsp butter, softened
1 cup superfine granulated sugar
3 large eggs
1 cup ground almonds
1¼ cups polenta or fine cornmeal
zest and juice of 2 lemons

10oz (300g) fresh raspberries
¾ cup heavy cream
¾ cup confectioner's sugar, plus
   extra for dusting

SPECIAL EQUIPMENT
 2 x 8in (20cm) round cake pans

1 Preheat the oven to 350°F (180°C). Lightly grease the pans and line with parchment paper.

2 In a large bowl, cream the butter and sugar with an electric whisk until pale and fluffy. Add the eggs, one at a time, beating well between additions. Add 1–2 tablespoons of the ground almonds with the last egg to prevent curdling. Add the remaining almonds, polenta, lemon zest and juice, and a quarter of the raspberries, and gently fold together.

3 Divide the mixture equally between the 2 prepared pans, scattering 10 raspberries over one of them; this will be the top layer. Bake for 25–30 minutes, until the cakes spring back when lightly touched in the center. Leave to cool for 5 minutes in the pans. Carefully remove from the pans, peel away the lining paper, and cool completely on a wire rack.

4 With an electric whisk, whip the cream and confectioner's sugar until peaks form. Fold in the remaining raspberries. Spoon it over the base cake, and top with the raspberry-topped cake. Dust with confectioner's sugar and serve. Once filled, this cake should be served within 4 hours.

SPICED HONEY CAKE

A great cut-and-come-again cake with a wonderfully moist crumb. Sprinkle sliced almonds on top, if preferred.

SERVES   12
PREP   20 mins
COOK   1 hour
FREEZE   3 months

GUIDELINES PER SERVING

● ● ○   Calories

● ● ○   Saturated fat

● ○ ○   Salt

STATISTICS PER SLICE

Energy 276kcals/1161kJ

Protein 4.75g

Fat 11.5g
Saturated fat 6g

Carbohydrate 38g
Sugar 23.5g

Fiber 0.8g

Salt 0.27g

²/₃ cup honey
8 tbsp unsalted butter, plus extra
  for greasing
½ cup light brown sugar
1¾ cups gluten-free all-purpose flour
1 tsp ground cinnamon
½ tsp ground ginger
1½ tsp gluten-free baking powder
1 tsp xanthan gum
1 tsp gluten-free baking soda
pinch of salt

3 large eggs
⅓ cup milk

TO DECORATE
⅓ cup honey
1oz (30g) pistachio nuts, shelled,
  skinned, and chopped

SPECIAL EQUIPMENT
8in (20cm) square or 9in (23cm)
  round cake pan

1 Place the honey, butter, and sugar into a small pan and heat, stirring until the mixture is smooth and melted. Set aside to cool slightly.

2 Preheat the oven to 350°F (180°C). Grease and line the pan with parchment paper. In a large bowl, sift together the flour, spices, baking powder, xanthan, soda, and salt. Add the cooled honey mixture to the bowl along with the eggs and milk and mix well with a wooden spoon. Pour the mixture into the prepared pan and bake for 1 hour or until the cake springs back when lightly touched in the center.

3 To decorate, place the honey in a small pan, bring to a boil, and boil for 1–2 minutes or until the honey darkens and thickens. Stir in the pistachios to coat, then pour over the top of the warm cake. Allow the cake to cool completely before removing from the pan.

HONEY
Honey attracts water, which makes it very good for baking as it keeps cakes moist for longer.

CARROT CAKE

Everyone loves a carrot cake, but if walnuts are not your thing, replace them with the same amount of raisins.

SERVES	12
PREP	20 mins
COOK	35–40 mins
FREEZE	3 months

1 cup light brown sugar

1 cup sunflower or vegetable oil, plus extra for greasing

1 tsp pure vanilla extract

3 large eggs

1½ cups gluten-free all-purpose flour

1 tsp gluten-free baking powder

½ tsp gluten-free baking soda

1 tsp xanthan gum

1 tsp ground cinnamon, plus extra for dusting

1 tsp ground ginger

8oz (225g) carrots, coarsely grated

2oz (60g) walnuts or raisins, finely chopped

a few walnut halves, to decorate

FOR THE FROSTING

2 tbsp unsalted butter, softened

2½oz (75g) full-fat cream cheese

1 tsp pure vanilla extract

1¾ confectioner's sugar

SPECIAL EQUIPMENT

2 x 8in (20cm) round cake pans

GUIDELINES PER SERVING

● ● ● Calories

● ● ○ Saturated fat

● ○ ○ Salt

STATISTICS PER SLICE

Energy 464kcals/1943kJ

Protein 5g

Fat 27g
Saturated fat 6g

Carbohydrate 52g
Sugar 38g

Fiber 1.6g

Salt 0.3g

1 Preheat the oven to 350°F (180°C). Lightly grease the pans and line with parchment paper. Beat the sugar, oil, vanilla, and eggs in a large bowl with an electric whisk until smooth and thick. Sift over the flour, baking powder, soda, xanthan, cinnamon, and ginger, then fold in until well combined. Fold in the carrots and walnuts (or raisins, if using).

2 Divide the mixture between the cake pans. Bake for 35–40 minutes or until golden and risen and the middle bounces back when lightly pressed. Cool in the pan for 5 minutes before transferring to a wire rack to cool.

3 For the frosting, place the butter and cream cheese in a large bowl and cream together using an electric whisk. Add the vanilla and mix. Sift the confectioner's sugar into a large bowl, then add to the cream cheese a little at a time, whisking well between additions.

4 Peel away the parchment paper from the cakes. Divide the frosting between the 2 cakes, spreading it evenly over the top. Stack the cakes, top with walnut halves, and dust with cinnamon.

GREAT FOR KIDS

RICH FRUIT CAKE

SERVES 12
PREP 20 mins
PLUS SOAKING
COOK 2 hours
FREEZE 3 months

GUIDELINES PER SERVING

●●● Calories
●●● Saturated fat
●○○ Salt

STATISTICS PER SLICE

Energy 460kcals/1932kJ

Protein 6.5g

Fat 21g
Saturated fat 9g

Carbohydrate 61g
Sugar 53g

Fiber 2.2g

Salt 0.13g

This fruit cake matures over time and it's worth baking it 2–3 months ahead. If you like, make holes with a skewer and spoon over some brandy every 2–3 weeks.

1lb 5oz (600g) mixed dried fruit, such as vine fruits, dates, prunes, and figs
4oz (115g) candied cherries, halved
zest and juice of 1 lemon
1 tsp apple pie spice
2 tbsp brandy
12 tbsp unsalted butter, softened, plus extra for greasing
1 cup light brown sugar
3 large eggs

1 cup gluten-free all-purpose flour
¼ cup ground almonds
1oz (30g) chopped walnuts
65 whole blanched almonds, approx. 2½oz (75g) in weight (optional)

SPECIAL EQUIPMENT
8in (20cm) round or 8in (20cm) square cake pan

1 Place the dried fruit, candied cherries, lemon zest and juice, spice, and brandy in a large bowl. Mix well, cover, and leave to soak for at least 4 hours or preferably overnight.

2 Preheat the oven to 325°F (160°C). Lightly grease and line the pan with parchment paper. In a large bowl, cream the butter and sugar together until pale and fluffy using an electric whisk. Add the eggs, whisking well between additions.

3 Add the flour, almonds, walnuts, and soaked fruit, and stir until evenly mixed. Spoon into the prepared pan and level the surface. Top with the whole almonds (if using), arranging them in a pattern of decreasing circles. Alternatively, omit the almonds and decorate after baking with approximately 1¼lb (550g) each of store-bought gluten-free marzipan and gluten-free icing.

4 Bake in the center of the oven for 2 hours or until the top is golden and a skewer inserted into the middle comes out clean. Check the cake halfway through and if it's browning too quickly, cover loosely with parchment paper. Cool in the pan, then remove the parchment, rewrap in clean parchment and foil, and store in an airtight container until ready to use.

CRANBERRY AND APPLE CAKE

Choose a red-skinned apple with a little tartness to it for this cake—Jonathan apples work well.

14 tbsp unsalted butter, softened,
 plus extra for greasing
1lb (450g) apples, cored and sliced
3oz (85g) dried cranberries
2 tbsp lemon juice
1 cup light brown sugar
3 large eggs, beaten
1¼ cups gluten-free all-purpose flour

2 tsp gluten-free baking powder
½ tsp ground cinnamon
⅔ cup sour cream
1 tbsp coarse sugar

SPECIAL EQUIPMENT
 9in (23cm) round springform cake pan

1 Melt 2 tablespoons of the butter in a large frying pan, add the apples, and sauté for 4–5 minutes, or until just softened. Stir in the cranberries and lemon juice and set aside to cool. Preheat the oven to 350°F (180°C). Lightly grease and line the pan with parchment paper.

2 Cream the remaining butter and the brown sugar until fluffy using an electric mixer. Gradually add the eggs, beating well between additions. Sift the flour, baking powder, and cinnamon together, add half to the bowl along with the sour cream, and whisk again. Repeat with the remaining flour mix, then fold in two-thirds of the apple and cranberry mixture.

3 Spoon the mixture into the pan, leveling the surface. Arrange the remaining fruit on top and sprinkle with the coarse sugar.

4 Bake in the center of the oven for 1–1¼ hours until golden and springy to the touch and a skewer inserted into the middle comes out clean. Cool in the pan for 10 minutes before transferring to a plate. Serve warm as a dessert with sour cream, or cold in slices.

SERVES	12
PREP	20 mins
	PLUS COOLING
COOK	1–1¼ hours
FREEZE	3 months

GUIDELINES PER SERVING

⬤⬤⬤ Calories
⬤⬤⬤ Saturated fat
⬤⬤◯ Salt

STATISTICS PER SLICE

Energy 327kcals/1377kJ

Protein 4g

Fat 18g
Saturated fat 11g

Carbohydrate 32g
Sugar 20g

Fiber 2.2g

Salt 0.3g

GREAT FOR KIDS

FRUIT STREUSEL CAKE

Pink rhubarb looks pretty in this dessert-style cake, but green rhubarb works just as well.

SERVES 12
PREP 25 mins
COOK 1¼ hours
FREEZE 3 months

GUIDELINES PER SERVING

●●● Calories
●●● Saturated fat
●● Salt

STATISTICS PER SLICE

Energy 310kcals/1306kJ

Protein 4.5g

Fat 16g
Saturated fat 9g

Carbohydrate 38g
Sugar 19g

Fiber 2g

Salt 0.2g

GREAT FOR KIDS

9 tbsp unsalted butter, softened, plus
  extra for greasing
½ cup light brown sugar
8oz (225g) rhubarb, sliced into
  ½in (1cm) pieces
4oz (115g) strawberries, chopped
2 large eggs
1⅓ cups gluten-free all-purpose flour
1 tsp gluten-free baking powder
½ tsp ground cinnamon
3 tbsp milk
gluten-free custard (see page 286)
  or crème fraîche, to serve

FOR THE TOPPING
½ cup gluten-free all-purpose flour
¼ cup brown sugar, plus 1 tbsp
  for sprinkling
½ tsp ground cinnamon
4 tbsp cold unsalted butter, cubed
1oz (30g) whole blanched hazelnuts,
  toasted and coarsely chopped

SPECIAL EQUIPMENT
9in (23cm) round cake pan

1 Melt 1 tablespoon each of the butter and brown sugar in a frying pan, add the rhubarb and sauté for 3–4 minutes, or until soft. Remove, stir in the strawberries, and set aside. The fruit should be cold before it's stirred into the mixture or it will sink to the bottom of the cake.

2 Preheat the oven to 350°F (180°C). Lightly grease the pan and line the base with parchment paper. For the topping, pulse the flour, brown sugar, cinnamon, and butter in a food processor until it resembles bread crumbs. Transfer to a bowl, stir in the hazelnuts, and set aside.

3 Cream the remaining butter and brown sugar using an electric mixer, until fluffy. Add the eggs, beating between additions. Sift together the flour, baking powder, and cinnamon. Add half the flour mixture and half the milk to the wet ingredients and beat; add the remaining flour and milk and beat. Stir in the rhubarb and strawberries. Spoon the mixture into the pan, scatter over the topping, and sprinkle with brown sugar. Bake for 1¼ hours, or until a skewer inserted into the cake comes out clean. Leave to cool in the pan for 10 minutes, remove, and cool on a wire rack. Serve with gluten-free custard or crème fraîche.

CHESTNUT BANANA BREAD

Sweet breads are easy cakes to prepare, as there is no need to beat in air and retain it with gentle folding—simply mix well, pour into the pan, and bake.

SERVES	12
PREP	15 mins
COOK	50–55 mins
FREEZE	3 months

1 cup gluten-free all-purpose flour
1 cup chestnut flour
1½ tsp gluten-free baking powder
1 tsp xanthan gum
1 tsp gluten-free baking soda
½ tsp ground cinnamon
½ tsp freshly grated nutmeg
pinch of salt

3 ripe bananas
8 tbsp unsalted butter, plus extra for greasing
½ cup light brown sugar
3 large eggs
⅓ cup milk

SPECIAL EQUIPMENT
9 x 5in loaf pan

GUIDELINES PER SERVING

● ● ○ Calories

● ● ○ Saturated fat

● ○ ○ Salt

STATISTICS PER SLICE

Energy 219kcals/918kJ

Protein 4.5g

Fat 10.3g
Saturated fat 5.7g

Carbohydrate 34.7g
Sugar 19.7g

Fiber 2.08g

Salt 0.7g

1 Preheat the oven to 350°F (180°C). Grease the pan and line with parchment paper.

2 In a large bowl, sift together the flours, baking powder, xanthan, soda, cinnamon, nutmeg, and salt.

3 Mash the bananas. Melt the butter, then stir in the sugar. Beat the eggs and milk together. Make a well in the center of the sifted ingredients, add all the wet ingredients, and mix well with a wooden spoon.

4 Pour the mixture into the prepared pan and bake for 50–55 minutes or until the cake springs back when lightly touched in the center. Leave to cool in the pan for 10 minutes before turning out. Cool on a wire rack. Store in an airtight container for up to 1 week.

Cook's Tip
If preferred, bake 2 loaves in 5¾ x 3 in mini loaf pans and freeze the second loaf.

GREAT FOR KIDS

APRICOT AND CARDAMOM TEABREAD

Earl Grey tea adds a lovely citrus note to this wonderfully moist teabread, but any other tea will work too.

SERVES 12
PREP 15 mins
COOK 1 hour 20-25 mins
FREEEZE 2 months

GUIDELINES PER SERVING

● ● ○ Calories

● ● ○ Saturated fat

● ○ ○ Salt

STATISTICS PER SLICE

Energy 225kcals/948kJ

Protein 4g

Fat 7g
Saturated fat 3.5g

Carbohydrate 36g
Sugar 23g

Fiber 2.4g

Salt 0.3g

GREAT
FOR KIDS

1 teabag, such as Earl Grey
8oz (225g) dried apricots, finely chopped
6 cardamom pods, split
1 cup light brown sugar
oil, for greasing
1$\frac{1}{3}$ cups gluten-free all-purpose flour
1 tsp gluten-free baking powder
1 tsp xanthan gum
1 tsp ground cinnamon
a pinch of salt

5 tbsp cold unsalted butter, cubed
2 large eggs, beaten
$\frac{1}{2}$oz (15g) sliced almonds
2 tbsp coarse sugar
butter, to serve

SPECIAL EQUIPMENT
9 x 5in (23 x 13cm) loaf pan

1 Pour 1$\frac{1}{4}$ cups boiling water over the teabag and leave to infuse for 5 minutes. Place the apricots in a small pan. Remove the teabag and add the hot tea, cardamom, and sugar to the pan. Bring to a boil, then simmer, uncovered, for 10 minutes. Leave until cold; the apricot mixture will cool quickly if poured into a shallow tray. Remove the cardamom pods.

2 Preheat the oven to 350°F (180°C). Lightly oil the pan and line the base with parchment paper. Sift the flour, baking powder, xanthan gum, cinnamon, and salt into a large bowl. Rub the butter into the flour mixture. Stir the cold apricots and their cooking liquid into the flour, add the eggs, and beat together. Pour into the pan and scatter over the almonds and coarse sugar. Bake in the center of the oven for 1 hour 20–25 minutes or until well risen and firm to the touch.

3 Cool in the pan for 10 minutes before transferring to a wire rack to cool completely. The teabread is even better the day after baking and will keep in an airtight container for up to 1 week.

GOLDEN RAISIN SCONES

A classic teatime treat. Serve split and spread with strawberry jam and clotted cream for extra indulgence.

MAKES   8
PREP   10 mins
COOK   15–20 mins
FREEZE   3 months

GUIDELINES PER SERVING

● ● ○   Calories

● ● ○   Saturated fat

● ● ○   Salt

STATISTICS PER SCONE

Energy 264kcals/1116kJ

Protein 4.5g

Fat 9g
Saturated fat 5.5g

Carbohydrate 40g
Sugar 18.5g

Fiber 1.3g

Salt 0.9g

GREAT FOR KIDS

1 cup gluten-free all-purpose flour
1 cup rice flour
¼ cup granulated sugar
4 tsp gluten-free baking powder
1½ tsp xanthan gum
pinch of salt
4 tbsp cold unsalted butter, cubed,
   plus extra for greasing

¾ cup buttermilk, or ½ milk
   and ½ full-fat plain yogurt
3oz (85g) golden raisins
1 large egg, beaten, to glaze

SPECIAL EQUIPMENT
2¾in (7cm) round metal cutter

1 Preheat the oven to 425°F (220°C). Sift the flours, sugar, baking powder, xanthan, and salt into a large bowl. Add the butter and rub it in with your fingertips until the mixture resembles fine bread crumbs; alternatively, pulse in a food processor.

2 Stir the buttermilk into the crumb mixture, add the golden raisins, then gently mix using your hands to make a soft dough. Knead briefly. On a lightly floured surface, roll out the dough to a thickness of ¾in (2cm) and press out 8 scones using the metal cutter, re-rolling the dough as necessary. Dip the cutter in flour before cutting out each round to achieve a clean cut. This will help the scones rise evenly.

3 Place the scones a little apart on a lightly greased baking sheet and brush the tops with egg. Bake near the top of the oven for 15–20 minutes or until risen and golden brown on top. Cool for 5 minutes, then serve warm or cold.

Variations

CHOCOLATE CHIP Omit the golden raisins and replace with an equal weight of milk chocolate chips.
CHEESE SCONES Omit the sugar and golden raisins, add 1 teaspoon mustard powder to the dry ingredients, then stir in 4oz (115g) grated mature Cheddar cheese with the buttermilk. Shape as before, dust the tops with a little paprika and more grated cheese, if desired.

FRESH BERRY SCONES

A lovely summery twist on the classic scone. Single berries, freshly-picked in season, taste stunning: strawberries in June, raspberries in July, and blackberries in August.

3oz (85g) strawberries, raspberries,
 or blackberries, or a mix
1 cup gluten-free all-purpose flour
1 cup rice flour
¼ cup granulated sugar
4 tsp gluten-free baking powder
2 tsp xanthan gum
pinch of salt
4 tbsp cold unsalted butter, cubed,
 plus extra for greasing

⅔ cup buttermilk, or ½ milk and ½
 full-fat plain yogurt, plus extra to glaze
 (see Cook's Tip)
sprinkle of coarse sugar, to glaze

SPECIAL EQUIPMENT
 2¾in (7cm) round metal cutter

1 Preheat the oven to 425°F (220°C). If using strawberries, cut them into halves or quarters. Sift together the flours, sugar, baking powder, xanthan, and salt into a large bowl. Add the butter and rub it in with your fingertips until fine crumbs form; alternatively, pulse in a food processor. Empty the mixture into a bowl, stir in the berries, add the buttermilk, and mix using a rubber spatula to make a soft dough. Knead briefly.

2 On a lightly floured surface, roll out the dough to a thickness of ¾in (2cm) and press out 6 scones using the metal cutter, re-rolling the dough as necessary. Dip the cutter in flour before cutting out each round to achieve a clean cut. Place the scones a little apart on a lightly greased baking sheet. Brush the tops with buttermilk and sprinkle over the coarse sugar. Bake near the top of the oven for 15–20 minutes or until risen and golden brown on top. Cool for 5 minutes, then serve warm or cold.

Cook's Tip
Depending on how juicy the berries are, you may need to add a little more or less buttermilk. The dough shouldn't be too soft and wet or the scones won't rise.

MAKES 6
PREP 15 mins
COOK 15–20 mins
FREEZE 3 months

GUIDELINES PER SERVING

● ● ○ Calories
● ● ○ Saturated fat
● ● ○ Salt

STATISTICS PER SCONE

Energy 280kcals/1175kJ

Protein 4g

Fat 9g
Saturated fat 5g

Carbohydrate 44g
Sugar 16g

Fiber 1.5g

Salt 1.1g

GREAT FOR KIDS

CHOCOLATE AND PECAN BROWNIES

MAKES	20
PREP	15 mins
COOK	15–18 mins
FREEZE	3 months

GUIDELINES PER SERVING

● ● ○ Calories

● ● ● Saturated fat

● ○ ○ Salt

STATISTICS PER BROWNIE

Energy 282kcals/1178kJ

Protein 4g

Fat 16.5g
Saturated fat 8g

Carbohydrate 30g
Sugar 24g

Fiber 1.5g

Salt 0.25g

If you are not a fan of nuts, omit the pecans and add 2oz (60g) dried cherries instead.

10oz (300g) dark chocolate (at least 60% cocoa solids), broken into pieces
12 tbsp cold unsalted butter, cubed, plus extra for greasing
1½ cups light brown sugar
5 large eggs
1¼ cups gluten-free all-purpose flour

¼ cup cocoa powder
3oz (85g) pecans

SPECIAL EQUIPMENT
9 x 13in (23 x 33cm) rectangular pan

1 Preheat the oven to 400°F (200°C). Lightly grease the pan and line with parchment paper.

2 Put the chocolate in a large heatproof bowl with the butter and place over a pan of gently simmering water, stirring occasionally until melted and smooth. Stir in the sugar and allow to cool slightly.

3 Gradually add the eggs, beating well between additions. Sift the flour and cocoa over the mixture, add the pecans, and then fold together. The mixture should be thick and glossy.

4 Spoon the mixture into the prepared pan and bake for 15–18 minutes or until the top is firm to the touch, but the center is still slightly sticky when tested with the tip of a knife. Leave to cool in the pan. Once cold, remove from the pan and cut the brownies into about 20 squares.

GREAT FOR KIDS

Cook's Tip
If you overcook the brownies, you'll end up with chocolate cake. You want them to be crusty on the top but gooey in the center. They firm up as they cool.

SHORTBREAD COOKIES

These cookies have a wonderfully buttery flavor and short, crumbly texture.

12 tbsp unsalted butter, softened,
  plus extra for greasing
¼ cup granulated sugar, plus extra
  to dust
1¼ cups gluten-free all-purpose flour
½ cup rice flour

¼ cup cornstarch
1 tsp xanthan gum

SPECIAL EQUIPMENT
 8 x 8in (20 x 20cm) rectangular pan
 or 7in (18cm) round pan

1 Preheat the oven to 350°F (180°C) and lightly grease the pan. Use an electric whisk to cream together the butter and sugar in a large bowl until light and fluffy. Sift over the flours and xanthan, then fold in very gently with a wooden spoon to form a smooth, stiff dough; stop as soon as the flours are mixed through. Bring the dough together with your hands.

2 Press the dough into the bottom of the pan. Level and smooth it with your fingertips, then prick all over with a fork. Bake for 25–30 minutes or until pale golden and firm to touch. Remove from the oven and, using a sharp knife, cut it into 16 fingers and sprinkle generously with sugar. Cool in the pan. Use a spatula to remove the squares and store in an airtight container.

Variations
LEMON Add the finely grated zest of 1 lemon to the butter and sugar when creaming it.
LAVENDER Instead of ordinary sugar, use lavender sugar. You can make your own by mixing whole dried lavender flowers with sugar and leaving to infuse for 2 days; you need about 1 teaspoon flowers per 2¼ cups sugar.

Cook's Tips
Choose good-quality butter for this recipe; margarine just won't do. It's also very important to let the shortbread cool in the pan, otherwise it will crumble and break easily. If freezing, leave to cool completely and wrap the cookies in foil.

MAKES	16
PREP	10 mins
COOK	25–30 mins
FREEZE	3 months

GUIDELINES PER SERVING

- ● ● ○   Calories
- ● ● ○   Saturated fat
- ● ○ ○   Salt

STATISTICS PER BISCUIT

Energy 166kcals/699kJ

Protein 1.5g

Fat 9g
Saturated fat 6g

Carbohydrate 19g
Sugar 5.5g

Fiber 0.6g

Salt trace

GREAT FOR KIDS

CHOCOLATE CHIP COOKIES

MAKES 14
PREP 10 mins
COOK 15 mins
FREEZE 3 months

GUIDELINES PER SERVING

● ● ○ Calories
● ● ○ Saturated fat
● ○ ○ Salt

STATISTICS PER COOKIE

Energy 204kcals/858kJ

Protein 2.3g

Fat 9g
Saturated fat 5.5g

Carbohydrate 28g
Sugar 16g

Fiber 0.8g

Salt 0.2g

For an even more chocolatey treat, replace ¼ cup of the flour with cocoa powder.

8 tbsp unsalted butter, softened
⅔ cup granulated sugar
1 large egg
1 tsp pure vanilla extract
1¼ cups gluten-free all-purpose flour

1 tsp baking powder
½ tsp salt
⅓ cup gluten-free rice flour
3oz (85g) chocolate chips, or chocolate broken into small chunks

1 Preheat the oven to 375°F (190°C). Line the baking sheets with parchment paper.

2 Cream together the butter and sugar until fluffy, using an electric whisk. Add the egg and vanilla and whisk again.

3 Sift the flours, baking powder, and salt into the mixture, add the chocolate chips, and mix well with a wooden spoon. Heap 14 tablespoons of the mixture onto the prepared baking sheets; place them well apart since they will spread as they bake. Flatten them with your fingertips.

4 Bake for 15 minutes or until golden brown. Use a metal spatula to transfer the cookies to a wire rack and leave until cold. Don't worry if the cookies are soft when you take them out of the oven; they crisp as they cool.

GREAT FOR KIDS

CHOCOLATE
You could use dark, milk, or white chocolate chips or chunks in these cookies. If making for children, avoid dark chocolate, which doesn't seem to appeal to younger palates.

OAT AND RAISIN COOKIES

Crunchy on the outside and lightly chewy in the middle, the whole family will love these easy-to-make cookies. Omit the raisins if you prefer.

MAKES	18
PREP	10 mins
COOK	15 mins
FREEZE	3 months

8 tbsp unsalted butter, softened, plus extra for greasing
1½ cups brown sugar
1 large egg
1 tsp pure vanilla extract
½ cup gluten-free all-purpose flour

1 tsp ground cinnamon
½ tsp gluten-free baking soda
pinch of salt
2 cups rolled oats
2oz (60g) raisins (optional)

1. Preheat the oven to 375°F (190°C). Lightly grease the baking sheet or line with parchment paper.

2. Cream together the butter and sugar until fluffy, using an electric whisk. Add the egg and vanilla and whisk again.

3. Sift the flour, cinnamon, soda, and salt into the mixture, add the oats and the raisins (if using), and mix well with a wooden spoon.

4. Roll the mixture into 18 walnut-sized balls and place them well apart on the baking sheet. Flatten them with your fingertips and bake for 15 minutes or until the cookies are golden brown. Leave to cool on the baking sheet for 2 minutes, then use a metal spatula to transfer the cookies to a wire rack to cool completely.

GUIDELINES PER COOKIE

● ● ○ Calories

● ● ○ Saturated fat

● ○ ○ Salt

STATISTICS PER COOKIE

Energy 160kcals/677kJ

Protein 2g

Fat 7g
Saturated fat 3.5g

Carbohydrate 24g
Sugar 14g

Fiber 1g

Salt 0.2g

GREAT FOR KIDS

VIENNESE COOKIES

These swirly, chocolate-dipped cookies look as good as they taste.

MAKES   9
PREP   10 mins
COOK   15–20 mins
FREEZE   6 months

GUIDELINES PER SERVING

● ● ○ Calories

● ● ● Saturated fat

● ○ ○ Salt

STATISTICS PER SERVING

Energy 254kcals/1063kJ

Protein 2g

Fat 16g
Saturated fat 10g

Carbohydrate 26g
Sugar 14.5g

Fiber 1g

Salt 0.2g

9 tbsp unsalted butter, softened,
   plus extra for greasing
½ cup powdered sugar
1 cup gluten-free flour
2 tbsp cornstarch
2 tsp xanthan gum
¼ tsp gluten-free baking powder

½ tsp pure vanilla extract
4oz (115g) dark chocolate (at least 60%
   cocoa solids), broken into even pieces

SPECIAL EQUIPMENT
   piping bag fitted with a ¾in (2cm) star
   nozzle

1 Preheat the oven to 375°F (190°C) and lightly grease two large baking sheets. Place the butter and powdered sugar in a large bowl and use an electric whisk to beat until pale and fluffy.

2 Sift over the flours, xanthan, and baking powder. Add the pure vanilla extract, then beat again with the whisk until a soft dough forms.

3 Spoon the dough into a piping bag and, holding the nozzle with one hand while squeezing with the other, pipe nine cookies in a zigzag fashion onto the baking sheets. Space them well apart as they will spread during baking.

4 Bake for 15–20 minutes or until pale golden brown. Leave to cool slightly before transferring to a wire rack to cool completely.

5 Place the chocolate in a heatproof bowl set over a pan of simmering water. Heat gently until the chocolate melts, stirring occasionally. Dip one half of each cookie in melted chocolate and leave to set on parchment paper.

Cook's Tips
To fill a piping bag easily, stand it in a tall drinking glass and pull the sides of the bag over the glass to open it up. Store the cookies in an airtight container for up to 5 days.

STEM GINGER COOKIES

With little chunks of stem ginger baked into them, these spicy cookies are very addictive!

MAKES 24
PREP 10 mins
COOK 15 mins
FREEZE 3 months

GUIDELINES PER SERVING

● ● ●   Calories
● ● ●   Saturated fat
● ● ●   Salt

STATISTICS PER COOKIE

Energy 93kcals/391kJ

Protein 1g

Fat 4g
Saturated fat 2.5g

Carbohydrate 12g
Sugar 5g

Fiber 0.4g

Salt trace

3 balls of preserved stem ginger, finely chopped, and 1 tbsp syrup from the jar
8 tbsp unsalted butter, softened, plus extra for greasing
½ cup light brown sugar
1 large egg

1¼ cups gluten-free all-purpose flour
1 tsp baking powder
½ tsp salt
⅓ cup rice flour, plus extra for dusting
1 tsp ground ginger

1 Preheat the oven to 375°F (190°C). Lightly grease 2 baking sheets and line with parchment paper.

2 Place the butter, sugar, and ginger syrup in a large bowl and cream together using an electric whisk, until light and fluffy. Thoroughly whisk in the eggs. Sift over the flours, ground ginger, and salt, then fold into the mixture along with the chopped stem ginger.

3 Heap 24 tablespoons of the mixture onto the prepared baking sheets. Place the dollops well apart as they will spread during baking. Flatten the dollops with your fingertips; if the mixture is too sticky, dust your fingers with rice flour before flattening.

4 Bake for 15 minutes until golden. Cool for 5 minutes on the baking sheets and, using a metal spatula, transfer to a wire rack and leave to cool completely. You can store them in an airtight container for up to 3 days.

Variation
For a citrus tang, add the finely grated zest of 1 lemon to the mixture.

AMARETTI COOKIES

These crunchy Italian-style macaroons are highly versatile. Use them for a cheesecake base, in a trifle, with ice cream or mousse, or on their own with coffee or dessert wine.

MAKES   20
PREP   10 mins
COOK   15–20 mins
FREEZE 3 months

vegetable oil, for greasing
2 large egg whites
¾ cup granulated sugar

2 cups ground almonds
1 tbsp amaretto liqueur
  (see Cook's Tips)

GUIDELINES PER SERVING

● ● ○ Calories

● ○ ○ Saturated fat

● ● ● Salt

STATISTICS PER COOKIE

Energy 104kcals/436kJ

Protein 2.5g

Fat 6g
Saturated fat 0.4g

Carbohydrate 11g
Sugar 11g

Fiber 0.2g

Salt trace

1 Preheat the oven to 350°F (180°C). Lightly grease 2 baking sheets and line with parchment paper.

2 In a clean bowl, whisk the egg whites using an electric whisk until they form stiff peaks. Add the sugar and whisk again until glossy. Sprinkle over the ground almonds and liqueur and gently fold in, using a large rubber spatula, until well mixed.

3 Divide the mixture into 20 portions and roll each into a ball. Place them on the baking sheets, well apart as they will spread during baking. Bake for 15–20 minutes or until golden brown. Use a metal spatula to transfer the cookies to a wire rack and leave to cool completely.

Cook's Tips

If you prefer, omit the amaretto liqueur and add 1 teaspoon almond extract with 1 tablespoon water. The cookies will store in an airtight container for up to 3 days.

GREAT FOR KIDS

INDEX

Page numbers in *italics* refer to nuggets of information about individual ingredients (e.g., their nutrient content). Variations on the main recipe on a page are indicated by *(V)*.

H

I, J

K

L

ABOUT THE AUTHORS

HEATHER WHINNEY is an experienced food writer and home economist. She has worked as a food editor and freelance food writer for several magazines, including *BBC Good Food, Family Circle, Good Housekeeping, Prima*, and *Woman and Home*. She is the author of DK's *The Illustrated Quick Cook* and co-author of *The Diabetes Cookbook*. Her food philosophy has always been to write simple recipes for the everyday cook.

JANE LAWRIE has been baking ever since she could stand on a chair. As an experienced food stylist and food writer, she has worked for numerous food and women's magazines, including *BBC Good Food, Bella, Best*, and *Good Housekeeping*. Jane also works as a consultant for the British Egg Information Service. She has worked on several DK books, including *Preserve It!* and *The Kitchen Garden Cookbook*.

FIONA HUNTER is a food writer and nutritionist with over 25 years' experience. With a degree in Nutrition and a postgraduate degree in Dietetics, she began her career as a dietitian for the NHS before going on to write for magazines, including *BBC Good Food, Good Housekeeping*, and *Health and Fitness*, as well as making many appearances on television and radio. She is the co-author of several books, including DK's *The Diabetes Cookbook*.

ACKNOWLEDGMENTS

Dorling Kindersley would like to thank:

RECIPE EDITORS Jane Bamforth, Holly Kyte

RECIPE TESTERS Rebecca Blackstone, Anna Burges-Lumsden, Amy Carter, Jan Fullwood, Laura Fyfe, Katy Greenwood, Anne Harnan, Catherine Rose, Rachel Wood

PROOFREADER Sue Morony

INDEXER Sue Bosanko

PHOTOGRAPHY ART DIRECTION AND PROPS STYLING Luis Peral-Aranda, Katherine Raj

FOOD STYLISTS Marie-Ange Lapierre, Emily Jonzen

Charis Bhagianathan and David Fentiman for editorial assistance. Mahua Mandal for design assistance. Danaya Bunnag for hand modeling.